"Resendez's brisk historical narrative cries out for novelisation."
—*Times* (U.K.)

"Reséndez ... shows how Cortez, de Soto and other would-be conquistadors schemed for their kingdoms in the New World like investors jockeying for IPOs." —*Wall Street Journal*

"An extraordinary adventure story (which) offers a very different sort of paradigm for Europe's encounter with the Americas."
—*The Scotsman*

"Andrés Reséndez's new interpretation of this uncanny ordeal of human survival comprehensively reveals the adventure in almost seamless, highly readable prose. He provides a clear background of the politics of the Spanish Conquest, then spins a yarn of unimaginable hardship and a testament to endurance that elicits head-shaking disbelief on almost every page. Amazingly, all of it is true ... Mr. Reséndez's new telling of this astounding tale entertains and captivates from the first page."
—*Dallas Morning News*

"[Reséndez's] voice is original, his writing lucid and gripping."
—*Miami Herald*

"[I]t is Reséndez's clever rewriting of his ordeal—as a survivor's tale—that is most memorable." —*Texas Monthly*

"Reséndez creates a gripping narrative of one of the most amazing survival stories of all time."
—*Library Journal* (starred review)

"[Resendez] misses nothing in telling this riveting quest for gold and glory: prickly pears, pecan nuts, and other plants new to Europeans; migrant tribes in the daily search for food; massacres and treks of naked men across hundreds of miles; and the jealousies and cabals among men like rich fat Diego Velazquez of Cuba; the fierce adventurer and expedition commander Panfilo de Narvaez (who died at sea on a makeshift raft after his coastal 'invasion' of Florida killed virtually all of his men); the rapacious Hernan Cortes who decimated the Aztecs; and various greedy bishops and friars . . . This is must and wonderful reading for anyone interested in our mutual histories at a time when Europeans came upon a new world and found themselves irrevocably transformed." —*Providence Journal*

"Resendez is a marvelous storyteller who makes you feel like you are there—even if you're really just lying on the couch."
—*American Way magazine*

"One of [the survivors], Álvar Núñez Cabeza de Vaca, the royal treasurer for the trip, wrote a narrative of his adventures, published in 1542. He survived along with two other Spaniards and an African slave. The three Spaniards also issued what became known as the *Joint Report*. The story that Reséndez (a history professor at the University of California at Davis) tells is woven largely from these two famous accounts, although he interprets them with fresh eyes. He also brings a breadth of knowledge to his story, stopping often for welcome excursions into such subjects as the weather patterns of the period or how one navigates (or in Miruelo's case, fails to navigate) by dead reckoning. The generous elaborations in his endnotes almost form a second narrative." —*American Scholar*

"Reséndez's graceful tale of four men who came to accept a new land on its own terms is itself a marvel to behold."
—*Houston Chronicle*

"Reséndez proves a patient storyteller, employing effective prose hand in hand with the tools of a scholar, including many maps, excellent footnotes and a terrific Further Reading section. The experiences of one of the first outsiders to see the American Southwest still prove fresh and pertinent." —*Kirkus*

"A riveting account of the epic journey . . . Told from an intriguing and original perspective, Reséndez's narrative is a marvelous addition to the corpus of survival and adventure literature."
—*Publishers Weekly* (starred review)

"The accidental journey of Cabeza de Vaca and his companions across North America is one of the epics of the Age of Exploration. Andres Resendez recounts the story in broad context and riveting detail, capturing the lofty, base, cunning, fatuous, cowardly, and heroic actions and motives of an improbable cast of astonishing characters."
—H.W. BRANDS, author of *The Age of Gold: The California Gold Rush and the New American Dream* and *Andrew Jackson: His Life and Times*

"Andres Resendez has written a definitive account of the remarkable overland journey of Cabeza de Vaca across 16th-century America. This important book brings a seminal yet neglected historical figure into a broad perspective. Displaying impressive skills as one of a new generation of narrative historians, Resendez tells a compelling story about a little-known chapter in American history. *A Land So Strange* is destined to become the standard work on the extraordinary journey of this courageous explorer."
—BRIAN FAGAN, author of *The Little Ice Age* and *Fish on Friday*

A LAND SO STRANGE

A Land So Strange

THE EPIC JOURNEY OF
Cabeza de Vaca

The Extraordinary Tale of a
Shipwrecked Spaniard Who Walked
Across America in the Sixteenth Century

ANDRÉS RESÉNDEZ

BASIC
BOOKS

A Member of the Perseus Books Group
New York

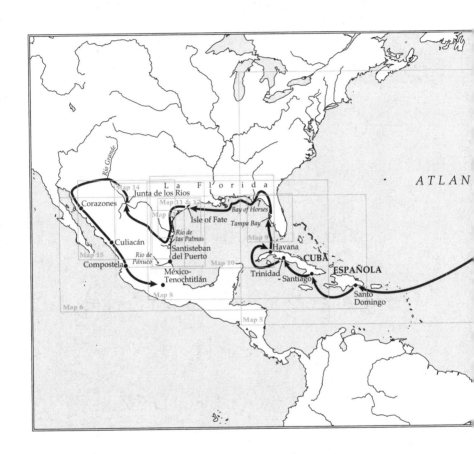

ATLAN

La Florida

Map 14
Junta de los Rios

Map 11 & 12

Corazones

Map
Isle of Fate
Bay of Horses
Tampa Bay

Culiacán

Rio de
las Palmas

Map 15

Map 9
Havana

Santisteban
del Puerto

Rio de
Pánuco

CUBA

Compostela

ESPAÑOLA

México-
Tenochtitlán

Map 10
Trinidad
Santiago

Santo
Domingo

Map 6

Map 8

Map 5

Rio Grande

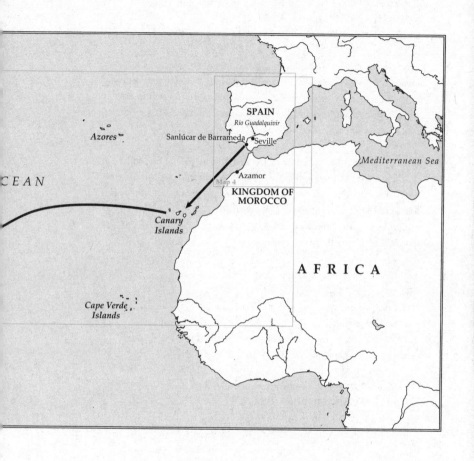

Hardcover edition first published in 2007 by Basic Books,
A Member of the Perseus Books Group
Paperback edition first published in 2009 by Basic Books

Books published by Basic Books are available at special discounts for
bulk purchases in the United States by corporations, institutions, and
other organizations. For more information, please contact the Special
Markets Department at the Perseus Books Group, 2300 Chestnut
Street, Suite 200, Philadelphia, PA 19103, or call (800) 810-4145,
ext. 5000, or e-mail special.markets@perseusbooks.com.

Library of Congress Cataloging-in-Publication Data

Reséndez, Andrés.
    A land so strange : the epic journey of Cabeza de Vaca : the
extraordinary tale of a shipwrecked Spaniard who walked across
America in the sixteenth century / Andrés Reséndez.
        p. cm.
    Includes bibliographical references and index.
    Hardcover ISBN: 978-0-465-06840-1
    Paperback ISBN: 978-0-465-06841-8
    1. Núñez Cabeza de Vaca, Alvar, 16th cent. 2. Explorers—
America—Biography. 3. Explorers--Spain—Biography. 4. America—
Discovery and exploration—Spanish. 5. Indians—First contact with
Europeans. 6. Indians, Treatment of—America—History. I. Title.

E125.N9R47 2007
970.01'6092--dc22
                                    2007037052

LSC-C

Printing 16, 2022

To Andrés Reséndez Medina in memoriam

CONTENTS

ILLUSTRATIONS

MAPS

MAPS

Introduction

IN THE SPRING OF 1536, A POSSE OF EUROPEAN horsemen ventured north from Culiacán. Barely one generation after Columbus they were, quite literally, the advancing edge of Spain's empire in North America. They were still becoming familiar with this region, now part of northwestern Mexico. The riders could gaze at the lush slopes of the Sierra Madre Occidental on the right. The Pacific Ocean with its loud crashing waves lay to the left. Straight ahead, a narrow coastal plain seemed to extend forever. On this strip of land, at once tropical and open, they could roam as far as they wished without ever expecting to find another white person—only Indian prey.

The horsemen were busy. Rounding up human beings was unpleasant but profitable. And they looked to an entire continent teeming with natives who could not move faster than their own legs would carry them. Even a small cavalry detachment could turn into an extremely efficient enslaving machine. And thus the posse burned villages and ran down men, women, and children.

One day, four of the slavers caught sight of thirteen Indians walking barefoot and clad in skins. In the distance the natives must have seemed ordinary to the horsemen except for one thing: rather than scurrying away, the Indians headed straight toward them. A sense of unease must have spread through the Christians. But they stayed put because the approaching Indians did not seem to harbor ill intentions. At closer range the unexpected details began to emerge. One of the natives seemed very dark. In fact, he was black. Was he an Indian too, or an African emerging from the depths of North America? The horsemen's unease must have turned into shock when they realized that one of the others in the group was a white man. He had gone completely native. His hair hung down to his waist, and his beard reached to his chest. The man's skin was leathery and peeling.[1]

As the two parties approached, the slavers could hear that the haggard white man spoke perfect Spanish. They became dumbfounded. "They remained looking at me for a long time"—Álvar Núñez Cabeza de Vaca would later recall—"so astonished that they neither talked to me nor managed to ask me anything."[2]

Cabeza de Vaca had to do the talking. He first asked to be taken to the slavers' captain. Next he wanted to know what the Christian date was and requested to have it officially recorded. The precise date has not reached us in spite of Cabeza de Vaca's insistence, but it must have been April 1536. After these formalities were out of the way, Cabeza de Vaca and his African companion—a resilient slave named Estebanico—began to tell their story of wandering adrift in a completely alien continent, a tale that had begun eight years earlier with a flawed leader in search of redemption.

FOR SHEER DRAMA and excitement, the journey of Cabeza de Vaca and his companions remains unrivaled, even by the adventurous standards of the Age of Exploration. Out of 300 men who set out to colonize Florida in 1528, only four survived: Cabeza de Vaca, two other Spaniards, and Estebanico. They became stranded. And to reenter European-controlled territory, they were forced into a harrowing passage on makeshift rafts across the Gulf of Mexico, years of captivity in what is now Texas, and a momentous walk across the continent all the way to the Pacific coast.

This small band of men thus became the first outsiders to behold what would become the American Southwest and northern Mexico, the first non-natives to describe this enormous land and its peoples. Conversely, innumerable natives living in the interior of the continent experienced the passage of the three Spaniards and the African as an extraordinary portent, a first brush with the world beyond America. The natives called the four travelers "the children of the sun" because they seemed to have come from such unimaginably remote lands.

It is tempting to narrate their journey as an extreme tale of survival: four naked men at the mercy of the natural elements, facing an extraordinary array of native societies. Comparisons to Joseph Conrad's *Heart of Darkness* are difficult to avoid. It was certainly a hellish journey. But it was also much more. At its heart, it is the story of how a handful of survivalists, out of necessity, were able to bridge two worlds that had remained apart for 12,000 years or more. Deprived of firearms and armor, the castaways were forced to cope with North America on its own terms. They lived by their wits, mastering half a dozen native languages and making sense of social worlds that other Europeans could not even begin to fathom. Incredibly, they used their knowledge of native cultures to escape from enslavement and refashion themselves into medicine men. Eventually, their reputation as healers preceded them wherever they went, as they moved from one group to the next in their quest for deliverance.

The castaways' insight into native North America is especially poignant at a time when Europeans debated whether the natives of America were fully human and crown officials reexamined Spain's conquests. In just five decades since Columbus, Iberians had rushed headlong into the New World. Men and women of enterprise and ambition had explored and ultimately devastated the islands of the Caribbean. More recently, Hernán Cortés and Francisco Pizarro had subdued millions of Indians in Mexico and Peru. These conquests constituted fantastic feats of daring. But they had been achieved at a great human cost, prompting a determined group of friars and crown officials to launch a reformist movement to change Spain's methods of conquest and convince colonizers of the essential humanity of Indians. The ensuing debate resonated throughout the empire. If it turned out that Indians did not possess human souls, then ruthless conquistadors would be permitted to enslave them by the millions. But if, however, these natives were endowed with God's spirit, then they would have to be painstakingly Christianized and their rights respected.[3]

Against this backdrop, the journey of the four castaways constitutes a rare turning point in the history of North America, every bit as momentous and full of possibilities as the landing of the *Mayflower* Pilgrims or the arrival of Cortés on the shores of Mexico. The experience of Cabeza de Vaca and his companions afforded Spain an opportunity to consider a different kind of colonialism. These four pioneers had revealed the existence of many native cultures north of Mexico and the availability of precious metals, buffalo, and other resources. But instead of advocating a conquest in the traditional mold, Cabeza de Vaca and the others proposed a grand alliance with the native inhabitants. Over the course of their long odyssey, they had come to recognize the natives of North America as fellow human beings. Their life-changing experience had persuaded them that a humane colonization of North America was possible—a far cry from the views held by most of their contemporaries in the Old World. Their journey thus amounts to a fork in the path of exploration and conquest, a road that, if taken, could have transformed the brutal process by which Europeans overtook the land and riches of America.

THERE WAS A time when the adventures of these four resilient travelers were well known in America and Europe. Two extraordinary texts made the castaways' story available to anyone interested. One was the testimony provided by the three surviving Spaniards upon their return. This document is often referred to as the *Joint Report*. Although the original testimony was lost at some point, a near-complete transcription has survived until today, thanks to the assiduous work of fellow explorer and chronicler Gonzalo Fernández de Oviedo (1478–1557), who included it as part of his massive *Historia general y natural de las Indias, islas y tierra firme del mar océano.*[4]

The second source is a first-person *Narrative* written by Cabeza de Vaca and first published in 1542, six years after he completed his journey. Cabeza de Vaca's humble and self-reflective account circulated widely in the Spanish empire and even beyond it. Contemporary explorers pored over the *Narrative*, looking for even the most casual mention of metals or simply to learn about the terrain and human landscape of the interior of North America. More pious readers drew transcendent lessons from this text, recasting the four survivors as Christ-like figures; a seventeenth-century friar, for instance, matter-of-factly stated that Cabeza de Vaca and his companions "performed prodigies and miracles among innumerable barbarous nations" and "healed the Indians by making the sign of the cross over them." In either case, colonial Spaniards were well aware of this tale.[5]

More recently, however, the odyssey of Cabeza de Vaca and the others has fallen into relative oblivion. In the United States, the Florida expedition has received surprisingly scant public attention, even though historians and archaeologists have passionately sparred over the survivors' probable route across the continent for well over a century. These scholars have felt sufficiently motivated to venture into rugged lands and onto forgotten trails. A courageous writer even tried to "fix" Cabeza de Vaca's latitude by sleeping naked outdoors until he could not bear it any longer! Clearly, the Florida expedition has stirred powerful emotions among some enthusiasts and specialists. But beyond this circle, its impact has been modest.[6]

The survivors' saga is somewhat better known in Mexico. In the early 1990s an entire generation of moviegoers went to see a film bearing the slightly disorienting title of *Cabeza de Vaca*, or "Cow's Head." The film is mesmerizing as much for the plot (the world of conquistadors turned upside down) as for the surreal atmosphere (complete mutual incomprehension in the midst of a magical world). Although the film takes considerable liberties with the facts, it played a crucial role in bringing the story to a wide audience. Nevertheless, Mexico's narrative of conquest is still dominated by the towering figure of Cortés and the downfall of the Aztec empire; the Florida expedition remains something of a minor curiosity or a diversion.

Modern boundaries have further obscured the significance of this venture. Cabeza de Vaca, Estebanico, and the others walked across the continent long before the border between Mexico and the United States came into being. But now the route of their journey is bisected by this national boundary, relegating their story to the fringes of both countries—neither a wholly American story nor a Mexican one.

Finally, the story of this extraordinary expedition has become less well known to us simply because the passage of time has rendered *Joint Report* and Cabeza de Vaca's *Narrative* increasingly difficult to read. Many passages within both texts are downright perplexing to modern readers. Since they were written for sixteenth-century Spaniards, they offer little by way of context. They tell us nothing about how the expedition was conceived, why the leaders became involved in this venture, and what exactly they intended to do upon reaching Florida. Context is even more sorely needed once the expedition lands on the continent and begins interacting with Native Americans.

Understanding the *Joint Report* and the *Narrative* is also complicated by the fact that both are very public and official documents. In casting their narratives, Cabeza de Vaca and the other survivors engaged in self-conscious scripting. They wrote their reports in part to establish their virtues and merits and thereby curry royal favor. They thus avoided controversial subjects. For instance, neither source contains a single word about intimate relations between the castaways and native women, even though other evidence suggests that it occurred. Similarly, to avoid problems with the Inquisition, Cabeza de Vaca studiously refrains from using the word "miracle" to describe his incredible healings.[7]

And yet despite the fact that both documents were shaped, in part, by the agendas of their authors, they remain extraordinary historical sources. Both are remarkably detailed and complement each other well, except in some minor but significant points. But to fully understand them, one must also resort to scraps of information buried in many other sources and avail oneself of recent findings on the archaeology, climate, geography, botany, and population history of North America. The most daunting aspect of writing this book has been the quest to locate all sorts of elusive information to help me explain the curious behavior of sixteenth-century Spaniards and their often perplexing interactions with very different native groups. In spite of my best efforts, I am far from having succeeded in every case. I can only say that I have gained an enormous appreciation for the craft of the storyteller.[8]

CABEZA DE VACA and his companions were the first outsiders to have lived in the immense territories north of Mexico. Their accounts give us the rarest of glimpses into precontact North America. These pioneers were able to see the continent before any other outsiders, prior to European contact.

But the lands visited by Cabeza de Vaca and the others were by no means static or prelapsarian; North America was changing profoundly and irreversibly even during the half a century since Columbus. The population of the Americas was already declining with startling speed due to epidemic diseases introduced by Europeans. In the course of the sixteenth century, many indigenous groups disappeared from the face of the earth. Even those who survived had to change beyond recognition or merge with larger groups in order to endure.[9]

What the castaways saw and recorded constitutes our very first and frequently our only window into a continent before and during this great devastation. They depicted a world that was alive. Wherever the survivors went they found Native Americans, all vigorously exploiting the environment by setting fires to hunt deer or replacing large tracts of North American Eden with plots of corn. These groups moved about in deliberate circuits to take advantage of different edible sources, possessed intricate trading networks, and waged war on one another with the same cunning and vindictiveness of their European counterparts. Tantalizingly, the castaways also reported dramatic instances of population decline. America was changing before their very eyes.

By the time English, French, and Spanish colonists penned their impressions in the seventeenth and eighteenth centuries, the indigenous populations had been greatly diminished, and the flora and fauna had reclaimed the abandoned lands. It is no wonder that such writers were prone to conjuring images of a wild, virgin North America only sparsely populated by bands of Indians who were themselves primeval and incapable of conquering nature. This perception has endured to the present time in what one scholar has aptly called "the pristine myth" of America. In this sense, the castaways offer a much-needed corrective to a seductive but ultimately distorted image.[10]

And beyond these insights into pre-Columbian North America, the story of the castaways constitutes an extraordinary instance of first contacts between peoples whose ancestors had remained apart for at least 12,000 years. When these two peoples finally came face to face with one another, they did it from the perspective of vastly different cultures, lifestyles, technologies, and expectations. Yet, no matter how outwardly different they appeared from each other, they were still ordinary humans trying to come to terms with one another as best as they could.

Too often, the human dimension of these encounters is lost in the crucible of grand imperial narratives. The script is predictable: gold-crazed conquistadors confront either savages or unsuspecting exemplars of paradise on earth. The outcome of such encounters is never in doubt. The odyssey of the Florida survivors reminds us that first contacts were in fact far more interesting. Not all voyages of exploration were equal, just as not all Native Americans were the same. Early encounters were intensely personal affairs guided by the personalities of those involved and resources available to them. The Florida expedition makes this point powerfully. Here are conquerors who were themselves conquered and Indians who became masters and benefactors, all the while acting in deeply human ways.

At its most elemental, the castaways' tale constitutes in microcosm the much broader story of how Europeans, Africans, and natives set out to bridge the enormous cultural distances separating them. It is, in essence, the story of America. The journey of Cabeza de Vaca, Estebanico, and the others was thus spiritual as much as physical. Their life depended on their ability to understand the basic humanity of their indigenous masters and hosts. Time and again, as the survivors came within sight of a new native group, they had to find a middle ground. They were European and African by birth but were becoming American by experience. So profound was the survivors' spiritual journey that fellow conquistadors could scarcely recognize them on the radiant spring day when they finally reemerged from the depths of the continent.[11]

CHAPTER 1

The Prize That Was Snatched Away

T HE STORY OF CABEZA DE VACA AND HIS COMPANIONS has its origins in the Caribbean archipelago, that immense arch of green gems set against a turquoise sea that was Spain's first foothold in America. There, at the edge of an unexplored continent, two partners dreamed of ruling a vast and wealthy colony on the mainland. They nearly succeeded. But a heartless betrayal caused their venture to unravel in the end. The Florida expedition was a direct consequence of this failure. It was a second and even more desperate bid for a continental possession and a last-ditch effort to remake a life.

The older and more influential of the two partners was Diego Velázquez, a widower beloved for his banter and constant talk of pleasure and mischief. During his long career as a colonist in the Caribbean, he had witnessed a good deal of human misery. But he also liked to laugh and often found himself surrounded by eager listeners. He had taken his chances by accompanying Columbus on his second voyage in 1493 and by staying on a God-forsaken island that turned out to contain the largest gold deposits anywhere on those islands. Velázquez was also resourceful at waging war and getting the vanquished natives to

Diego Velázquez, the jokester and plump master of Cuba who was first-in-line to conquer Mexico.

work in his mines. In a little more than a decade, he emerged as the richest resident of Española, the island shared today by Haiti and the Dominican Republic.[1]

Yet, more than his gold, Velázquez's network of allies and acquaintances constituted his greatest asset. From Española a wave of conquests radiated in all directions, so Velázquez summoned his influence within the imperial bureaucracy and relied upon his contacts at the Spanish court to secure colonization rights. His playful demeanor belied great ambition. By 1511 he had obtained the crown's authorization to occupy Cuba, the largest island of the archipelago and potentially even richer than Española.

The conquest of Cuba would require much help, so Velázquez sought out the kind of men who could make this undertaking a reality. Most crucially, he struck up a partnership with a fierce-looking adventurer named Pánfilo de Narváez. The two men got along well from the start. They hailed from nearby towns in Spain's central plateau and complemented each other admirably. Velázquez may have been well connected, but he was getting old, and his expanding waistline was already the butt of jokes. Narváez, by contrast, was still in his thirties and looked every bit the part of the Spanish conquistador: tall and muscular, with light hair turning to red, a ruddy beard, and a deep, booming voice, "as if it came from a vault."[2]

The genial administrator and the intrepid adventurer imposed their will on Cuba rapidly, leaving no doubt that their alliance worked well. Velázquez wrote letters to the King and prudently surveyed the southern coast with a fleet of canoes. Meanwhile, Narváez cut an east-west swath right through the middle of Cuba at the head of 100 Europeans and perhaps 1,000 Indian porters. In just four years, this band of outsiders crushed all native resistance, turning a lush island into a sordid outfitting station and a brave new colonial experiment.[3]

Buoyed by their success, the two partners felt sufficiently confident to set their sights even higher. For a time the possibilities seemed unlimited.

USING CUBA AS a base, Velázquez ventured farther west. Early in 1517 he dispatched an expedition that drifted onto the Yucatán Peninsula, probably blown off course and not intending to go so far. What the Christian sailors saw there astonished them: large temples made of stone and mortar, Indian nobles adorned with extravagant headdresses, exquisitely designed ornaments of gold and silver. They had come in contact with the Maya. They also brought back to Cuba two natives from Yucatán; "Old Melchor" and "Little Julián," who were able to elaborate on first impressions.[4]

Velázquez, ordinarily a man of steely patience, seems to have been overcome with excitement. He hastily cobbled together a second expedition, which departed in January 1518 under the

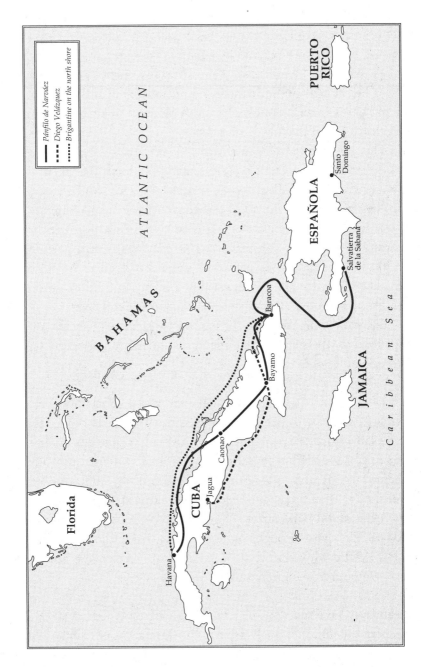

command of Velázquez's nephew, Juan de Grijalva. The spring and summer months of 1518 seemed interminable for Velázquez as he waited for word from his relative. At last, in the fall, this second exploratory party returned to Cuba carrying precious objects obtained by barter with the Indians of Yucatán. In their possession was gold valued at between 16,000 and 20,000 pesos, considerably more than what the Spaniards had been able to extract from Cuba in an entire year. The stuff that made dreams of El Dorado seem all too real.

But Diego Velázquez was now in a bind. Although faced with a colossal opportunity, he had exhausted his financial resources by launching two expeditions in two consecutive years. He could not wait too long to launch yet another expedition, for rumors of the wealth of Yucatán were already reaching the ears of potential competitors. The plump master of Cuba desperately needed to find a partner, someone who would captain a third fleet to claim these new lands for the greater glory of Spain, and for his own.

There is little doubt that Velázquez's first choice would have been Pánfilo de Narváez, his old partner and trusted right-hand man. But, alas, Narváez was in Spain at the time, serving as a representative of the island of Cuba at court. Within Cuba itself there were very few settlers wealthy enough for a venture of this magnitude. So in spite of some misgivings, Velázquez decided to send Hernán Cortés.[5]

Cortés was one of the original conquerors of Cuba. He was vivacious, likable, and literate; he could even pepper his speech with Latin. Velázquez promptly recognized these qualities and made Cortés his personal secretary in 1512 or 1513. For several months Cortés acted as Velázquez's confidant and most trusted representative in matters that required diplomacy and tact.[6]

But the two men had a falling out. It appears that Cortés began to chafe under Velázquez's command. In 1514 Cortés, ever the man of action, tried to make his way back to Española bearing a load of letters that detailed Velázquez's abuses for members of the *audiencia* of Santo Domingo (a high court with jurisdiction over Cuba). As fate would have it, Cortés was seized before leaving Cuba. At first Velázquez wanted to have his secretary hanged, but, with the passing of time, and after many residents interceded on Cortés's behalf, his rage subsided. Eventually Velázquez relented and turned Cortés loose but refused to restore him as secretary.

For Cortés it was a defining moment. From then on he did his utmost to regain Velázquez's trust, "behaving so humbly and seeking to please even the lowliest of Velázquez's servants." In this, he had some success. Cortés asked Velázquez to be a godfather witness in his wedding. The two men became compadres. When Cortés learned of Velázquez's proposal to jointly explore Yucatán, it must have seemed to him like the culmination of a long and arduous process of social rehabilitation.[7]

At the threshold of a new phase in his life, Cortés seized his destiny like a possessed man. He talked to friends and neighbors; bought a carvel and a brigantine; and used his formidable powers of persuasion to procure wine, oil, beans, and chickpeas on credit. But as the months of preparation wore on, Velázquez began to worry over Cortés's independence of character. At the eleventh hour he attempted to relieve his old secretary of command. By then, however, Cortés was too deeply involved to be stopped. In the early hours of November 18, 1518, he gathered his ships, crews, and soldiers and left Cuba in haste. When Velázquez was notified that Cortés had taken to sea, he hurried to the shore at daybreak. With Velázquez beckoning to him, Cortés got on a small boat and rowed within earshot. Velázquez reportedly shouted to him: "Why, compadre, are you going so? Is this a good way to say farewell to me?" Cortés could barely respond.[8]

It was not an auspicious beginning to the expedition. Velázquez, the great leader of Cuba, the astute administrator who still claimed powerful backers at all levels of the imperial bureaucracy, would seek his revenge. He would eventually launch a *fourth* armada, larger and better supplied than the previous three, to extend his authority over the mainland and bring back the outlaw Cortés—in chains, if necessary. This time he would entrust the task to his old partner, Pánfilo de Narváez.

BY THE TIME Cortés took to the sea, leaving Velázquez shouting from the shore, Narváez had been absent from Cuba for three years. He had spent this time in Spain following the court. It should have been a pleasurable tour of duty, a welcome respite from the rustic New World. Instead it turned into a hellish experience.

Narváez had traveled to Spain to act as Diego Velázquez's representative at court and secure some privileges for his fellow European settlers in Cuba. Narváez had plans for himself as well. Being already at court, and at great expense, he intended to get the King's permission to lead an expedition, either to present-day Colombia or to Central America.[9]

Yet Narváez never quite made himself at home at the court. He found many reasons to complain, beginning with the transient lifestyle. The Spanish court in the sixteenth century was perpetually on the move. It resembled a roving circus of eccentrics, traveling at times on dignified ships and carriages but more often than not on donkeys or by foot on dusty roads. The King's duties took him everywhere, and his unceasing wandering exacted a heavy price of those forced to follow him.[10]

When the court resided in sizable cities the logistics were straightforward, but numerous problems arose when it passed through small towns. For instance, a man at court had to give out generous tips to the *aposentadores*, the court officials charged with making the lodging arrangements. In the absence of such a bribe, the courtier was liable to wind up in a bleak inn far from the ear of the King and his ministers. It was only the first of a great many expenses. The courtier was responsible for paying a veritable army of service providers: butchers, bakers, and winemakers for supplies; woodcutters for fuel to stay warm; shoemakers and tailors for elegant clothing; doormen who controlled access to the King; royal servants who eased matters in his presence; secretaries who controlled the pace of the business being transacted; and so forth. None of this came cheaply. Bishop Antonio de Guevara, a seasoned courtier and author of a *how-to* manual for those wishing to join the court, put it very eloquently: "Where the court resides nothing is sold and everything is resold."[11]

In addition to money, a petitioner like Narváez needed a thick skin. Individuals wishing to join the court were subjected to constant scrutiny and mockery. They could be ridiculed for dressing too extravagantly or too plainly, for being too eager to get on with their business or too timid and roundabout in approach, or for lacking proper manners or affecting manners above their station. The hapless courtier could only smile at such humiliation and turn the other cheek. One angry word was enough to jeopardize his painstaking lobbying effort. Courtiers spent their nights devising schemes to approach this or that minister and their days solving the innumerable problems posed by an extravagant lifestyle on the trail. It went on for months at a time, driving all but the most determined men to desperation. A nobleman who left his family believing that he would be back in two months quite frequently spent six at court without obtaining any appreciable results, other than having wasted a good portion of his estate.[12]

Shrewdly, Narváez and his companions began to lobby for favors by delivering to the monarch the first large consignment of Cuban gold, totaling 12,437 pesos. Nothing could have been more persuasive to King Ferdinand than the promise of similar remittances in the future. The Cuban delegation also enjoyed the support of some influential court members, chief among them the bishop of Burgos, Juan Rodríguez de Fonseca. The good bishop was a mercurial man of striking contrasts worthy of a novel. Although a man of God, he was exceedingly savvy in worldly affairs. Bishop Rodríguez de Fonseca had helped to organize Columbus's second voyage and had made a career out of mustering armadas, an occupation "more suitable for ruffians than bishops," as one contemporary insightfully noted. The bishop also happened to preside over the royal committee that administered all of Spain's New World possessions, the powerful Council of the Indies. He ran the council from the comfort of his home and as he saw fit. As it turned out, this influential figure was notoriously—even scandalously—partial toward Diego Velázquez. It was rumored that the bishop wanted to marry one of his spinster nieces, Mayor de Fonseca, to Velázquez, a widower whose previous marriage had lasted barely a week. It was also said that Velázquez, in return, had granted a substantial stake of Indian servants from Cuba to the bishop. Whether all the rumors were true, Narváez could expect to be warmly received by Rodríguez de Fonseca.[13]

Narváez's lobbying campaign could have succeeded, if not for two extraordinary and unforeseen complications. The first was the death of King Ferdinand. Just as Narváez was getting settled at court as it traveled through western Spain, Ferdinand fell seriously ill and promptly died in late January 1516. The court was thrown into disarray and all negotiations had to be suspended.[14]

The King's death must have impressed Narváez profoundly. Ferdinand's long and portentous reign, first jointly with Queen Isabella, had spanned Narváez's entire life. During that time Spaniards had lived through their most heroic and hopeful days as the Catholic monarchs unified their realms, drove the last Muslim enclaves out of the Iberian Peninsula, and sponsored the expedition of an obscure Genoese that culminated in the discovery of America. In five decades Ferdinand and Isabel had managed to parlay a collection of disheveled kingdoms at the tip of Europe into the most promising empire in the world.

Yet for all their successes, the Catholic monarchs had failed to prepare an orderly succession. By 1516 Ferdinand's most direct heir was his daughter, Juana, a woman who had remained secluded in the castle of Tordesillas in central Spain for seven years. She refused to bathe or change her clothes and would not eat in the presence of others. Her behavior was so erratic and contrary to prescribed royal protocol that she became known to history as Juana the Mad. This condition was brought about (or at least exacerbated) by her tumultuous marriage to Philip the Fair, an archduke from the Low Countries who enjoyed the company of other women. Juana's possessiveness and jealousy lingered even after Philip's death in 1506. Some accounts state that Juana had her husband's coffin repeatedly opened to make sure that the body had not been snatched away and describe how she knelt down and kissed Philip's feet immediately after the shrouds were removed.[15]

After Juana, the next in the line of succession was her eldest son, Charles. At the time of Ferdinand's death Charles was still a gangly sixteen-year-old, born and raised in the city of Ghent in Belgium. He was quiet, indolent, somewhat awkward, and very much the tool of his ambitious Flemish advisors. In the eyes of many Spaniards, Charles of Ghent represented a foreign intrusion, as he did not even speak Spanish. But the mental condition of his mother thrust him onto the throne—and he took it. After bidding adieu to the Flemish Estates in July 1517, Charles and his entourage journeyed first to Tordesillas, to obtain the endorsement of Queen Juana, and then around Spain to meet his new subjects.[16]

For Narváez, the unfolding of this stately drama only resulted in delays, as months of waiting turned into years.[17] In the meantime, he had to contend with a second unforeseen complication. One day in late 1515, a friar by the name of Bartolomé de Las Casas joined the court. Las Casas had been Narváez's chaplain during the conquest of Cuba, but now he was a much changed man. Friar Las Casas had experienced an epiphany that would propel him to devote the rest of his life to the passionate defense of the natives of America. According to his own account, this flash of moral insight occurred when he was preparing a sermon to celebrate Pentecost in 1514. While perusing the *Ecclesiasticus* he stumbled on these words:

> The bread of the needy is their life: he who defrauds him thereof is a man of blood.
>
> He who takes away his neighbor's living slays him; and he who defrauds the laborer of his hire is a bloodshedder.[18]

Las Casas began his remarkable transmutation by returning to Diego Velázquez the Indians that had been apportioned to him as reward. Within months Las Casas became notorious throughout Cuba for preaching that God intended the natives to be free. More threateningly still, he took to warning his fellow Europeans that enslaving Indians or reducing them to servitude constituted a mortal sin.

From Cuba the embattled priest took his crusade to the Spanish court, where he found many sympathetic ears. He aired his views and regaled court members with horrific stories of New World ruthlessness and uncontrolled greed. Narváez's exploits figured prominently among them. In 1516 Las Casas introduced three *Memoriales* (formal petitions or requests) detailing various atrocities perpetrated against the Indians in Cuba and elsewhere in the Caribbean. Narváez was forced to respond, disputing some of Las Casas's claims and stating that his former chaplain was "an irresponsible man of little authority and credibility who speaks of things that he did not see." Still, the reformist movement at first succeeded so well that it not only put Narváez on the defensive but also undermined the power of Bishop Rodríguez de Fonseca, a principal backer of Cuba's conquerors and chief proponent of a system that was based on the exploitation of Indian labor.[19]

Las Casas pressed ahead with his campaign. His solution to the Indian problem was both disarmingly simple and extremely radical: "The Indians need to be placed beyond the grasp of the Spaniards, because no remedy that leaves them in Spanish hands will stop their annihilation." He further explained that the Spaniards already living in the New World, who would be unable to sustain themselves, "had to be helped to make a living without committing sin and on the basis of their own industry." A group of Indian-holders and representatives from the Indies that included Narváez resolutely opposed the movement to set the Indians free, dryly claiming that the Indians "do not have the capacity to remain by themselves" and warning that any effort to deprive New World colonists of Indians would constitute a serious breach of the terms under which they had agreed to go to the new lands.[20]

This quarrel reflected a long-smoldering controversy within the empire that would continue to rage for decades. Las Casas would go on to publish a brief but incendiary treatise in 1552 entitled *The Devastation of the Indies* that would expose Spain's abuses and establish its reputation as a cruel colonial power around the world. Yet, from Narváez's perspective, the battle over the treatment of the Indians constituted an unfortunate distraction. By the beginning of 1518, he had little to show for a stay of more than two years in Europe.

It was the news of Diego Velázquez's discoveries in the Yucatán Peninsula that finally brought an end to Narváez's frustrating sojourn in the Old World. Reports of Velázquez's discoveries reached the court in late 1517 or early 1518, changing completely the nature of Narváez's embassy. His most pressing concern now was to help Velázquez secure the administration of these new lands. In a matter of months his efforts bore fruit, perhaps owing to the excitement over the discoveries or to the influence of Bishop Rodríguez de Fonseca, who was able to reassert his power in the nascent administration of King Charles.[21]

Narváez got most of what he wanted. In November 1518, the King named Velázquez *adelantado* (civilian authority) of Yucatán and appointed Narváez as *contador* (comptroller). The King also ordered that Narváez be paid his full salary as an advocate of Cuba for the entire period that he had spent in Spain, surely a most welcome relief. King Charles even took the time to write to Diego Velázquez, praising Narváez for his services and recommending him highly. Thus Narváez ended his torturous experience in the Spanish court on a high note, a fact that would weigh heavily on his future plans.[22]

In early 1519, Narváez returned to Cuba. He arrived just a few weeks after Hernán Cortés had brashly made off with the ships, which raised questions about the fate of the Yucatán that Narváez had just secured for Velázquez.

REMARKABLY, VELÁZQUEZ had not immediately appreciated the extent of Cortés's treachery and the seriousness of his challenge. In complete control of Cuba and now also secure in his lifetime appointment as *adelantado* of Yucatán, he could scarcely imagine that a servant (*un criado*), with no court backing to speak of, could turn into a serious rival. Certainly Cortés had left in a hurry, but he had done so out of fear that he would be relieved of the command of the expedition to Mexico. Velázquez still hoped that Cortés would act as his agent. Indeed, from November 1518 (when Cortés left) to August 1519, Velázquez was content to wait for news from his spirited envoy. He even sent additional supplies.[23]

Cortés did not waste his time during these months. His fleet first sailed west toward the Yucatán Peninsula and then coasted along the Gulf of Mexico, finally stopping in San Juan de Ulúa, a little island in close proximity to the mainland with a good harbor. There Cortés and his men came in contact with the most powerful indigenous kingdom on the continent. They learned that the center of this fabulous empire—the city-state of Mexico-Tenochtitlán—lay not on the coast, but 200 miles inland on a high plateau, and that its ruler was a magnificent lord named Moctezuma. Thus began an epic exchange conducted with runners, couriers, and spies. Cortés explained to Moctezuma's emissaries—from a relentlessly European perspective that must have surely mystified them—that King Charles, "ruler of the largest part of the world," had sent him to pay his respects; that he and his men intended to begin their ascent toward Mexico-Tenochtitlán; and that they wanted an audience with the powerful Moctezuma.[24]

Moctezuma's first impulse was to avoid contact with these odd strangers. He lavished presents on the Spaniards instead (carried by as many as 100 porters), hoping to induce them to return contentedly to wherever they had come from. Little did Moctezuma know that his extraordinary gifts, far from dissuading Cortés and his men, only fanned the flames of their greed. The Spaniards were delighted to receive several gold samples that were the size of garbanzo beans and lentils; necklaces of jade set in gold; golden bells; scepters studded with precious stones; gold rings; a roomful of breastplates and shields of gold and silver; human figurines of jugglers, dancers, and hunchbacks; statues in solid gold of jaguars, monkeys, and armadillos; two wooden disks as large as carriage wheels, one covered with gold and the other one with silver; many cotton blankets and cloaks with intricate chess-like patterns of white, black, and yellow; magnificent headdresses of large and shiny feathers unknown in Europe; and two screenfold books, or codices, made of bark and containing stylized drawings of humans and animals. It was a treasure trove that easily dwarfed *anything* that had been previously found in the New World.[25]

Cortés decided to use these astonishing riches to open a direct line of communication with the King of Spain. From the coast of Mexico, Cortés dispatched a ship that was to skip Cuba entirely and go to Spain, avoiding the most common sailing routes. In addition to the treasure, the ship transported two representatives from Cortés whose charge was to negotiate directly with King Charles, circumventing Velázquez's authority.[26]

Although the plan was to sail on to Spain, the vessel ultimately touched on Cuba in August 1519. One of Cortés's agents, Francisco de Montejo, suggested a brief landfall at his *estancia* in northwestern Cuba to take on some provisions before crossing the Atlantic. At least one startled resident was allowed to go on board and gaze at the Indian objects and hear some of the stories about the Aztecs and their lord Moctezuma. Although the witness had been sworn to secrecy, he revealed that the booty on the ship was so enormous that "there was no other ballast than gold."[27]

Velázquez became livid when he learned of Cortés's treachery. He immediately sent two ships in hot pursuit to seize the treasure on the high seas or at least warn Spanish authorities of Cortés's fraud and request that the objects be confiscated. Velázquez and Narváez also vowed to stop Cortés and press their claim on a land that promised fabulous wealth. No resources were spared. With the two most powerful men on the island working side by side, an armada of eighteen ships, eighty horses, and more than 1,000 men and a few women was assembled by early 1520. The armada was roughly twice as large as that of Cortés. So many Europeans became involved in this expedition and so few would remain in Cuba that the island would become vulnerable to being reclaimed by the Indians.[28]

Velázquez considered leading the expedition to Mexico himself. But he was already too old and, as some playfully observed, too fat for such an undertaking. Narváez would lead it. He must have relished the staggering stakes involved. In uncharted lands, Narváez and his men would face not one but two enemies: a renegade band of Europeans and the most powerful indigenous polity in the hemisphere, possibly making common cause with each other. Yet Narváez remained confident. In the presence of Velázquez he boastfully declared that "even with half as many people, I am certain to imprison Cortés so you can do with him as you please . . . when the time comes I will know how to treat Cortés, he will respect me and come back as a son, and I will send him to you so he'll never raise his head again." Narváez's overconfidence would resurface again and again in the course of his life, at last with tragic results.[29]

By February of 1520, Narváez and his fleet were prepared to leave Cuba. However, before the army could sail, Velázquez and Narváez had to deal with one last nettlesome bureaucratic affair. Authorities in Española had gotten word of the brewing conflict between Velázquez and Cortés, and the likelihood of a civil war among Spaniards in Mexico had them worried. Wishing to prevent the spilling of blood among brothers in the new lands, a most disastrous precedent, the *audiencia* of Santo Domingo hurriedly dispatched one of its own as a mediator, the *licenciado* Lucas Vázquez de Ayllón. Sailing on two ships put at his disposal, this resourceful fifty-year-old man met both Narváez and Velázquez and did his best to dissuade them from their plan of direct confrontation. Instead of initiating hostilities, the *licenciado* reasoned, Velázquez and Narváez would gain more by simply sending two or three ships with provisions for Cortés, along with some discreet agents who could find out more about his intentions and remind him of his duties and royal orders. More menacingly, the *licenciado* Vázquez de Ayllón notified Narváez that he would face a penalty of 50,000 ducats if he insisted on taking his armada to Mexico.[30]

The proud conquerors of Cuba refused to recognize the authority of the *audiencia* of Santo Domingo and, undaunted, proceeded with their preparations. The *licenciado* made arrangements of his own to follow Narváez to Mexico, where he would continue his mediating role.

Narváez's fleet (including the *licenciado*'s two ships) first crossed the Straits of Yucatán in March 1520. Following Cortés's route, the expedition continued along the Gulf Coast of Mexico, skirting the modern states of Campeche, Tabasco, and Veracruz. The gulf is a relatively small and self-contained body of water, but sailing it can be treacherous. During the winter months the gulf is buffeted by a series of polar air masses known as *northers*. These unstable fronts of cold air come down from Alaska, barreling through North America, and descend on the gulf's warm waters, producing gusty winds and pouring rain that can last for days at a time. They seem to materialize out of

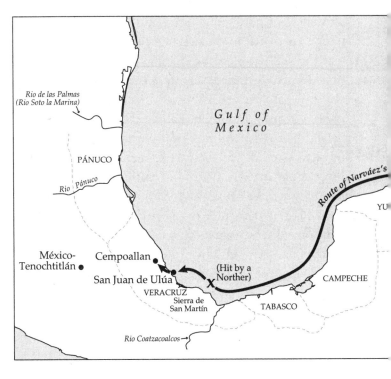

nowhere and hit with great force. Although the *norther* season lasts from October to March, it is possible to get caught in one even in the spring. Near Veracruz, Narváez's difficulties began when a *norther* caught up with them in early April as they sailed under the shadow of the Sierra de San Martín. One ship capsized, six others were damaged, and 40 men drowned. It was the first recorded shipwreck in the Gulf of Mexico.[31]

Narváez's problems would only continue. Wishing to spare 60 ailing men as well as all of the women on board from the impending showdown with Cortés, Narváez put them ashore at the Río de Alvarado, where the armada had briefly paused to reassemble. The sick men and the women were to remain as guests of the indigenous people of Tuxtepec until Narváez could assess

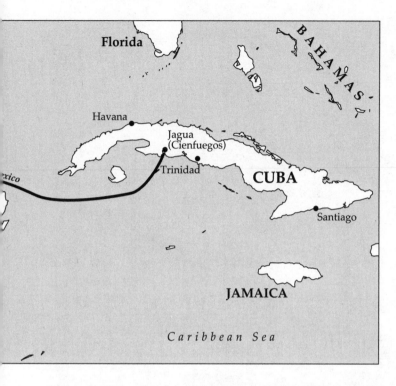

the level of danger the mission faced. Unfortunately the group left behind outlived its welcome and was massacred by the hosts some weeks later.[32]

The rest of the fleet was able to reach San Juan de Ulúa in late April 1520. Some of the ships were badly in need of repairs. Aztec lookouts on the coast promptly spotted the Spanish armada. They made a drawing on a cloth of eighteen vessels, five of them wrecked on the beach, and sent it to Moctezuma with fast runners. It did not take long before Narváez and Moctezuma were exchanging messages. Narváez sent word that he had come to Mexico to apprehend Cortés and his soldiers, who were bad men with no license from the King of Spain, and that after capturing Cortés they would all go back to Castile. Encouragingly,

Drawing of the landing of Cortés on Veracruz in April 1519. Florentine Codex, Volume III, folio 406 r.

Moctezuma confirmed that Cortés was in Mexico-Tenochtitlán and, as he had done earlier, showered Narváez with valuable presents. Evidently, the Aztec leader was playing the two sides against each other.[33]

Having learned of Cortés's whereabouts, Narváez disembarked his men and horses and established a permanent settlement on the mainland. The veteran captain conducted a formal ceremony of possession—an act that must have seemed to him like the culmination of his lobbying efforts in Spain. He then founded the town of San Salvador, probably where the modern city of Veracruz now stands. In a matter of weeks San Salvador grew into a substantial settlement of some eighty or ninety houses surrounding a plaza, a church, and a jail. It also boasted city officials and magistrates appointed by Narváez but whose authority derived ultimately from the King of Spain himself.

Although peaceful on the surface, the small settlement was divided against itself. Certainly there were those who supported the Velázquez-Narváez faction, but many others in the expedition were either indifferent or sympathetic toward Cortés. Some of the rank and file, for instance, had consented to go to Mexico only under duress, as Velázquez's vigorous recruiting in Cuba had involved strong-arm tactics and veiled or explicit threats. After weathering a severe storm, these reluctant "volunteers" had little appetite for battling a group of fellow Europeans just to settle a personal score in which they had no stake. Others were less loyal still: a group of hardened adventurers who enlisted merely as a means of leaving Cuba and reaching the "new world of gold" that they had heard so much about. Far from wanting to antagonize Cortés, these pragmatists were more inclined to join him to secure a place at the victor's table when the spoils were distributed.[34]

And into this combustible mix, the *licenciado* Vázquez de Ayllón and his staff had inserted themselves. Here was a royal judge from Española who had opposed Narváez's enterprise all along, and who had objected to the decision to disembark the men and found San Salvador on the grounds that it would upset the neighboring Indians. Worse still, Vázquez de Ayllón was gaining a following among expedition members who wished to avoid a clash. When Narváez's determination to deal harshly with Cortés became clear, the *licenciado* and his followers turned defiant. Narváez had the town crier in San Salvador proclaim that Cortés and his party were bad men. But the *licenciado* continued to speak favorably of Cortés and even exchanged letters and gifts with him.[35] Narváez reacted to Vázquez de Ayllón's betrayal by having the *licenciado* seized and locked up on his ship along with his secretary and servants, and another ship loaded with his supporters. The masters of both vessels were ordered to sail back to Cuba. Narváez would come to regret his heavy-handed treatment of the royal judge. En route, the *licenciado* was able to bribe and threaten the ship's master into changing their destination from Cuba to Española. Upon rejoining his colleagues at the *audiencia* of Santo Domingo, Vázquez de Ayllón gave vent to his long-suppressed frustration and anger with Velázquez and Narváez, and the ever-changing constellation of influences and powers swirling around the Spanish court began to tilt against Velázquez and in favor of Cortés.

Yet back in Mexico it appeared as though Narváez's decisiveness and sheer manpower would prevail. Four defectors from Cortés's army walked into Narváez's camp one day, offering crucial information. Over food and wine they told how Cortés and his band had boldly made their way to Mexico-Tenochtitlán, where they had lived for months as "guests" of the Aztecs and their lord, Moctezuma. That was an incredible feat, but one that also put them in extreme peril. Mexico-Tenochtitlán was nothing short of a deathtrap. It was a wonder of a city, built on an island in the middle of a lake, connected to the shore only by drawbridges, and home to perhaps 250,000 Indians. But at any moment the bridges could be lifted, the Indians could turn into fierce warriors, and Cortés's party would be lost forever without any hope of help. "Just how much better it is to be here"—the four defectors mockingly exclaimed in front of Narváez—

"drinking good wine and beyond Cortés's grasp who had us all so overwhelmed day and night as we awaited our deaths from one day to the next." The red-bearded commander surely hoped that these four men were merely the first of a raft of defectors pushed to the brink by a megalomaniac leader.[36]

Above all, Narváez felt reassured by the good reception of his large expedition by the natives of Mexico. Contrary to what the *licenciado* Vázquez de Ayllón had feared, the Indians were immediately impressed by the number of men, ships, and horses at Narváez's disposal and became quite friendly. It must have been especially pleasing to Narváez to learn that the Totonac Indians of the city-state of Cempoallan, the largest and most powerful community in the area near Narváez's settlement, as well as Cortés's first indigenous ally, had now decided to throw in their lot with this second and more impressive contingent of Europeans. The ruler of Cempoallan—an individual named Tlacochcalcatl but whom the Spaniards for the sake of expediency called the "fat cacique"—warmly welcomed Narváez and invited him to come forward. Narváez obliged. Hoping both to secure the approach to San Salvador and take advantage of the chief's hospitality (i.e., food), he moved his troops and weapons into Cempoallan, located 20 miles inland. Narváez established his command and artillery right on top of the pyramids and temples of Cempoallan. From these elevated positions he was able to dominate the plains that extended in front of this large city-state.[37]

When Cortés learned of Narváez's arrival, he had little choice but to divide his expedition. He left about 200 men in Mexico-Tenochtitlán to preserve a precarious standoff with the Aztecs. With the balance of his forces—fewer than 350 men—Cortés retraced his steps to Cempoallan to face a far superior force. But Cortés had a tool than Narváez lacked: gold. Cortés excelled when it came to bribery: he had put together his expedition and kept it together in the face of overwhelming danger by rewarding his men with booty and promising further riches. Now he employed the same tactics with Narváez's men. As Cortés approached Narváez's camp, he sent negotiators, spies, and plenty of gold.

A sagacious priest, Friar Bartolomé de Olmedo, and his namesake, Bartolomé de Usagre, were Cortés's two most crucial advance men. Accompanied by a mare loaded with gold, the two envoys approached Narváez's camp and sought to win over key members of his expedition. Usagre met with his own brother, who was in charge of Narváez's artillery, and gave him gold chains. Friar Olmedo spoke in confidence with Rodrigo Martín, Narváez's other artilleryman. Martín would receive more than 1,000 pesos for blocking the main cannon with wax. Cortés's envoys also carried letters addressed to virtually all of Narváez's principal captains and civil authorities of San Salvador; each one was offered 20,000 *castellanos* should they join Cortés. It appears that Narváez's camp was soon awash with Cortés's gold.[38]

During much of the month of May 1520, Narváez and Cortés spun fantastic webs of intrigue and counter-intrigue. Cortés sent at least three delegations into Narváez's camp, each composed of operators like Friar Olmedo and Usagre, bent on neutralizing and subverting the enemy. Narváez also sent his own intermediaries and attempted to bribe some of Cortés's lieutenants by offering future authority, since he did not yet possess Mexico's gold. Narváez even set up an elaborate trap by consenting to a face-to-face encounter with Cortés, along with ten men from each of their camps. Narváez's plan was to hide a cavalry unit behind a hill that was to fall on Cortés and his delegates, instantly capturing or killing them. In the end, Cortés gained the upper hand because he had a larger stash of gold and appeared to be in control of the fabled Mexico-Tenochtitlán, "the richest city in the world," facts that hard-nosed conquistadors could hardly ignore.[39]

After frantic weeks of negotiations without an amicable solution, Cortés's men started their advance on Cempoallan on the night of May 28–29, 1520, in the midst of a raging storm. Narváez had never believed that Cortés would dare to fight a force that was four times as large; Cortés may have been attempting to make a show of force to improve the terms of his surrender, but nothing more. Even after one scout informed Narváez that Cortés's forces were about 3 miles from camp, the leader could not bring himself to take the threat seriously. Tlacochcalcatl, the "fat cacique" who had taken refuge in Narváez's quarters, feared Cortés and understood him far better than Narváez. He predicted that Cortés would attack when least expected. But Narváez's lieutenants only laughed: "Do you take 'Cortesillo' to be so brave that, with the three cats which he commands, he will come and attack us just because this fat chief says so?"[40]

He did. Cortés's forces closed in on Cempoallan so rapidly that Narváez's artillery, already compromised by bribes and secret agreements, was able to inflict only minimal damage. As the rain let up and the moon and the fireflies appeared, one of Cortés's detachments surrounded the base of the pyramid where Narváez had set up his command. They ascended the steps, wielding long pikes with iron tips and challenging Narváez's crossbowmen on the upper platform.[41]

The fight intensified as Cortés's men reached the top steps and approached a shrine of wood and thatch from which Narváez and some thirty men had been firing guns and arrows. As Cortés's detachment drew near, Narváez's warriors reverted to swords and pikes. Narváez himself emerged swinging a two-handed broadsword, and a pitched battle ensued.

After hours of hand-to-hand combat, Narváez's cavernous voice rose above the murmur of war: "Holy Mary, they are killing me and have shattered my eye!" A pike thrust had emptied his right socket. Narváez's men were brought even closer to surrender when one of the attackers set fire to the thatched roof, leaving them completely exposed and surrounded. It was just a matter of time before Cortés's soldiers were able to quell all resistance on the pyramid and elsewhere in Cempoallan. During the wee hours of the night after the battle, Narváez pleaded for medical attention. His doctor was eventually found, and he and his captains were placed in irons in a nearby temple.[42]

It was not an ordinary victory. Cortés won over Narváez's men and with his combined forces would go on to topple the Aztec empire. Even today, schoolchildren learn about Hernán Cortés's exploits in Mexico. Yet hardly anyone remembers Diego Velázquez or Pánfilo de Narváez. It is hard to believe that there was a time when the opposite was true.[43]

NARVÁEZ SPENT YEARS "shackled and in chains," according to one witness, and rotting away in the moist, warm, and mosquito-infested coast of Veracruz. He nearly escaped once by offering to buy a ship in which to escape to Cuba, but the ploy was discovered and his accomplice was summarily tried and sentenced to death. For a man so proud and accustomed to victory, imprisonment must have been indescribably bitter: Narváez surely brooded over every mistake he had made and every man who had betrayed him. He also had to cope with life with one eye.[44]

At least Narváez was able to console himself with the thought that Cortés had been a formidable adversary. In 1522 Narváez was transferred from Veracruz to Mexico-Tenochtitlán and on the way had occasion to gaze at a part of Mexico that thus far had eluded him. When Narváez came into Cortés's presence in Coyoacán, overlooking Mexico-Tenochtitlán, he could not suppress a tinge of admiration: "I have seen the many cities and lands that you have tamed and subjected to the service of God and our Emperor, and I say that Your Lordship must be praised and honored." No small compliment, coming from Cortés's archrival.[45]

Back in Cuba, Velázquez was doing everything possible to neutralize Cortés through legal and political means. But his star was on the wane and his life was at an end. He died in June 1524. In his testament Velázquez recounted how he had outfitted the expeditions that discovered Mexico, had honored Hernán Cortés by naming him captain of one of them, and then had been ignominiously cheated out of the big prize. Velázquez believed that his heirs were entitled to at least 45,000 to 50,000 pesos in gold from Cortés. No such payments were ever made.[46]

María de Valenzuela, Narváez's wife, was more levelheaded. Showing greater insight into Cortés's soul, she pleaded with the conqueror of Mexico to spare her husband's life. But knowing that pleading might not be enough, she also prepared to offer a rich ransom for his release. It did not come to that. Sometime in 1524 Pánfilo de Narváez, no longer the threat that he once had been, was allowed to return to Cuba. Without his right eye, and scarred forever from his experience in Mexico, he rejoined his family.[47]

During the months that he spent in Cuba surrounded by family and friends, Narváez had ample time to meditate on the entire arc of his life. His successful career as a colonist and conquistador was now overshadowed by the embarrassing debacle in Mexico. And even though Narváez was approaching fifty—already an old man by the exacting standards of his age—

he might still have time to lead one last expedition. Pride must have played a distinct role in his deliberations. One of his friends counseled him to desist of his foolish plan and "retire peacefully to his house into the bosom of his family, giving thanks to God for the sufficiency he possessed to go through this stormy world so full of troubles."[48]

But the veteran conquistador could not be dissuaded. In Spain Pánfilo de Narváez would seek retribution from Cortés. And in a final gamble, he would also try to restore his life.

CHAPTER 2

A Voyage of Redemption

IN SIXTEENTH-CENTURY SPAIN, ALL NEW WORLD explorations originated in Seville, that marvel of a city-port on the Guadalquivir River. As Spain's only port licensed to do business with the American colonies, Seville became a protagonist in the history of discovery, the starting and end point of all transatlantic voyages. As one contemporary so aptly put it, "Seville is the common homeland, the endless globe, the mother of orphans, and the cloak of sinners, where everything is a necessity and no one has it." In the 1520s many sevillanos could still recall the stir caused by Columbus's triumphant entrance in the spring of 1493. The Admiral of the Ocean Sea had paraded around town followed by ten natives and a few resilient parrots that he had brought from the newly discovered lands. The people of Seville had more recent memories of that cantankerous Portuguese commander, Ferdinand Magellan, who had departed in 1519 with five good ships. Three years later a lone vessel with tattered sails and twenty-one famished survivors pulled up into harbor after having circumnavigated the entire globe.[1]

But far from being a backdrop or a silent witness, Seville was a beehive of activity, its workforce specializing in the procurement, outfitting, and manning of fleets bound for the New World, activities that drew men and women from all over Europe and North Africa. The main action centered on a stretch of beach that joined the left bank of the river to the city. Measuring 800 yards long and 350 yards wide, this area, commonly referred to as El Arenal (the Sandy Beach), functioned much like a surgeon's operating table. On any given day, one could see dozens of ships crowding each other, all floating perpendicularly to the waterline to make the most of the work space. Many of these vessels were surrounded by swarms of carpenters, caulkers, riggers, stevedores, boatmen, pilots, accountants, royal officials, aspiring passengers, and the many other characters that populated this vibrant maritime community. Since the average lifespan of sixteenth-century ships that plied the transatlantic routes was a mere four years, repair crews were ubiquitous. Caulkers skillfully laid ships on one side by shifting the ballast and taking advantage of low tides to expose parts of the hull. They had a few frantic hours to scrub the bottom and add tarred oakum between the planks before the tide turned again. Loading a vessel required less skill but far more stamina. There were no piers or wharves at El Arenal, so the entire cargo—fifty, seventy, 120, or more tons— had to be taken by smaller boats and lifted up with ropes onto the deck, or carried on the backs of stevedores who staggered from shore to the ships over narrow planks.[2]

It took about ten minutes to walk from El Arenal to the city center, where the imperial and ecclesiastical powers resided and expedition leaders wrestled with the overwhelming logistics of raising armadas. Human rivers flowed between the rowdy port scene and the august downtown through two main streets. The principal thoroughfare, a cobblestone street flanked by high stucco walls and wrought-iron grilles, began in the heart of El Arenal and ended at the steps of the Cathedral of Seville. Shipmasters recruited crew members and volunteers from these steps, and in the cool shade of the surrounding archways. Fit-

The busy port of Seville in the sixteenth century, the gateway to the New World

tingly, the street was named La Calle de la Mar ("The Street of the Sea"), as it was here that crews bid their last farewells and caught their last glimpses of the city before boarding the ships.[3]

A second avenue, less crowded but even more important, connected El Arenal to the royal palace. Along this route Cortés's lavish gift and many other riches from the Americas were hauled by oxcart to the heavily protected coffers of the House of Trade, the royal agency that regulated all commerce between Spain and her American colonies. On these two streets, as in many others, one could find throngs of merchants, shop owners, brokers, and intermediaries eager to satisfy the needs of those headed for the Americas. They offered every conceivable item, from wine, hardtack, olive oil, and salted cod to swords, breastplates, chickens, and horses.

The availability of these commodities was important, but Seville's principal asset was its large population that enabled it to provide crews for expeditions of any size. Even prior to the discovery of America, it ranked among Spain's largest ports. Propelled by its monopolistic position in the transoceanic routes, Seville emerged in the course of the sixteenth century as one of the most populous cities in all of Europe. Signs of this prodigious growth were visible everywhere, especially across from El Arenal, on the right bank of the river, in the famous neighborhood of Triana. A modest and nondescript section of town in the mid-fifteenth century, by the 1520s it had become a bustling and overcrowded neighborhood, harboring more than its share of paupers, children leading uncertain lives, abandoned women, African slaves, and incurable dreamers with schemes to match. Seamen of all ranks made their homes here. Captains and masters owned one- or two-storied buildings, while sailors lived in communal residences called *corrales*. Triana attracted scores of transients from all over the Iberian Peninsula and the wider Mediterranean world, all avid to learn the latest rumors of future expeditions. Miguel de Cervantes found Seville so compelling the he characterized it as "the asylum of the poor and the refuge of the outcasts" and wrote about the lives of some of its denizens, like the two scruffy, streetwise youngsters, *Rinconete* and *Cortadillo*, and their protector, *Monipodio*, the master of Seville's underworld.[4]

❊ ❊ ❊

NARVÁEZ TRAVELED FROM Cuba to Spain sometime in the summer of 1525 and proceeded to spend a year and a half following the Spanish court from Toledo in central Spain to Seville in the south. He was nothing if not persistent. He spoke out against Cortés at every opportunity and sought to discredit the famous conqueror of Mexico.

But Narváez was also a realist. As time went on, he shifted his strategy and used his influence more productively by proposing to lead an expedition to the vaguely known lands north of Mexico. During his time as a prisoner in Mexico City, Narváez had already heard about Cortés's eagerness to explore the north by sending various scouting parties. There would have been no sweeter revenge for Narváez than to cut short Cortés's advances. Cast in this light, Narváez's proposed enterprise constitutes a continuation of an epic rivalry that had started with the conquest of Mexico.[5]

Narváez cast himself as a wealthy man and a longtime resident of the New World with a clear vision of what he could accomplish. He no longer counted on the formidable patronage of Bishop Rodríguez de Fonseca, who had died the previous year. But the veteran colonist was on speaking terms with other court members, including King Charles (who had also become emperor of the Holy Roman Empire, adopting the name of Emperor Charles V) himself. Narváez's petitions to the Emperor, although somewhat formulaic like all such documents, reveal his confidence: "To serve God and Your Majesty it will be my pleasure to go in person to discover the islands of Tierra Firme . . . without Your Majesty having to make any commitments or expenditures whatsoever." In another petition, almost a threat, Narváez urged the emperor to avoid delays, for it would "weigh greatly on your royal conscience if it hindered the conversion of the Indians to our holy Catholic faith and postponed the benefits to your royal patrimony."[6]

In the early days of December 1526, during a stay in Granada, the newly married emperor and his Council of the Indies signed off on the venture. Narváez was to organize and outfit the expedition at his own expense. It would have to depart within a year. The goal of the expedition was nothing less than the permanent occupation of Florida and the adjacent territories. Narváez was allowed to establish two towns and three fortresses in these lands. It was a great victory for Narváez: the Crown could have opted for a far more restrictive charter allowing trade with the Indians but forbidding the planting of permanent settlements.[7]

However, Narváez's broad mandate entailed its own complications. For starters, it would make the expedition costly. Each settlement had to consist of at least 100 men (and eventually some women as well), and therefore Narváez would have to offer passage to 200 settlers at a minimum, not counting the friars to look after the spiritual well-being of the natives, and a handful of royal officials to make sure that the imperial coffers received a share of the proceeds. In return, Narváez would receive some tax exemptions, a large piece of land measuring ten square leagues, as well as the titles of governor of Florida, captain-general, *alguacil mayor* or chief law enforcer (this last titled bestowed for life and transferable to his descendents for all eternity), *adelantado* or civilian authority, and superintendent of the projected fortresses. Each of these offices entailed the prospect of wealth, preeminent social status, and genuine political power.

With the royal charter in his pocket, Narváez went to Seville and began preparations in earnest. For six months, Narváez's daily life must have revolved around chartering vessels, purchasing provisions at less-than-outrageous prices, recruiting crew members and colonists, and gathering whatever geographic information he could find about his destination.

Even though Seville's very existence was geared toward the out-fitting of armadas, setbacks were inevitable. During 1527–1528 there was an acute shortage of flour. To feed the city, officials is-sued orders preventing millers from selling to the fleets. Narváez's expedition must have been affected by this order.[8]

Narváez also struggled mightily to find a pilot familiar with the coast of Florida. It was a grave matter that he must have dis-cussed repeatedly with royal officials. One of the most vital functions of the House of Trade was to keep a stable of "royal pilots." The Crown retained these experts to deploy them in im-portant expeditions like Narváez's. The core of this group was comprised of the famous pilots who had accompanied Colum-bus in his voyages of discovery—the Pinzones, Niños, Ledesmas, and others—and their descendants, but these dynasties of navi-gators were hardly enough. The Spanish Crown had to go to great lengths to procure additional pilots wherever they could be found, especially in that other precocious maritime power, the neighboring kingdom of Portugal. King Ferdinand had made no secret of his intensions: "You know all too well the acute neces-sity of mariners who are experienced in matters of navigation," the monarch wrote to the officials of the House of Trade in 1514, "therefore, if any Portuguese pilot arrives in that city [Seville], I order you to treat him well and try to lure him as best you can." It was not uncommon for pilots to find themselves embroiled in acrimonious disputes between competing courts. Narváez must have pursued leads in all Seville, but, as can be de-duced from subsequent events, to no avail.[9]

In spite of such difficulties, for Narváez this must have been a time of exhilaration and renewal. By the late spring of 1527 he had purchased five ships that together were able to transport as many as 600 passengers. For weeks a crier must have advertised Narváez's colonization venture. Understandably, expedition captains gave preference to relatives, friends, and neighbors in their recruiting efforts. It is possible that the *adelantado* of Florida may have tried to lure volunteers from his hometown of Cuéllar, although no record of such an effort has come to light. Considering that Narváez's pressing responsibilities in Seville made travel difficult, the bulk of the recruiting effort almost certainly must have taken place right on the cathedral steps. It is also here where Narváez must have first met Cabeza de Vaca, Estebanico, and the others.[10]

AT A DISTANCE of nearly five centuries, we have only scraps of information about the colonists bound for Florida: people like Pedro Lunel, a rich man who would not go without taking his four black slaves; Mari Hernández and Francisco de Quevedo, a couple that had been to Mexico with Cortés, but after quarreling with him had returned to Spain, only to enlist in the Florida expedition; Doroteo Teodoro, a resourceful Christian from Greece; don Pedro, an Indian lord from the city-state of Texcoco in central Mexico, traveling with a Franciscan friar; Juan Velázquez de Salazar, a well-connected man who was to serve as councilman of the first town to be founded in Florida; and many others about whom we know even less.[11]

None of the colonists were cardboard figures, no gold-crazed conquistadors madly brandishing their swords, but rather ordinary men and women with their own struggles and fears and dreams. The overwhelming majority were Spanish, with a sprinkling of Portuguese, Greeks, and perhaps some other nationalities. All of them were Catholic (with the exception of some of the African slaves) and from families that had likely professed the same faith for generations. In fact, Narváez's charter included a pointed but somewhat cryptic order preventing him to recruit individuals "forbidden to go to those places [the New

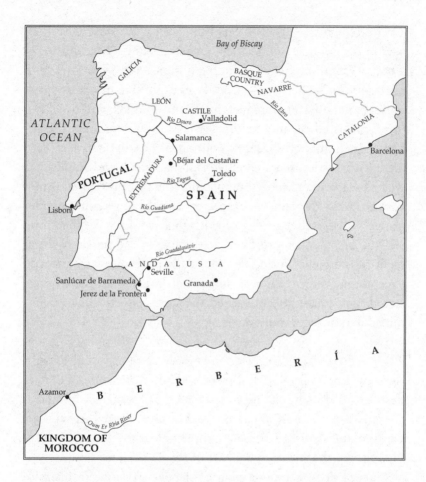

World]," most probably an interdiction aimed at Muslims and Jews who had recently converted to Catholicism. Such converts were euphemistically referred to as *New Christians*, and were often the target of discrimination in an empire that had become unified on the basis of a militant religiosity.[12]

The settlers were not marginal characters, vagabonds, or criminals bent on unleashing their social frustrations on American Indians. As the partial listing above shows, they comprised a veritable cross section of Spanish society. Of those who took part in the conquest of Mexico, an astonishing 11 percent were *letrados* (men of letters), including notaries and secretaries (and not counting other professionals like physicians and friars); more than a quarter were merchants and artisans; and roughly a third consisted of men of the sea (sailors, pilots, pages, etc.). Similarly, Francisco Pizarro's contingent at Cajamarca in Peru included notaries, merchants, working artisans, and soldiers, as well as seamen and more humble individuals of urban and rural backgrounds. Captains went to great lengths to recruit individuals who possessed a variety of skills that would make the group self-sufficient and more likely to survive in the harsh environment of the New World. The Florida expedition was hardly an exceptional venture. It was somewhat larger than the average expedition, but it still possessed the same assortment of determined and hopeful individuals.[13]

THE HIGHEST-RANKING members of the Florida expedition, rivaling even Narváez, were a handful of royal appointees destined to become the new aristocracy of Florida. Royal Treasurer Álvar Núñez Cabeza de Vaca and Captains Alonso del Castillo and Andrés Dorantes—three out of the four main protagonists in the story—were part of this exalted group.

Cabeza de Vaca was a man of slender physique in his midthirties. He hailed from Jerez de la Frontera, a parched but attractive Andalusian town about 50 miles due south of Seville. To this day Jerez is famous for its sweet wines (the English, not especially noteworthy for their faithful pronunciation of foreign names, rendered Jerez into "sherry"). Cabeza de Vaca's contemporaries were first struck by his amusing last name, meaning "cow's head," which nonetheless carried a ring of nobility in the sixteenth century. Cabeza de Vaca's extended family included such luminaries as the *maestro* Luis Cabeza de Vaca, who had been Charles's tutor during his Flemish days before his elevation to the Spanish throne and the holy Roman emperorship. This illustrious Cabeza de Vaca may well have helped his young relative gain access at court. But Álvar Núñez Cabeza de Vaca's most obvious role model was his paternal grandfather, Pedro de Vera Mendoza. This larger-than-life figure had led the conquest of the island of Gran Canaria in the 1480s, an episode that paved the way for Spain's conquests in the New World. Young Álvar became quite familiar with his famous forebear when the latter relocated to Jerez in old age. Time and again Álvar would invoke his grandfather's accomplishments in the Canaries as evidence of his family's service to the Spanish Crown.[14]

Cabeza de Vaca's ancestry may have been illustrious, but his circumstances growing up in Jerez were far from opulent. The household finances had taken a turn for the worse in the wake of the premature deaths of his father in 1506 and his mother in 1509, which left six youngsters to fend for themselves. The children were forced to leave home and move in with their maternal aunt. Cabeza de Vaca was the oldest son and must have been around eighteen when he and his siblings were orphaned. But by then he had started to blaze his own way in the world. Since he was twelve or even before then, he had worked for the dukes of Medina Sidonia, the most prestigious house of nobles in Andalusia, and had embarked on a distinguished military career. He must have been barely twenty-one when he enlisted with the Spanish forces fighting in Italy during the campaigns of 1511–1513. In 1520–1521, before he turned thirty, Cabeza de Vaca fought against the so-called Comuneros. The towns of Castile, tired of having their autonomy assailed by centralized rule, rose up to defend themselves. Cabeza de Vaca, siding with the Crown and the nobility against the rebels, helped put down the movement. Around this time, Cabeza de Vaca also got married to a woman from a *converso* family (a Jewish family recently converted to Catholicism) named María Marmolejo.[15]

We know little about the specific circumstances leading to Cabeza de Vaca's appointment as Royal Treasurer of the expedition to Florida. His powerful sponsors within the house of Medina Sidonia, the influential members of his own extended family, and fifteen years of distinguished military service surely made him an attractive choice. Although Narváez had great latitude in choosing the members of his expedition, there were a handful of royal appointees that he simply had to accept. It is likely that Narváez had little say in Cabeza de Vaca's appointment. What is certain is that the Royal Treasurer owed his primary allegiance not to Narváez but to the emperor. His main duties consisted of overseeing all economic transactions and making sure that the Crown received its rightful share of the profits.[16] As a royal treasurer, and therefore an extension of the Crown itself, Cabeza de Vaca had to be capable of challenging the authority of self-assured colonization entrepreneurs like Narváez.[17]

Captains Andrés Dorantes and Alonso del Castillo were nearly as prominent as Cabeza de Vaca. In the rigid hierarchy of early expeditions, these two men stood somewhat below the Royal Treasurer in that they did not oversee Narváez but rather were his partners and subsidiary captains. Socially, however, they were Cabeza de Vaca's equals. Andrés Dorantes came from the town of Béjar del Castañar in Old Castile. He was only in his mid-twenties but already bore a scar on his face from a wound that he had received during the Comunero rebellion. Like Cabeza de Vaca, Dorantes had fought on behalf of the king and against the townsfolk. His loyalty would not go unrewarded. While on a trip to Seville to visit the duke of Béjar in 1527, Dorantes found out about Narváez's projected expedition to Florida. He must

Coat of Arms of the House of Cabeza de Vaca. After Joseph
Pellicer de Tovar, *Genealogía de la noble y antigua casa de
Cabeza de Vaca sacada del teatro genealógico de los reyes,
grandes, títulos, y señores de vassallos de España.* Madrid,
1652. Courtesy of the Houghton Library, Harvard University.

have found considerable merit in the undertaking for, in short
order, he decided to enlist. Through the good offices of his influential host in Seville, Dorantes received from the emperor an appointment as captain of infantry of the Florida expedition.[18]

Alonso del Castillo, the last in this trio, had a more scholarly
background than Dorantes or Cabeza de Vaca. He was a native of
the city of Salamanca, home to Spain's foremost university. His father was a physician, a very respectable and coveted profession.
Castillo's social background and education at the University of

Salamanca would have all but guaranteed him a comfortable life in Spain. Several of his relatives already occupied city and municipal offices in major cities. Instead, he decided to seek his fortune in the New World. As many other aspiring Spaniards of substantial means, Castillo looked to America as a way to propel himself into the highest social and economic ranks. He sold a portion of his estate in Salamanca to buy arms and supplies, became a partner in Narváez's expedition, and, like Dorantes, secured an appointment as captain. Two decades later he would be described as "a caballero and one of the most socially prominent persons on the Narváez expedition." Undoubtedly, Castillo, no less than Cabeza de Vaca and Dorantes, wanted to expand his sterling pedigree to the New World and contribute with his assets, talents, and sense of noblesse oblige.[19]

All three were men of faith. They were pious adventurers whose belief in their Christian God would not waver. However, none of them had ever set foot in the New World.

ALONGSIDE THESE THREE caballeros, a microcosm of Spanish society was to travel to Florida. The expedition must have included a full complement of *letrados*, physicians, merchants, artisans, sailors, all the way down to lowly peasants seeking a fresh start. Five Franciscan brothers were to introduce the Indians to the mysteries of the Catholic faith. Their leader was Fray Juan Suárez, a New World veteran who had been among the "First Twelve" Franciscan missionaries dispatched to Mexico as early as 1524. With his appointment as "bishop of the Rio de las Palmas and Florida," he had reached the pinnacle of his profession. He was accompanied by at least one other member of the "First Twelve," a friar named Juan de Palos.[20]

The Florida expedition included women as well. Women were a fixture of early voyages of discovery and settlement. Ac-

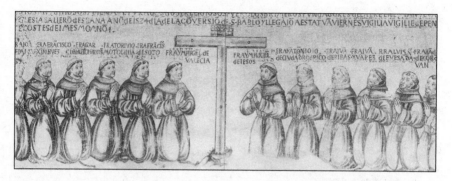

Friars Juan de Palos (first from left) and Juan Suárez (third from right) are the only likenesses of members of the Narváez expedition that have come to light. In this mural they are included among the "First Twelve" Franciscan friars who reached Mexico. Mural at the Sala de Profundis of the Monastery of San Miguel de Huejotzingo. Huejotzingo, Puebla, Mexico.

cording to one estimate, they comprised around 10 percent of all licenses issued to departing passengers from Seville during much of the sixteenth century. In certain years they accounted for as much as 20 percent and even close to 30 percent of all European migrants to the New World. The majority of these pioneering women were married to members of the expeditions, but unmarried women traveled too, including the daughters of families, female servants, and prostitutes.[21]

The lure of the Americas was all too evident for those women interested in marriage. In Spain there was an overabundance of women due to male migration and early death from war. According to the ambassador of the Republic of Venice, in the 1520s Seville appeared to be "very nearly under the control of women," many of whom earned their living in manly occupations like peonage, masonry, and roofing. The situation was the exact opposite in the Indies, where European women were notoriously scarce and greatly appreciated by affluent but lonesome conquistadors.[22]

Azamor, the prosperous and substantial north African port where Estebanico came from. From Georg Braun and Franz Hogenberg, *Civitates orbis terrarum*, volume 1. Cologne, 1572.

Not surprisingly, most women traveled to parts of the New World already settled by Europeans; they were far less likely to risk voyages of exploration and conquest headed for unknown lands. Some expedition captains refused to take females altogether. But Narváez was not among them. The first European women in Mexico had traveled with Narváez in the imposing armada that was to confront Cortés. In the Florida expedition there were ten women, all of whom were married and traveling with their husbands.[23]

ESTEBANICO, A BLACK slave, was the fourth and final protagonist in the story. He came from Azamor, a substantial coastal town of some 5,000 inhabitants in the kingdom of Morocco in northwest Africa. The people of Azamor spoke Arabic and were largely Muslim. A contemporary traveler described them as "civil and decently appareled," living at the mouth of the Oum Er Rbia River amidst fig orchards. Azamor was blessed by an extraordinary abundance of shad fish (shebbel or *clupea alosa*). Every year, fish sales brought in about 6,000 or 7,000 ducats to this Mediterranean town.[24]

It was precisely Azamor's wealth that attracted a powerful Portuguese armada in 1513 (an expedition that included a young Ferdinand Magellan). After taking possession of the town, the Portuguese began acquiring slaves and shipping them to the Iberian Peninsula. Azamor remained a fortified Portuguese outpost until 1541. Through the vagaries of the slaving business, Estebanico was taken to Spain and perhaps sold by Portuguese merchants in Seville's slave market. As his name implies—Esteban as in St. Stephen—this young man was forced to abjure Islam and convert to Christianity at some point during his early experience as a slave. His eventual purchaser was none other than Captain Andrés Dorantes.[25]

Estebanico's provenance from a racially mixed, prosperous town put him already on a higher plane than the slaves from the sub-Saharan interior. The latter were mostly black, whereas roughly half the slaves from *Berbería*—as this "more advanced" coastal region was known—were white and only one-quarter were black. Thus sixteenth-century Spaniards could not make any assumptions about the skin color of the slaves coming from Berbería. That is why Cabeza de Vaca described Estebanico somewhat convolutedly as a "black Arab from Azamor" (*negro alárabe, natural de Azamor*), a depiction that contains several important clues to his background and identity. He was a vivacious, outgoing, and curious young man with a remarkable facility for languages.[26]

African slaves in these early voyages of exploration were the chattel of their European masters. In other words, they could be punished, sold, or used in any way deemed appropriate. Any payments derived from their efforts would be pocketed by their owners. Their utter subordination meant that the danger and harsh living conditions that affected all expeditioners were worse for the slaves.

And yet by going to the New World in the company of conquerors, early Africans also enjoyed freedoms denied to their

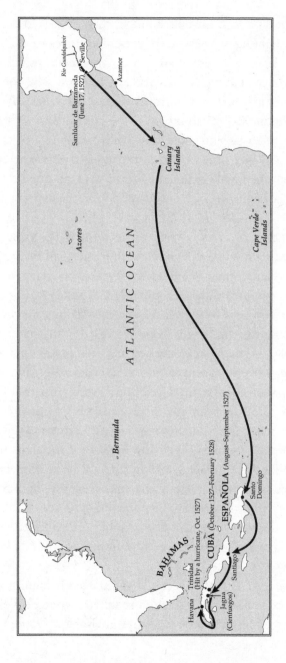

counterparts back in Europe. Some of them, enslaved because of their very fighting prowess, were permitted to bear arms and ride horses. Indeed, there are examples of African slaves who struck out on their own in the New World and led successful conquering expeditions in Mexico, Central America, Venezuela, Peru, and Chile. Without seeking to minimize the bleak reality of slavery, it is important to bear in mind that the lives of African slaves involved in voyages of discovery and conquest were markedly different from the highly regimented form of plantation slavery that would later define the peculiar institution in the new continent.[27]

NARVÁEZ'S SHIPS MUST have been partially loaded in Seville and then sailed downriver for 56 miles, all the way to the sea. The Guadalquivir is a tidal river with some dangerous shallow areas caused by the accumulation of sand. In those heady days it had come to resemble a long, meandering graveyard. As the transatlantic shipping volume increased in the sixteenth century, so too did the wrecks strewn along the river's course—thus rendering it even more difficult to navigate. Rotting, wooden carcasses served to remind pilots at every turn that many a happy venture had been cut short just as it was getting started or, worse, when it had nearly reached its final destination.[28]

It took two excruciatingly slow weeks for the ships to travel from Seville to the ocean; walking would have been faster, as one scholar has noted. The initial phase of the journey mercifully ended with the arrival at Sanlúcar de Barrameda, where the river met the sea. Narváez's fleet would have gathered at Sanlúcar to pass one final inspection, top off provisions, and board all passengers.[29]

Crossing the Atlantic Ocean in the sixteenth century was not an inconsequential undertaking. It required a good deal of preparation and endurance. It was always advisable to settle one's affairs permanently, as there might well be no return. Prior to departure, many passengers felt compelled to go to church to receive the sacraments of confession and communion, and to attain a state of grace because "a sea passage entailed mortal danger," according to one contemporary authority. Other travelers, more focused on their bodies than their souls, fasted or swallowed purgatives to empty their stomachs or, conversely, purchased chickens and pigs to have access to fresh meat during the passage. And yet, according to Antonio de Guevara, the experienced traveler and author of a guide entitled *Arte de marear*, most first-time passengers had but few inklings of the ordeal that lay ahead.[30]

The Florida expedition left the Spanish coast on June 17, 1527. The novelty of sea travel, the anticipation of life in another continent, and a natural curiosity for the vessels and their occupants would have made the eight- to ten-day journey to the Canary Islands bearable. Fleets headed for the New World normally stopped briefly at Gran Canaria or La Palma to restock with water, wood, live animals, and some other provisions.[31]

An entire month of open-ocean sailing across the Atlantic began when the ships departed the Canaries. By now the passengers would have had a very good idea of the level of endurance needed for the journey. The most aggravating factor was overcrowding. By our modern standards, sixteenth-century ships were appallingly small, measuring around 20 yards in length by 5 yards across by 2.7 yards of depth. All told, there were between 1,615 and 2,153 square feet of habitable space—roughly the surface area of a good-sized apartment. Within the confines of this space, some 100 to 120 human beings commingled day and night for weeks, using the most rudimentary latrines, and with no privacy at all except in the rarest of cases. On average, each person on board had a suffocating 1.8 square yards to himself. The luggage made the limited space more unbearable still. Travelers brought a variety of chests, boxes, and personal effects that inevitably ended up scattered all over the deck, cluttering every nook and cranny. Fights sometimes erupted when someone moved a chest just a few inches, unavoidably encroaching on a neighbor's area. Voyagers were also forced to share their precious space with numerous animals, some deliberately transported and others uninvited. Chicken coops abounded, and pigs, goats, sheep, cows, and horses were also included in these voyages. From a distance, the decks of some of these vessels must have looked like veritable floating farms. The uninvited guests were surely the worst, however—rats, fleas, and lice roamed freely through the ships and mingled with everyone on board, recognizing no distinctions of social rank.[32]

Overcrowding affected every single facet of life. Food and drink, for instance, were made available in a centralized, regimented fashion to all but the privileged few. Ordinary travelers could expect three square meals consisting mostly of water, wine, and hardtack (unleavened bread), with occasional meat and soup dishes. Unfortunately, the large number of mouths to feed put a premium on expediency rather than quality or flavor. Passengers found many reasons to complain. They noted the murkiness and smelliness of water; wine, even the cheap and watered-down kind, was always far more popular. The hardtack was dependably dry, blackened, rancid, and often bitten by rats and covered with cobwebs. Neither did the passengers have much praise for the salty, leathery, half-cooked meats that only increased the pangs of thirst. Polite eating manners were out of the question. Two, four, or more individuals shared big platters that were placed on the floor since there were no tables. Everyone took food liberally with his or her hands and passed around knives as necessary (conditions were not necessarily much better on land, as spoons and forks were just becoming widely used in

Europe, amid some skepticism. Objecting to the use of forks, one German preacher remarked that God "would not have given us fingers had he wanted us to use this instrument.").[33] An acerbic passenger left a vivid description of the method for feeding a crew over the Atlantic:

> With the sun already on high, I saw two of the said pages bring from below deck a certain bundle that they called tablecloths, arranging them in the waist of the ship . . . ; then they heaped on this table some small mountains of ruined hardtack, so that the hardtack on the tablecloths looked like heaps of dung in a farmer's field. . . . After this they put three or four large wooden platters on the table, filled with stringy beef joints, dressed with some badly cooked tendons. . . . In the twinkling of an eye, all the mariners arrived, saying "Amen," and seated themselves on the ground . . . one with his legs behind him, another sticking his legs forward; this one squatting; that one reclining. . . . And without waiting for grace to be said, they took out their knives . . . of diverse fashions, some made to kill pigs, others to flay lambs, others to cut purses, and they grabbed the poor bones in their hands, separating them from their nerves and sinews.[34]

The crowding was felt most acutely at night. The privileged few had cots and even beds, but the vast majority of passengers had to resign themselves to spending the night wrapped in simple blankets. With no fixed sleeping places, passengers lay down wherever they found reasonably level, unoccupied surfaces, inevitably much too close to other sleepers. In his traveling guide, Guevara advised readers to tolerate the proximity of others by pretending that everything had been a dream: the startling screams, the awful smells, even the unwanted sexual advances would vanish with the new day. In cases of extreme necessity, one could always opt to pay "good money" for the privilege of sleeping in a *ballestera* (crossbow holder), which at least was flat and somewhat more removed. It was always preferable to sleep on the deck, even if passengers were exposed to the elements and occasionally awakened by crew members trimming sails or changing shifts. Below deck the temperatures became infernal, and the overpowering odors that ascended from the depths of the ship's hold made every single night a wretched ordeal. Slaves were frequently forced to sleep below deck.[35]

AFTER A MONTH of such daily and nightly sufferings, it is no wonder that voyagers would greet the sighting of the first Caribbean islands with unrestrained and overwhelming joy. The Florida expedition first stopped at Española, where it remained for about a month and a half, from late July through September of 1527. The fleet must have pulled into Santo Domingo's excellent harbor. It is easy to imagine the passengers' sense of relief and wonderment when they were finally permitted to stagger out of the vessels, perhaps after some final bureaucratic delays, and meet the commotion created by their arrival in Santo Domingo.[36]

Narváez's objectives in Santo Domingo were limited to purchasing provisions and acquiring horses. Shipmasters must have scurried around town procuring specific items. In the meantime, passengers and crew members enjoyed their leisure. They walked around town exchanging news with the locals about relatives, friends, and acquaintances. These conversations inevitably veered toward the economic prospects in America and, just as inevitably, often ended in business and employment propositions. As the weeks went by, an astounding 140 men— nearly one out of every four expedition members—deserted.

They chose to remain at Española "because of the favors and promises that the men of that land made to them."[37]

There was some irony to this attrition. In his petition to the emperor, Narváez had offered to refrain from enlisting men from the Caribbean islands so as not to contribute to their further depopulation. Yet, far from depopulating the islands, he appeared unable to prevent his own men from staying in them.[38]

In hindsight, the 140 deserters were extremely fortunate, though of course they had no way of knowing what lay in store for those who continued on toward Florida. Those who stayed behind made their decisions based on a cold assessment of the economic potential of Española. During the month and a half that they stayed at Santo Domingo, the Florida expeditioners must have noticed the constant coming and going of vessels. Santo Domingo was the gateway to the New World and afforded a variety of provisioning and trading opportunities.

Some of Narváez's men must have also heard about the gold mines. Although the local Indians had been worked to death in the mines, a more resilient workforce consisting of African slaves had taken up their place. The transition had been disruptive and costly but, in the end, successful. An official report written in 1525 cheerfully noted that "more gold is now obtained than in earlier times." Dreams of gold lived on at Española.[39]

Other voyagers must have decided to skip Florida altogether after learning about the pearls. Española was the hub of a veritable pearl rush that extended all along the eastern coast of Venezuela, an area grandly known as "the pearl coast." Canoes carried slave-divers to the massive oyster beds in that area. The slaves were thrown overboard into the crystalline, blue waters with stones fastened to their shoulders plunging as deep as forty-nine to fifty-two feet and reemerging one minute later with pouches full of oysters. Each year some 26,000 pounds of pearls were obtained in Cubagua alone and then sold in Seville "on heaps," as if they were seeds.[40]

Finally, Española was thriving because of the sugar plantations. The first speck of land controlled by the Europeans in the New World, Española was now pioneering a formula that in time would revolutionize the entire continent and cause the enslavement of millions of Africans. A surgeon in Santo Domingo by the name of Gonzalo de Vellosa humbly launched this transformation in 1515–1516 by importing sugar masters from the Canary Islands and building the first commercially viable sugar mill of the Americas. The experiment turned out to be enormously successful. During the 1520s sugar mills sprouted all over the island along the Nigua, Nizao, and Ocoa rivers; by the 1530s there were no fewer than thirty-four mills in operation. Sugar production had not yet become an economic juggernaut, but it was already sufficiently promising that it may well have tempted some of Narváez's men into staying. Perhaps in the brownish, sweet residue left after squeezing the canes, some of Narváez's expeditioners went on to gain the riches that eluded their more adventurous and far less fortunate shipmates.[41]

FROM ESPAÑOLA THE fleet sailed to Cuba. Narváez intended to make some final arrangements in his home turf and then proceed immediately to his *adelantamiento* before the onset of winter. But his carefully laid plans were shattered by the natural elements.

During September and October 1527, at the height of the hurricane season, the fleet sailed unconcerned along the southern coast of Cuba. It traveled first to Santiago, Cuba's capital and principal settlement on the eastern side. There Narváez continued his provisioning work, relying on a network of associates, acquaintances, and friends.

Narváez must have been delighted to receive an offer of additional supplies from a "gentleman" named Vasco Porcallo. Vasco Porcallo was easily one of the richest and most prominent men on the island. Indeed, rumors of Porcallo's fabulous wealth had already (or would soon) reach the Spanish court. Just two years later, in 1529, the Queen of Spain (Charles's wife) expressly solicited a loan from Porcallo to fight a series of Turkish and Moorish incursions on the coast of Andalusia. An offer to the Florida expedition coming from such a distinguished figure would have constituted a vote of confidence and a most welcome injection of resources at a time when the venture had suffered some setbacks. The only problem was that the provisions had to be retrieved from the town of Trinidad on the western side of the island at a distance of about 280 miles from Santiago. The entire fleet started sailing west, but about halfway to Trinidad Narváez decided to stop at a port called Cabo de Santa Cruz. Two ships were sent ahead to receive the promised victuals.[42]

Unbeknownst to the expeditioners, somewhere in the Caribbean Sea or the Gulf of Mexico, billowing clouds and localized thunderstorms began to clash and combine with each other, and this mass of clouds, rain, and wind started to rotate around a low-pressure center due to the earth's spinning motion. In the course of two or three weeks the wind must have picked up steadily, until the system developed into a tropical storm and finally a hurricane. And it drifted toward Cuba.[43]

Narváez's two lead vessels arrived at Trinidad on a Thursday. The next morning the weather began to turn bad, with occasional squalls and high surf. Since the town was located about 3 miles inland, Vasco Porcallo, Juan Pantoja (one of the vessel captains), and some men went ashore to receive the provisions. Cabeza de Vaca remained aboard in command of the two ships. He waited all of Friday and part of Saturday as the storms continued to increase in intensity. The pilots were worried because the anchorage was poor and exposed and the weather was not letting up. Sometime in the course of Saturday morning a canoe reached Cabeza de Vaca's ship; a messenger carried a letter requesting him to go to town to oversee the transfer of provisions. The Royal Treasurer refused to move, explaining that he could not leave his post under the circumstances. By noon the canoe had returned, this time with a horse and another letter urging Cabeza de Vaca's immediate presence. At last Cabeza de Vaca relented and headed toward Trinidad.[44]

Then the hurricane hit.

The great majority of the Florida expeditioners had never experienced such a towering, rotating giant, shuffling erratically from place to place and smothering everything in its path. Because hurricanes require tropical heat and high humidity to form, they do not occur anywhere in the Mediterranean or the northeastern Atlantic. Columbus was the first to report one during his second voyage. European residents of Española and Cuba had some encounters with them in the early decades, adopting the Taíno word for them, *hurakan*, meaning "big wind."[45]

Cabeza de Vaca could not hide his astonishment:

At this time the sea and the storm began to swell so much that there was no less tempest in the town than at sea, because all the houses and churches blew down, and it was necessary for us to band together in groups of seven or eight men, our arms locked with one another, in order to save ourselves from being carried away by the wind. We were as fearful of being killed by walking under the trees as among the houses, since the storm was so great that even the trees, like the houses, fell. In this great storm and continual danger we walked all night without finding an area or place where we could be safe for even half an hour.[46]

Throughout the night, the natives of Trinidad chanted and played bells and flutes and tambourines to appease Guabancex, the female spirit that "moves the wind and water and tears down the houses and uproots the trees." Interestingly, Spaniards, not unlike the natives, understood hurricanes as manifestations of the Devil. In the wake of two devastating hurricanes in 1508 and 1509, Española residents set out to protect themselves by building stone churches endowed with large crosses. As one early chronicler explains, "devout Christians affirm, and experience has shown, that after the Most Holy Sacrament has been placed on the churches and monasteries of this city [Santo Domingo] and other towns of this island, the hurricanes have ceased."[47]

The following day, on Monday, Cabeza de Vaca and about thirty survivors of the expedition who had remained in Trinidad went to the shore to find out what had happened to the ships. There were only a few traces of them at the anchorage: some buoys but nothing more. Search parties moving along the coast found a rowboat atop a tree close to 1 mile away. At a distance of more than 25 miles, they recovered two bodies so bludgeoned that they were impossible to identify. They also found a cape and some blanket rags. All in all, that day the Florida expedition lost two ships, twenty horses, and sixty men to the strange ways of the New World. The God-fearing survivors could only interpret this violent storm as a divine warning, an unmistakable omen.[48]

CHAPTER 3

Landfall

THE HURRICANE LEFT THE FLORIDA EXPEDITION in disarray. The departure date had to be postponed to replace the lost ships and replenish the dwindling colonists. Meanwhile, Narváez had a brewing insurrection on his hands. According to Cabeza de Vaca, "The men . . . became so terrified by what had happened [in Cuba] that they greatly feared embarking again in winter, and they begged the Governor to spend it there." Such a delay would have constituted a considerable financial setback. But Narváez ultimately relented because he, too, needed more time. Ever since the one-eyed Captain-General had begun raising his armada in Seville, he had been unable to find a pilot familiar with Florida and the northern Gulf Coast. It was no small hindrance. As any experienced explorer knew well, "a pilot is to the ship what the soul is to the human body." Without one, the entire venture would be in grave danger.[1]

Experienced pilots were quite simply indispensable in an age when the contours of a new continent were just becoming visible to Europeans. Aided only by basic compasses and charts, they navigated through treacherous waters relying on sea lore and their own painstakingly acquired experience. Pilots had to be able to recognize coastlines, read the weather for signs of impending storms, and learn to estimate depth by only looking at the color of the sea: deep-blue was safe; light-blue meant a sandy bottom but not much depth; brown was the ominous color of coral. Their worth was all too evident in the enormous salaries they commanded, the size of which kept increasing throughout the sixteenth century.[2] Yet good pilots were notoriously scarce. During his stay in Seville, Narváez had been unable to locate a pilot familiar with Florida and the Gulf Coast. The situation was not better at Española, and the Captain-General was forced to leave the island empty-handed. Cuba offered a final opportunity. Over the winter of 1527–1528, Cabeza de Vaca stayed with the ships at the spacious and protected port of Jagua (present-day Cienfuegos) on the southern coast of Cuba, while Narváez traveled about looking for a suitable navigator.[3]

When the Captain-General rejoined his party in February, he brought along a man by the name of Diego Miruelo. Miruelo had a reputation as "a very fine pilot of the northern Gulf coast." Most importantly, he was reputed to have been to the Rio de las Palmas. Little is known about Miruelo and about the true extent of his experience as a pilot, but he had quite likely traveled through some portions of the Gulf Coast and could claim some competence. Unfortunately, as Narváez would soon discover, Miruelo's skills as a pilot were inadequate to the mission ahead.[4]

NARVÁEZ'S CHARGE WAS to settle the land "between the Rio de las Palmas and Florida." Florida constituted the northern end of this region. By the 1520s it was still an enigma. Only a handful of European fleets had actually visited this flat, subtropical peninsula; even these early explorers had seen it mostly from the decks of their ships. Spanish slavers operating in the Bahamas were among the first to drift into Florida, as the scarcity of natives on the islands propelled them to extend their activities farther west. Some of these traffickers were surely the first Europeans to behold Florida.[5]

The glory of Florida's discovery belongs to a veteran explorer named Juan Ponce de León. In 1513 he set out to discover an island called "Bimini" thought to exist north of the Bahamas. Some early chroniclers claim that Ponce de León was looking for the "fountain of youth," although he never said so explicitly. Nonetheless, such a quest would not have been unthinkable. Early explorers cast off into distant lands, driven by gold but also by a wellspring of legends that included mermaids, Amazon warriors, pygmies, the Seven Cities of Cíbola, the mines of King Solomon, the rich kingdom of Prester John, and many other wondrous sites and creatures.

Ponce de León found neither "Bimini" nor the *fons juventutis*, but he did reach Florida's Atlantic coast somewhere near what is now Cape Canaveral. Since this first official sighting occurred during the *Pascua Florida*, or "Flowery Festival" (as Easter was known), Ponce de León called this new land *La Florida*. His three ships then sailed southward, surveying the peninsula to present-day Miami and around the Florida Keys. Other Europeans, particularly slavers, must have made their way there in the 1510s and 1520s. But none of them had the authorization, or the inclination, to plant permanent settlements. Narváez's enterprise was intended to establish three forts and two towns somewhere in this area.[6]

But it was not Florida proper that Narváez was after, but rather the riches farther south. Narváez's first objective was the Rio de las Palmas. This river, today's Rio Soto la Marina, runs parallel to the Rio Grande some 125 miles to the south. It served as the demarcation between Narváez's territory to the north and the province of Pánuco to the south. In the early

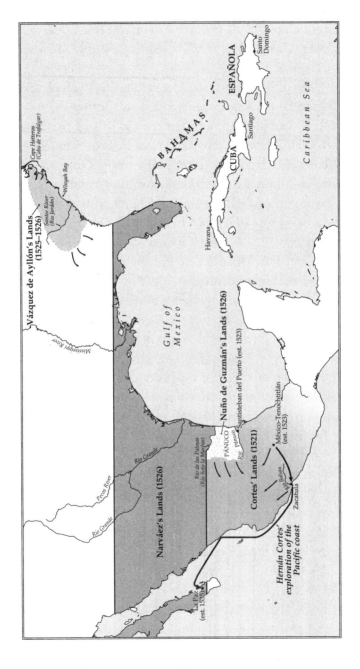

1520s, Pánuco had been the object of intense rivalry, as it was both well populated and easily accessible by sea—in other words, immensely appealing to anyone involved in the slaving business. The Rio de las Palmas constituted an obvious gateway into this economically attractive area. The river itself was rumored to contain fabulous riches, despite the fact that earlier explorers had found nothing of the kind. It also had strategic value. The river is navigable and constitutes a visible geographic feature on the Gulf Coast. Its delta had been considered an auspicious site for a European settlement since the first Europeans arrived. Exploring and controlling the Rio de las Palmas was Narváez's top priority.[7]

Narváez would also have to decide what other areas to explore and colonize within the lands apportioned to him. It was an immense area. According to a 1527 report that sought to clarify the political divisions of North America, Narváez's *adelantamiento* included everything between the Rio de las Palmas and the northern boundary of Florida *going west all the way to the other sea.* This expansive interpretation amounts to a swath of land measuring more than 470 miles from north to south and 2,500 miles across from the Atlantic to the Pacific, encompassing portions of today's Florida, Georgia, Alabama, Mississippi, Louisiana, Texas, Tamaulipas, Nuevo León, Coahuila, Durango, Chihuahua, New Mexico, Sinaloa, Sonora, Arizona, and Baja California. Spaniards of the 1520s knew practically nothing about these territories, but they already had inklings of their enormity. The 1527 report ruefully implied that the Emperor had been much too generous with Narváez as it would take "three princes, each of them with a large armada" to subdue and rule this immense space. In fact, the area in question is four times larger than Spain.[8]

But Narváez was not alone in laying claim to the territories north of Mexico. Well-connected, resourceful, and ambitious conquistadors were already engaged in a headlong race for the occupation and control of large portions of North America. At the top of the list of potential rivals was the richest man in the New World and Narváez's old nemesis, Hernán Cortés. As early as May 1522, an exultant Cortés had written to Charles V informing him that he had reached the Pacific Ocean: "and I have already begun building ships and brigantines to explore all the secrets of this coast that is ninety leagues from here [Mexico City] and which undoubtedly will reveal marvelous things." Cortés established a shipyard on the Pacific coast and started launching fleets to the north that would eventually reach Baja California and other areas that Narváez could claim. It seemed as though the two men were destined to clash once again in the distant Pacific coast.[9]

In addition to the looming threat of Cortés, Narváez faced two fierce competitors on either side of his *adelantamiento* on the Atlantic side. To the north, Narváez had to contend with none other than the *licenciado* Lucas Vázquez de Ayllón, the mediator sent by the *audiencia* of Santo Domingo to prevent a showdown between Narváez and Cortés in Mexico. The ubiquitous Vázquez de Ayllón was a man of "great learning and gravity" for whom twenty-four hours was not enough time in the day for his multiple occupations, beginning with his colorful private life. Although married, he had one or more illegitimate children and quite possibly kept a neighbor's wife in his house as a concubine. Beyond his romantic pursuits, Vázquez de Ayllón owned a sugar plantation and was also an enthusiastic participant in the slave trade. He sponsored slaving expeditions to the Bahamas, but his ships were so poorly provisioned that many of the captives died in transit.[10]

Vázquez de Ayllón's interest in North America stemmed from this last facet of his career. One of his slaving expeditions drifted far to the northeast, eventually reaching the coast of South Carolina. This serendipitous discovery enabled Vázquez de Ayllón to travel to Spain and request a patent to explore and colonize this region. In the summer of 1526, when Narváez was still lobbying in the Spanish court, the *licenciado* sailed to the coast of America with approximately 600 colonists. That set the stage for a head-on collision with Narváez's future settlements in Florida. There was no love lost between the two leaders. The confrontation was averted only because Vázquez de Ayllón became ill and died in October 1526. Factional disputes following the *licenciado's* death eventually compelled everyone to abandon the settlement.[11]

Narváez faced a far more significant threat to the south of his *adelantamiento*, in the province of Pánuco. Pánuco had attracted powerful figures since the early 1520s. In 1525, two years before Narváez embarked on his own expedition, the Crown had appointed an independent-minded governor of Pánuco named Nuño de Guzmán. Reputed to be a great villain, Guzmán arrived at Santiesteban del Puerto, Pánuco's only non-Indian settlement, with a head start of more than a year over Narváez. A drab community of perhaps sixty or seventy Spaniards, Santiesteban del Puerto was at the time Europe's northernmost foothold on the continent, and an excellent base for further exploration. Guzmán began his tenure by exploring the famous Rio de las Palmas.[12]

Guzmán's subsequent career reveals how much of a risk he posed to Narváez. In the early 1530s, he would go on to conquer the northwest coast of Mexico all the way to Sinaloa and Sonora while maintaining an iron grip over Pánuco. He then attempted to join his two coastal domains into one single territorial and political entity stretching from one coast to the other. Guzmán was a serious threat.[13]

HAVING SPENT THE winter in Cuba, the expeditioners resumed their journey in February 1528. But they ran into trouble almost immediately. Only three or four days after the expedition set sail from the port of Jagua, the new pilot, Miruelo, revealed worrying signs of incompetence when the ships began running aground in the archipelago of Canarreo. Comprised of some 350 verdant islets in the Gulf of Batabanó to the southwest of Cuba, Canarreo is surrounded by a treacherous maze of reefs, shallows, and jagged rocks. Navigating these shallows was a nightmare for shipmasters and pilots, and Miruelo was not up to the task. "And we were in this predicament for fifteen days, the keels of the ships frequently touching bottom," Cabeza de Vaca writes, "after which time a storm caused by the south wind brought so much water into the shallows that we were able to get out, although not without great danger." Embarrassingly, the expedition was about to meet its end right at Cuba's doorstep.[14]

The problems continued. At Guaniguanico a storm overtook the fleet. "[We] were nearly shipwrecked," recounts Cabeza de Vaca. At Cabo de Corrientes, the expedition encountered another tempest that lasted for three days. After rounding Cape San Antón, Cuba's westernmost tip, the fleet sailed upwind along Cuba's northern coast, where it was caught by yet another storm before entering Havana's harbor sometime in late February or March. Many explorers feared that God was bent on destroying the fleet, citing as proof the hurricane, the shallows of Canarreo, and the three consecutive storms. Everyone, but especially the pilot Miruelo, must have felt a sense of enormous relief upon reaching port.[15]

In early spring of 1528, Narváez's reconfigured expedition finally headed toward the mainland. Their destination was the critical Rio de las Palmas. During their passage across the Gulf of Mexico, Miruelo's skill was put to the test once again—this time with disastrous results. After several days of sailing, the pilots saw land and convinced themselves that they were close to the Rio de las Palmas, when in fact the expedition had drifted only to present-day Tampa Bay on the west coast of Florida. They were still within Narváez's enormous *adelantamiento*, but at the wrong end. Miruelo had misjudged the fleet's location by more than 900 miles. It was a dramatic error with deadly consequences.

Miruelo's lack of skill may have been partly to blame for this colossal mistake, but so too were the limitations of sixteenth-century navigation, coupled with the peculiar challenges posed by the Gulf of Mexico.

In the sixteenth century, the basic method of ocean navigation was "dead reckoning." Pilots steered ships from an origination point or "fix" to a new position by estimating the direction and distance traveled. Any point on the globe could be specified by means of only direction and distance. To keep track of direction, navigators used a thirty-two-point magnetic compass. To judge the distance traveled, pilots estimated the speed of the ship by simply looking at the passing bubbles on the sea. During the Age of Discovery this disarmingly simple system was used with accuracy to negotiate even long ocean passages. Dead-reckoning navigation, for instance, enabled Columbus to sail four times from Spain to the Caribbean and back.[16]

Dead-reckoning navigation, in turn, was made possible by a new type of chart known as a portolan. Invented in the thirteenth century, the portolan chart caused a nautical revolution, first in the Mediterranean and later in the Atlantic. Unlike medieval mappaemundi with their fanciful renderings of land masses and distances, portolan charts are incredibly accurate. One can gain a sense of their accuracy by comparing conventional maps of the sixteenth century, which often exaggerate the length of the Mediterranean by nearly twenty degrees (a problem traceable to

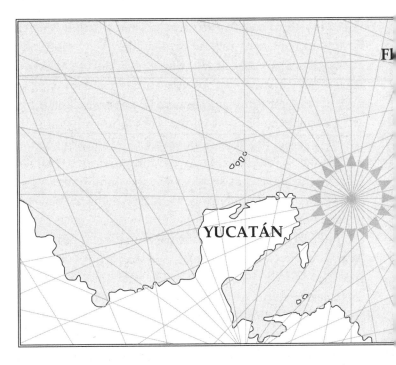

Ptolemy), with portolan charts, for which the comparable error seldom exceeds *one* degree.[17]

Intended for real, working seamen, portolan charts include only relevant geographic details like coastlines, islands, rivers, and mountains. But their most visually striking and useful feature is the series of lines bisecting the charts. These lines were the lifeblood of sixteenth-century navigators. Each one represents what pilots called a rutter (*derrotero* in Spanish) or technically a rhumb line—a path defined by a fixed compass direction. These were the lines that pilots strove to follow as they steered the ships through the oceans. Portolan charts thus gave pilots information about the distance between point A and point B, the precise direction that they needed to follow, and indications about any prominent geographic features along the way; all they needed to

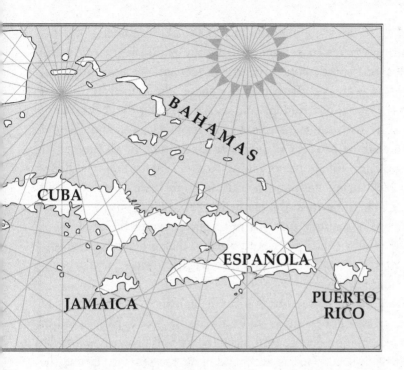

know, nothing more and nothing less. Crucially, portolan charts do not depend on latitudes or longitudes. Indeed, virtually no portolan charts contained such measurements prior to 1500. Moreover, they do not require the use of declination tables or any additional conversions or calculations, as these charts were drawn on the basis of the magnetic, rather than the true, north. Simply by maintaining a course with a magnetic compass and keeping track of the distance traveled on a portolan chart, an illiterate pilot—and roughly one out of four pilots in the sixteenth century was still unable to write his own name—could steer an expedition skillfully and safely to its destination.[18]

Like most pilots of his time, Miruelo must have navigated by the tried-and-true method of dead reckoning. It is entirely possible that Miruelo did not know the latitude (let alone the longitude) of the Rio de las Palmas and lacked the ability to determine his position except by reference to familiar land features. In the 1520s only some pilots were able to navigate by *alturas*, that is, by using a cross-staff to measure the angle formed by the sun and the horizon at midday and then correcting this "altitude of the sun" with tables of solar declinations. This method would have enabled Miruelo to pinpoint his latitude at all times. But the practical difficulties of taking an accurate reading on a heaving deck, using the published declination tables correctly, and being able to perform the mathematical calculations to reach an estimate of latitude put this procedure beyond the abilities of many pilots of the 1520s. And besides, this difficult exercise was pointless because dead-reckoning navigation was generally accurate and reliable.[19]

To go from Havana to the Rio de las Palmas, all Miruelo had to do was follow a rutter and estimate his speed, plotting all of this information on a chart to keep track of his progress across the Gulf of Mexico. That is all. Standing at the port of Havana, he would easily have imagined the circular Gulf Coast as an immense clock. Directly to the north, at 12:00 o'clock, lies Florida. The Rio de las Palmas is located due west at 9:00 o'clock. Yucatán lies to the southwest at 7:00 o'clock. Miruelo must have aimed his compass west at the Rio de las Palmas or somewhat north of it.[20]

Unfortunately for Miruelo, sailing from Havana to the Rio de las Palmas also meant that the ships had to brave the full force of the Gulf Stream, the fastest ocean current in the world.

The Gulf Stream enters the Gulf of Mexico from the south, in the opening between Cuba and the Yucatán Peninsula, and, after circling the Gulf, exits through the Florida Straits. The power of the Gulf Stream is staggering. It is equivalent to nearly 2,000 Mississippi Rivers flowing together (1.06 billion cubic feet per second), advancing through the ocean like an immense snake of warm water. It carries with it plants, fish, debris, and vessels at speeds that can top 100 miles in a day, or about 4 knots. At the Florida Straits the speed of the Gulf Stream ranges between 1.5 and 2.5 knots, depending on the time of year. It invariably affects the speed and direction of sailing vessels.[21]

In the 1520s European pilots were just getting to know this powerful ocean current. When Ponce de León's expedition met the Gulf Stream in 1513, the pilots were startled to realize that their ships were actually driven back even though they had a favorable wind. Two ships close to the shore had to drop anchors to stay in place, but a brigantine that found no bottom was carried out of sight. The Gulf Stream kept surprising pilots for decades. In 1565, thirty years after the Narváez expedition, an English merchant named John Hawkins navigating on the Cape of Florida suddenly ran into the Gulf Stream: "We felt little or none [of the current] till we fell with the cape, and then felt such a current, that bearing all sailes against the same, yet were driven backe againe a great pace." The Gulf Stream was fully charted only in the eighteenth century.[22]

Miruelo could only have had a very limited understanding of this current. Certainly no one at the time would have known just how much of a factor the Gulf Stream would be on the passage he was contemplating, as previous expeditions had taken more roundabout routes skirting the Gulf Coast. Because the Gulf Stream flows in a northwest to southeast direction as it exits the Gulf of Mexico, Narváez's ships would have run almost perfectly against it. The first effect would have been to dramatically reduce the fleet's speed over the ground, protracting the sailing time and giving the impression that the vessels had traveled a far greater distance than they had covered. If the ships were beset by light airs or headwinds, they would have actually been dragged backward by the current.

It is not clear how many days elapsed between the expedition's departure from Havana and its first sighting of land. But the pilots were clearly satisfied that they had sailed long enough to cross the entire Gulf of Mexico, when in fact they had traveled perhaps a third of that distance.

Just as importantly, the Gulf Stream would have pushed the ship to the east even if the pilots believed that they were following a more westerly course. The compass needles may have pointed to the west or a little north from there, but the powerful ocean current would have made the ships drift eastward in the direction of Florida.[23]

Narváez's party first saw the mainland on April 12, 1528. Believing that they were relatively near but to the right of the Rio de las Palmas, the pilots turned the ships to the left as they approached the coast and began looking for familiar geographic features. What they saw must have been unsettling. The coast on the starboard side seemed to run north instead of south, and the sun set on the sea rather than on land, as it would have occurred at the mouth of the Rio de las Palmas. Undoubtedly the pilots noticed these oddities, but probably dismissed them initially because judging the overall shape and direction of any coast is impossible at a single glance.

Even if Miruelo and the other navigators were seriously concerned, they would have been likely to keep the full extent of their consternation to themselves. They had already embarrassed themselves in the Canarreo shallows, after all, and could ill-afford any further loss of confidence on the part of Narváez. And they had the facts on their side. They could be certain only of the two cardinal elements of dead-reckoning navigation: direction and distance. They had traveled long enough to cross the Gulf of Mexico, and in the right direction. The Rio de las Palmas simply *had to be* farther up along the coast.

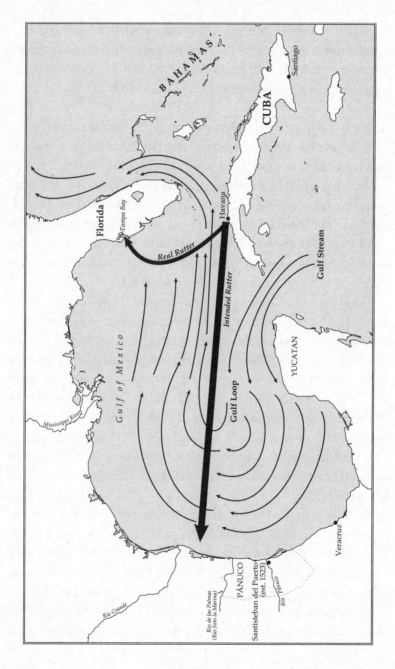

And so Miruelo and his fellow pilots made a bold and ultimately tragic proclamation. They declared "the Pánuco coast" not to be more than 10 or 15 leagues (30 to 45 miles) ahead of them. At that moment, they sealed the expedition's fate.[24]

AFTER THE FIRST sighting of land, the fleet spent two more days sailing alongside the coast, until it came upon a shallow bay, unsuitable as a port, but where the expeditioners spotted an Indian village. The settlement consisted mostly of ordinary thatched huts. Across the bay was an island that was also inhabited. The Royal Comptroller Alonso Enríquez went there, "and he called to the Indians, who came and were with him a considerable amount of time, and by means of exchange they gave him fish and some pieces of venison."[25]

On April 15, Narváez decided to have the colonists disembark. The ships pulled up as close to the shore as possible, and the sea-weary passengers began making their way to the land in small rowboats. The group had been significantly weakened in the course of the voyage from Havana. They had set forth with eighty horses, but nearly half of them had been unable to withstand the storms and died. The forty-two remaining horses were now so feeble and sick that they could hardly be mounted or used effectively. The Europeans would have to do without their most decisive and lethal military advantage over the natives.

But the horses were not needed. At the sight of the approaching ships the natives had prudently decided to evacuate. The explorers were able to wander freely through the dwellings. They found mostly fishing nets, but they did turn up one rattle made of gold, which must surely have been an encouraging sign.

Narváez lost no time in claiming the land for Spain and for himself. Even though the expeditioners did not know their exact location, at least they were certain to be within Narváez's enormous *adelantamiento*, somewhere between Florida and the Rio de las Palmas. As Cabeza de Vaca recounts, "[Narváez] raised the standard on Your Majesty's behalf and took possession of the land in Your royal name and presented his orders and was obeyed as governor just as Your Majesty commanded." For their part, the other high-ranking officers presented their own royal orders before Narváez, and he promised to obey them. Had there been natives on hand to witness the curious ceremony taking place in their own village, they would have been thoroughly mystified.[26]

After establishing a camp, the arrivals turned to exploring their surroundings. Over the following two weeks they mounted two reconnaissance expeditions. On their first foray, the marching Spaniards went north for much of the day, presumably following the coast, until, in the late afternoon, they stumbled on "a very large bay that seemed to us to go far inland"—Tampa Bay in all likelihood. The sight of this enormous body of water must have been as beautiful as it was disorienting. No European map contained any indication or reference to a large bay close to the Rio de las Palmas.[27]

The explorers returned to camp to share the news of their finding. Some days later, the reconnaissance party returned to the large bay and began rounding it. This time the Europeans surprised a group of Indians and took four of them. The captives ended up guiding the strangers to their village, which was also on the bay about 12 miles ahead. As the visitors seemed especially interested in maize, the natives showed them a cornfield that was not yet ready to be picked.

This first contact was volatile, with elements of coercion and cooperation, but ultimately resulted in a serious altercation. The bay Indians were in possession of "many crates belonging to

Castilian merchants, and in each one of them was the body of a dead man, and the bodies were covered with painted deer hides." They had clearly come from a shipwreck, as Narváez's men also found pieces of shoes, linen cloth, iron, and headdresses seemingly from New Spain. The Indians had evidently treated the deceased Europeans with great respect, carefully wrapping them in valuable painted skins. But Fray Juan Suárez, the would-be bishop of the Rio de las Palmas and Florida, quickly concluded that the Devil had inspired this idolatry and had the crates and the bodies burned. These outsiders had become downright abusive.[28]

The Indians of the large bay also possessed some gold pieces. Upon questioning, a laborious and uncertain task because there were no translators, the natives said that "very far away from there, there was a province called Apalachee in which there was much gold, and they made signs to indicate that there were very great quantities of everything we held in esteem." It is almost certain that the Indians were embellishing the truth in hopes that the intruders would leave.[29]

The explorers could see for themselves that the bay was poor and sparsely populated, so the mention of a rich indigenous province, perhaps another Aztec empire, inevitably piqued their interest. The leaders of the expedition now had to make a decision: They could go back to the ships to look for a more promising area to settle, or they could pursue this lead and march toward Apalachee.

Narváez did not hesitate. At camp he called aside the highest-ranking members of the expedition—the Royal Treasurer Cabeza de Vaca, Fray Juan Suárez, the comptroller, the chief inspector of mines, a mariner, and a notary. To this small group, the Governor revealed his intention to divide the expedition in two. All able-bodied men and horses would proceed on foot, going inland at times but keeping parallel to the coast until they reached the Rio de las Palmas. In the meantime, the ships would sail straight to the mouth of the river to wait for the overland party; only crew members and women would travel on the vessels.

It was a bold plan but not an outrageous one, given the claims the pilots had made about the location of the fleet with regard to the Rio de las Palmas. Certainly, it wouldn't be the first time such a plan had been used—other expeditions had resorted to this maneuver. Narváez himself had done so in Cuba. As the column led by Narváez had cut a swath from east to west through the middle of the island, a brigantine had sailed along the north coast while some canoes commanded by Diego Velázquez explored the south coast. This three-pronged advance proved very helpful as the ships carried provisions and provided intelligence, facilitating the work of the marching column. Fifteen years later, Narváez was proposing the same strategy as a way of surveying his new *adelantamiento*.[30]

Within the small group, a clear majority supported the Governor's plan. Fray Juan Suárez spoke in its favor, arguing that by keeping close to the coast it would be impossible for the land party to miss the river and a certain port that Miruelo knew existed nearby. The Pánuco coast could not be more than 30 or 45 miles away, according to the pilots. Suárez also reminded everyone of the many calamities that had befallen the expedition while at sea. Going back on board, he reasoned, would be tantamount to "tempting God." He was through with sea voyages: with the image of the crates stuffed with dead bodies still fresh in his mind, Suárez preferred to continue on foot. The comptroller, the chief inspector of mines, and the sailor also agreed with Narváez. They were either too tempted by Apalachee or too wary to go back to the ships.[31]

But there were dissenters as well. The notary quite sensibly observed that the land contingent would run a grave risk by letting the ships go without first identifying a secure port to which all could return. The land party would be literally cutting itself loose from its only means of return to the Spanish-controlled areas. Cabeza de Vaca was more adamant still, according to his own account. He echoed the notary's reluctance to leave the ships without first having established a secure port, but his concerns went further. The pilots were unsure about their whereabouts, he pointed out, and the horses were in such weakened condition that they could not be used in any hostile encounters with the Indians. Moreover, the expedition lacked interpreters and therefore had no certain information about the land that they were about to enter. Finally, Cabeza de Vaca pointed out that the expedition was running out of provisions: he estimated that each man could at most get a ration of no more than a pound of hardtack and another of salt pork.[32]

Cabeza de Vaca's is the only account of this gathering, and he wrote years later with the benefit of hindsight. Given what became of the expedition, it would have been very much in his interest to cast himself as the voice of reason in this decisive argument. Nonetheless, it is likely that either he or others did raise these points, and presumably they were discussed at some length.[33]

But in the end Narváez prevailed. The Governor was a skilled soldier, a veteran of the New World, and a commanding presence supported by a majority. The riches of the New World were there for the taking, but they were destined for the intrepid sort. Hadn't Cortés shown as much in Mexico? Narváez was determined to follow his star to Apalachee, even if he had to alienate his Royal Treasurer to do so.

Narváez ordered the men to pack their belongings and procure as much food as possible. He also saw an opportunity to shame his Royal Treasurer in public. In the presence of others, Narváez told Cabeza de Vaca to stay and take charge of the ships since he "objected so much and feared the inland expedition." That would have been a practical division of labor, but Cabeza de Vaca could not accept the implication of cowardice. He could not bear such an affront, and, as Cabeza de Vaca would later lament, "I preferred risking my life to placing my honor in jeopardy."[34]

The married women also opposed Narváez's plan. They would have to part with their husbands and face an uncertain destiny, fending for themselves on the ships. One of the ten women approached the Governor and flatly told him that he should not lead the men inland. She said that back in Spain, a Moorish woman from Hornachos had predicted that neither Narváez nor the others would ever escape from the land, and "if one of them were ever to come out, God would perform great miracles through him, but that she believed that those who escaped would be few or none at all." The woman on Narváez's expedition was so persuaded of the divination she had heard that she went so far as to advise her fellow women travelers to give up on their land-bound husbands and even urged them to seek protection immediately among the crew members, who would remain on the ships with them.[35]

The Governor felt compelled to respond. Narváez stated that those who entered the land with him would indeed need to fight "many strange peoples" and even conceded that many of the expeditioners might die. But he also expressed his conviction that those who remained would enjoy good fortune and would become very rich.[36]

With their nerves somewhat frayed, the members of the land contingent said their last goodbyes to those on the ships, never to see each other again. Some 300 Europeans, a sprinkling of Africans, and forty skinny horses became stranded in a completely alien world.

CHAPTER 4

Walking Through Florida

NARVÁEZ AND HIS MEN VENTURED INLAND, confident that Pánuco was no more than 30 or 45 miles away. After rounding Tampa Bay, they headed directly north. The Florida interior must have appeared to them like yet another kind of sea; the terrain was flat, endless, and, except for occasional rivers and marshes, mostly featureless. In every direction, the verdant expanse stretched as far as the eye could see. For two weeks the explorers walked through this enormous limestone platform covered in greenery. "During this entire time we did not find a single Indian," Cabeza de Vaca reported, "nor did we see a single house or village. And at the end we came to a river that we crossed by swimming because it had a very strong current." It took them one entire day to cross the river.[1]

Suddenly the long Florida peninsula had turned into a blind alley and a cruel irony: almost within sight of Spanish-controlled territory and yet so far from it. The tip of the peninsula lies barely 90 miles away from Cuba. On clear days it is even possible to make out the shape of the island just above the horizon. But crossing the strait was impossible without ships. The closest European outpost on the mainland itself was Santiesteban del Puerto in the province of Pánuco. To get there by land, Narváez's party would have to follow an excruciating, roundabout route through the length of the peninsula, around the northern rim of the Gulf of Mexico, and down the coast of what is today northeastern Mexico, a journey totaling some 1,500 miles to Santiesteban and 1,700 miles all the way to Mexico City. That was tantamount to the distance traveled by crusading knights as they crossed the entire European continent from Seville to Constantinople.

Food was constantly on the minds of the explorers. When the ships and the overland group became separated, every man had received 2 pounds of hardtack and half a pound of pork. Such measly rations could not have lasted more than a few days. The men were forced to rely for food on Florida's rich variety of flora and fauna. As Narváez's men skirted marshes or walked under canopies of pine trees, they spotted three different types of deer, rabbits, hares, bears, lions (the largest feline would have been the Florida panther), geese, night-herons, and "other wild beasts, among them one that carries its young in a pouch"—an unmistakable description of the opossum. Interestingly, they did not report seeing any alligators, creatures that would have been especially startling to New World newcomers like Cabeza de Vaca.[2]

But despite the natural bounty that surrounded them, the group was hard-pressed to find food. For weeks their paltry meals consisted almost exclusively of hearts of a certain palm tree (possibly the sabal palm) that appeared to the explorers to be similar to an edible palm that grew in Andalusia. It would take time before they learned to use the environment more effectively. For the moment, they lived like castaways in the midst of a green ocean.[3]

Despite their hunger, the explorers were still able to subdue other humans. As soon as they crossed the river "with a strong current"—possibly the Withlacoochee River in modern-day Citrus County—they found about 200 Indians. Cabeza de Vaca recounts how Narváez "went out to them, and after having spoken to them by means of signs, they gestured to us in such a way that we had to turn on them." The Indians were threatening the Europeans.[4]

In Florida, rivers served as important boundaries between different groups; these borders were guarded and enforced. As soon as they crossed the river, Narváez's men had entered into the territory of a new community. Here, they were treated as trespassers.

During the skirmish, the Spaniards captured five or six Indians who led them to a village about 1.5 miles away. This Indian community had plenty of ripe corn. It was a little oasis in the middle of the endless piney flatlands. Aching with hunger, the Spaniards devoured the corn ravenously; it must have tasted like salvation. "And we gave infinite thanks to our Lord for having aided us in so great a need," wrote Cabeza de Vaca, "because since we were most certainly new to these hardships, beyond the fatigue we suffered, we came very worn out from hunger." The intruders feasted here for several days.[5]

But all was not well. During this time, the rift between Narváez and Cabeza de Vaca deepened. The Royal Treasurer had wanted from the outset to remain close to the coast and reestablish contact with the ships as soon as possible. Yielding to the majority, he had been forced to march inland. After two weeks of arduous marches, Cabeza de Vaca had become evermore convinced that his plan was the right one. And now the friars and the other royal appointees had come to see the wisdom of Cabeza de Vaca's caution and began to close ranks behind him. They all beseeched the Governor to send scouts toward the coast, which was not too far from there, according to the Indians. The river "with a strong current" that they had only recently crossed could well turn out to be the elusive Rio de las Palmas, or perhaps a good anchorage would be found at its mouth. Or maybe they would find the port that Miruelo had said was near the Rio de las Palmas. The ships might even be waiting there![6] Narváez, however, had no interest in embarking on a long detour to the coast. He had his sights set ever-more firmly on Apalachee. The Governor had been questioning the Indians about this rich province, and they all pointed north. Finding the Rio de las Palmas was now only a secondary goal.

At first Narváez would not even hear of any plans to go to the coast. "We should not bother talking about this . . . it is too far," he replied to the pleas of his men. However, after much insistence, the Governor finally consented to sending a reconnaissance party. And since Cabeza de Vaca was the most adamant about surveying the coast, Narváez ordered him to go with forty men. They would have to go on foot.[7]

The next day Cabeza de Vaca departed for the coast, accompanied by Captain Alonso del Castillo and his company. They walked until noon, when they arrived at some sandbars and a shallow bay. Cabeza de Vaca, Castillo, and the men walked into the water to test its depth. They found no suitable anchorage or port; they walked for nearly 5 miles and the water never reached higher than their knees. Oyster reefs made the march especially difficult, cutting the soles and feet of the men. Narváez dispatched another party of exploration a few days later. This second group confirmed that the bay was shallow and contained no port. They saw no signs of the ships, although they did notice some Indian canoes crossing from one side to the other.[8]

Cabeza de Vaca's bid had failed, and now it was time to act on Narváez's plan. The expedition resumed its grueling march toward Apalachee. The specter of hunger returned; at times the trekkers went for 20 miles or more without finding any corn. They did not, however, encounter any hostile Indians, although indigenous lookouts must have monitored the Europeans care-fully throughout their journey. The long, monotonous march was only punctuated by occasional encounters.

One day, a group of Indians fearlessly made their way into Narváez's camp. They were led by a native lord, who was being carried on the shoulders of a porter and who was covered with a painted deer hide. Some other Indians in his entourage were playing reed flutes. To the Spaniards it must have seemed like an apparition or a dream. Narváez spent an hour in conversation with this lord, who was named Dulchanchellin. He and Narváez were able to communicate only through signs, and what conver-sation there was must have been painstaking as well as inaccu-rate. But Narváez was determined to question him about Apalachee. He gave the lord beads and bells, and in return, Dulchanchellin took off his precious hide and passed it to Narváez. The Spaniards understood that these Indians were sworn enemies of the people of Apalachee and were very willing to point the strangers in the right direction.[9]

The Indians and Spaniards walked together until they ran into another large river, perhaps the Suwannee River. An impa-tient cavalryman by the name of Juan Velázquez rode straight into the river. The current was so strong that he was swept off his horse, holding tightly to the reins, which caused the horse to drown too. Dulchanchellin's Indians told the Spaniards where to look for Velázquez's body. They also found the dead horse. The hungry explorers were able to feast on the carcass.[10]

After a month and a half of marches, the terrain began to change. The Spaniards had walked for so long since leaving Tampa Bay that the trees now appeared taller and more majes-tic, and the air had turned somewhat cooler as the tropical por-tion of Florida gave way to a more temperate climate characteristic of the continent.

At last, sometime in mid-June of 1528, the men came within sight of Apalachee. Everyone cheered. The hunger, exhaustion, and sore backs from carrying heavy weapons seemed to vanish. As Cabeza de Vaca wrote, "On finding ourselves where we desired to be, and where they told us there were so many foodstuffs and so much gold, it seemed to us that a great portion of our hardship and weariness had been lifted from us." It had been exactly one year since the Florida expedition had departed from Spain.[11]

APALACHEE WAS INDEED the largest and most complex chiefdom of the entire Florida peninsula. In fact, it was something of an anomaly. Thus far the Spaniards had encountered native peoples organized in small villages scattered over large areas. The size of these communities was dictated by the amount of food available. Although some of these groups cultivated maize, they were primarily hunters and gatherers. Their diet depended on a wide variety of animals, including deer, seabirds, turkeys, alligators, rays, and sharks. Indians who lived near the coast also feasted on oysters and other delectable mollusks. These food sources made for varied and delicious meals, but they also put a limit on the number of people who could reside at a single site. As communities grew in size, so did the strain on their immediate environments, eventually leading groups of families to move into unoccupied areas in search of more plentiful resources.[12]

Apalachee functioned in a very different way. This chiefdom occupied a surprisingly small area in the Florida panhandle, bounded by the Aucilla and Ochlockonee Rivers, yet it was a land most favored by nature. Although the people of Apalachee lived relatively close to the coast and had access to estuarine resources, most of their food came from rich upland soil known today as the Tallahassee Red Hills. This extraordinarily fertile

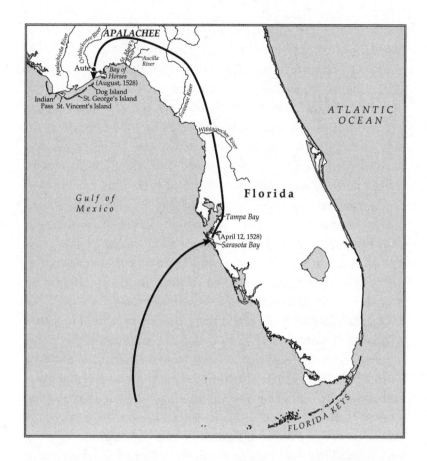

strip of land facilitated the intensive cultivation of maize. By the sixteenth century, the people of Apalachee had cleared large fields that stretched for miles and were regularly cultivated by communal labor. Corn sustained human communities many times larger than were possible anywhere else in Florida. It also fostered stability, large surpluses—and power.[13]

There was a dark underside, however, to this agricultural bounty. The need to coordinate and mobilize large numbers of people for the clearing, planting, and harvesting seasons inevitably led to greater centralization and inequality. Unlike the other Florida groups, who were relatively egalitarian, Apalachee sustained an intricate hierarchy. At the top was the paramount chief, a figure associated with the life-giving sun. He wielded the power of life and death over his subjects. He also exerted control over various village chiefs who ruled their own localities. In turn, each of these village chiefs was assisted by lesser officials charged with specific functions, down to the lowly farmers who constituted the vast majority of the people. This hierarchical arrangement also prevailed among settlements. Apalachee had a center, a capital city known as Anhaica where the paramount chief resided. From Anhaica he projected his influence over a series of outlying local capitals, which were more modest settlements. The village chiefs resided in these local capitals, ruling over their surrounding hamlets and farmsteads.[14]

Apalachee was only one among dozens of chiefdoms that flourished between A.D. 1000 and A.D. 1600 along the fertile floodplains of the Mississippi River, from the Great Lakes to the Gulf of Mexico. These chiefdoms were part of a remarkable cultural tradition along the mighty river and its tributaries. They practiced intensive agriculture, became organized as highly ranked societies, and took part in long-distance trading networks. They were the most powerful chiefdoms north of Mexico. Present-day scholars call them *Mississippian* societies; their temples, houses, and square-based pyramids proclaimed their might.

Once dominant, these centers began to falter. Some Mississippian centers, particularly those on the upper Mississippi, went into decline and in some cases collapsed prior to the arrival of Europeans. The site of Cahokia, the largest Mississippian chiefdom, just east of present-day St. Louis, was abandoned well before Columbus. Other centers experienced precipitous declines around

An example of the ancient buildings and mounds dotting the banks of the Mississippi and Ohio rivers. This site was found near Marietta, Ohio. After Ephraim G. Squier and Edwin H. Davis, *Ancient Monuments of the Mississippi Valley*. Washington, D.C., 1848.

the Age of Discovery. These societies were already wrestling with problems of endemic warfare and environmental degradation when the arrival of Europeans hastened their demise. By the time French and English colonists explored the upper reaches of the Mississippi in the seventeenth and eighteenth centuries, this remarkable cultural tradition had virtually disappeared. All that remained were the imposing, silent "mounds."[15]

Despite these earlier collapses, some chiefdoms on the lower Mississippi were still thriving by the sixteenth and seventeenth centuries. Centers like Natchez, within the present-day state of Mississippi, and Apalachee in Florida, carried on this centuries-old cultural tradition well into the colonial era. They persisted long enough to have to confront powerful and overbearing outsiders.[16]

Narváez's men came within sight of an Apalachee village without being seen. Comprising forty small houses, it was certainly more substantial than any other they had encountered along the way, but it was still quite disappointing when measured against their exorbitant expectations. The expedition had probably arrived at one of the outlying local capitals and not Anhaica proper, which would have contained 200 houses or more. The village that Narváez and his men found was surrounded by thick woods and many lagoons with trees sticking out of them.[17]

Narváez ordered Cabeza de Vaca to take nine cavalrymen and fifty foot soldiers and attack the village. As they made their way inside, they discovered that there were only women and children. All the indigenous men were gone. But some time later they returned and, having learned what had happened, shot arrows at the strangers and killed at least one horse before they withdrew. The Europeans kept the women and children as hostages. Two days later, the Indians asked for the release of their families. Narváez agreed, but in return demanded that the village chief be turned over to them. He was to remain as a hostage.[18]

Superior weapons gave the Spanish undisputed control of the settlement, but not much more. Native warriors reverted to guerrilla tactics to dislodge the intruders and force the release of their leader. They were unpredictable, skillful, swift, and relentless. On one occasion they even succeeded in setting fire to the houses where the Spaniards were staying. Outside the village, the chances of survival were minimal, as Cabeza de Vaca makes clear: "The Indians made war on us continually, wounding the people and the horses as we went to fetch water, shooting arrows at us from the safety of the lagoons where we could not retaliate."[19]

Narváez and his men stayed in this village for a full twenty-five or twenty-six days. They were well fed, at least; they found a large store of corn, along with mortars to grind it. Also scattered about were many deer hides and some cloth mantles of poor quality that indigenous women used as garments. And yet despite these spoils, these weeks must have been agonizing. The painful truth was inescapable: this was no Aztec empire, and there was no gold in sight. It was an ordinary indigenous town comprised of modest houses made of branches and grass. Narváez and his men had harbored dreams of riches kept alive by a rattle made of gold and the stories told to them by the Indians along the way. But in pursuing their goal so relentlessly, they had abandoned their ships. As the Spaniards prowled through the Indian village, the grave consequences of their actions must have dawned on them. There was plenty they did not know, and just posing the questions must have been hard. Had they been deceived by the Indian guides? Would they be able to rejoin the ships? How far could the Rio de las Palmas and the Pánuco coast still be?

During these weeks at the village, the trekkers mounted three reconnaissance expeditions to the surrounding areas, trying to find more substantial settlements. The return of each of these sorties must have been eagerly awaited, and the disappointment after each briefing must have been great. The land appeared to be sparsely populated and difficult to travel.[20]

Desperate, the explorers turned their attention to their hostages, including the village chief. The pressure on this man must have been enormous. Likely accustomed to being treated as a demigod (as were his ancestors before him, as these offices were hereditary), he was now being questioned and manhandled by these arrogant interlopers who had materialized out of thin air just a few days earlier. The village chief was not the sole hostage. En route to the village, the expeditioners had captured some Indian "guides" who were enemies of the people of Apalachee. The Spanish questioned each of these hostages separately.

The fate of the expedition hinged on what these captives had to say. Remarkably, their answers—or whatever their Spanish interlocutors understood of them—amounted to a consistent but deceitful picture: "They told us, each one by himself, that the largest village of that entire land was Apalachen, and that ahead there were fewer people, who were much poorer than they, and that the land was poorly populated and its inhabitants widely dispersed, and that going forward there were great lagoons and dense woods and great empty and unpopulated areas."[21]

It is easy to see how the indigenous "guides" from farther south may have conflated the *chiefdom* of Apalachee with the *town* where they were staying. To them Apalachee may have been an undifferentiated whole, perhaps *that* settlement. But the village chief knew better. No town called "Apalachee" existed within the chiefdom. Apalachee consisted of multiple settlements of different size and importance. Some of them were very substantial towns, including Anhaica, which likely lay to the west. Indeed, eleven years later another Spanish expedition traveled through the area and left a startlingly different portrayal. One source described Apalachee as "heavily settled" and named various villages along the way before reaching Anhaica. Similarly, early seventeenth-century witnesses gave population estimates for Apalachee ranging from 30,000 to 34,000 souls, at a time when it had been significantly reduced by military encounters with Europeans and epidemic diseases. Apalachee was hardly the "sparsely populated" land described by the hostages.[22]

By casting Apalachee as a small and impoverished chiefdom, the village chief cleverly discouraged the Europeans from traveling further into their territory. He was just as clever in advising the strangers on the best route to the coast. For after enduring weeks of constant guerrilla incursions and despondent about the seeming poverty of "Apalachee," Narváez's men had ceased to fantasize about gold and were now thinking only about saving themselves. They considered moving south toward the coast, where at least they would have some hope of being found by the vessels. The village chief knew well that there were other large towns on the northern portion of Apalachee's territory, along the flat ridge tops that were ideal for extensive horticulture. And if the Spaniards marched west, they would find sizable communities, plenty of maize, and eventually the capital of the chiefdom itself. In contrast, the sandy coastal plains to the south were lightly occupied and had been traditionally used mostly as a source of game and wild plant foods.[23] Along with some of the other hostages, the ingenious chief encouraged his captors to head south by offering them a series of lies and half-truths. He said that "going to the sea was a nine-day journey, and that there was a village there called Aute, and the Indians of that place had a great deal of maize and they had beans and squash, and that because of being so close to the sea they obtained fish, and that these people were their friends." Aute probably lay *outside* the sphere of influence of the Apalachee Chiefdom. If so, the hostage chief not only had rescued his fellow Apalacheeans from the destructive power of the Spaniards, but had also unleashed this scourge on an indigenous rival.[24]

The march to Aute was disastrous. After only two days on the trail, the trekkers ran into nearly impassable swamps so deep that the men had to wade through chest-deep waters and round submerged trees. Crossing these swamps was not only difficult but risky. As they waded through some lagoons, the men were ambushed by Indians who emerged from behind the trees on the shore and shot arrows that wounded several explorers and horses. The Indians also captured one of the "guides" whom Narváez's men had taken hostage weeks earlier.

The Royal Treasurer must have been taken aback, just like the other explorers. But he could also not help but admire the attackers' skill: "All the Indians we had seen from Florida to here are archers, and as they are of large build and go about naked, from a distance they appear to be giants. They are a people wonderfully well built, very lean and of great strength and agility. The bows they use are as thick as an arm [and] eleven or twelve spans long [as tall as a man] so that they can shoot arrows at two hundred paces with such great skill that they never miss their target." Two expedition members swore that they had seen two oak branches as thick as a man's lower leg pierced completely from one side to the other, "and this is not to be wondered at"—Cabeza de Vaca went on—"having seen the strength and skill with which they shoot them, because I myself saw an arrow in the base of a poplar tree that had entered it to the depth of a *xeme* [the distance between the thumb and the outstretched index finger]."25

After nine full days of hardships and danger, the Spanish reached Aute. They quickly learned that their exhausting journey had been for nothing; Aute offered scant relief or better prospects. It had been abandoned and burnt to the ground in advance of their arrival; obviously the natives were well aware of the intruders' movements and intentions. Worse still, many Spaniards became ill—typhus or typhoid was probably the culprit. Within days of their arrival, as many as a third of the expedition members were sick, Narváez among them. The affected found it difficult to move, let alone carry their equipment. Some forty men would never recover. The group was down to a little over 250.[26]

Aute had some maize, beans, and squash ready to be harvested, as the Apalachee Indians had reported, but the town offered no other advantages. It was still one day away from the coast. After considerable discussion and soul searching the Spaniards finally decided to push ahead to the shore, where at least they would have a slim chance of rescue. This last leg of the journey was taxing in the extreme. Every day more explorers fell ill, and the horses became insufficient to carry all of them. "It was a great sorrow and pain to see the necessity and hardship in which we found ourselves," Cabeza de Vaca recalls. "The men were in such a state that there were few from whom any service could have been obtained."[27]

As the trekkers traversed the last wooded swamps, their hearts were surely heavy. Dreams of gold had been dashed; many men had already perished. The once mighty and proud expedition had been reduced to a band of survivalists lost in the New World.

The coast near Aute was the expedition's final disappointment. The humbled explorers emerged somewhere between the St. Marks River and the Apalachicola Bay, an area of shallow inlets, coves, and swamps. Although this coiled estuary ultimately reached the Gulf of Mexico, much of it is separated by a chain of barrier islands. The expeditioners must have been disconsolate when they gazed at a large, shallow bay. The water was only waist-deep. At low tide the jagged edges of the massive oyster reefs must have been visible. There was no way a ship could ever penetrate this shallow maze.[28]

After brutal marches, brushes with Indians, and bouts with debilitating illnesses, the survivors had reached a cruel dead end. For some days they must have been overwhelmed by a sense of dejection and helplessness: "I refrain here from telling this at greater length,"—Cabeza de Vaca wrote, "because each one can imagine for himself what could happen in a land so strange and so poor and so lacking in every single thing that it seemed impossible either to be in it or to escape from it."[29]

BY THE TIME the land party regained the coast, it had been four months since they had separated from their fleet. The men and women aboard the ships had spent most of that time engaged in an all-out search for them. The maritime contingent numbered roughly 100 individuals, consisting of the most indispensable crew members and the ten women. Although less risky, their activities were dangerous all the same, and filled with anxiety. The ten women in particular faced uncertain futures, as the days went by and the prospects of never seeing their husbands again became ever-more real.

Narváez had ordered the ships to go to the Rio de las Palmas, where they were to wait for the overland party to catch up. Yet a few days of sailing must have persuaded the mariners that they had been utterly mistaken in claiming that the Rio de las Palmas was near. It was very far away. In fact, they were sailing on an altogether different coast than they had originally assumed. It must have been a horrifying realization—but it was already too late to make up for their error. The crew members were the first to understand that they might never reestablish contact with the overland group.

Distressing as all of this was, the men and women aboard the ships had even more pressing concerns. At the time of the separation, the maritime contingent had surrendered the lion's share of the food supplies to the land party. Within days, they must have faced severe food shortages, perhaps even starvation. Without more provisions, they would have been unable even to go back to the Caribbean islands. Only a lucky break saved them from a tragic end. Just prior to the separation of the expedition, Narváez had sent the pilot Miruelo back to Cuba on the lead ship. He was to get additional supplies and return promptly. Somehow, this time he was able to accomplish his mission. Miruelo rejoined his fleet after some days, bringing back badly needed victuals that sustained a search effort that would last for nearly a year.

The search began right at present-day Tampa Bay. One of the vessels sailed inside the bay, where the crew noticed a cane deliberately stuck in the ground. It was split at the top and a letter perched in the cleft. The group concluded that this piece of paper contained crucial information, possibly left by Narváez himself. The Spaniards spotted a group of Indians who were walking along the beach and called out to them to bring the piece of paper out to the ships. They refused and instead motioned for the Spaniards to come ashore.

It was a tremendously risky proposition, but the letter could hardly be ignored. Two men, an eighteen-year-old from Seville named Juan Ortiz and an older man whose name is not known, got in a rowboat and made their way to the beach. The Indians seized them immediately. The older man was killed in the ensuing scuffle. Juan Ortiz survived but was taken hostage.

Apparently the split cane and the letter constituted a trap astutely laid out by the Indians. It appears that when Narváez and his men rounded the bay, they had abused the Indians and had cut off the nose of a native lord called Hirrihigua. This native leader had not forgotten this ignominy. When Hirrihigua saw the lone Spanish vessel in the bay, he carefully set up his bait with the cunning of someone bent on revenge.[30]

The older explorer who died on the beach could count himself fortunate. Juan Ortiz was kept by the Indians for eleven years before he was rescued by another Spanish expedition. His captivity was horrendous. On feast days, the natives apparently forced Ortiz to run from sunrise to sunset on a plaza. A group of warriors watched over him. Whenever he slowed, they shot arrows at him to amuse themselves. On another occasion, the Indians tied him over a fire and released him only after he had been badly burned. According to a later writer who interviewed some explorers who knew Juan Ortiz, the poor captive "had wished to die because he was forced to carry wood and water all the time and was given little food or sleep; every day he was cruelly beaten with sticks, slapped in the face, or whipped and was subjected to other torments especially during their days of celebration; had he not been a Christian he would have taken his life with his own hands."[31] (Unfortunately, we have only indirect testimonies of Ortiz's captivity. Although some of the tortures were probably real, it is also possible that Ortiz may have exaggerated his ordeal to reclaim a place among his Spanish rescuers. He would not have been the first European to feel the need to repudiate his life as "a native," nor would he be the last.)

After leaving Tampa Bay, the ships continued to search for the land party. They scouted the interminable coast to the north but found not even the slightest trace. The man in charge of the maritime contingent, a captain simply identified as Carvallo, had a momentous decision to make. The fleet could either venture farther north or return to the point of debarkation. Not unreasonably, Carvallo chose to go back, hoping that Narváez and his men would also realize that the Rio de las Palmas was too far away. The ships waited at the point of debarkation for months, but the land party appeared to have vanished. Florida had swallowed each and every one of them.

After a year, the growing conviction was that the land party had perished. At some point Carvallo and his crew must have decided that Narváez and his men had died. The ten women too had begun to think of themselves as widows. Some had already established new relationships with fellow shipmates. There were more pressing concerns as well. The provisions brought by Miruelo were running out. The fleet finally returned to Cuba, where some residents blamed Carvallo for being "too fearful" in his searches and for having "forsaken" the Florida coast "without waiting longer for the return of their Captain General and Governor."[32]

Only one person had resources and interest sufficient to revive the search: Narváez's wife, María de Valenzuela. She was a woman of "virtue and rank" and a property owner in her own right, who did not think twice about using the courts to get her way. During Narváez's prolonged absences, she had managed his estate as well as hers, shrewdly directing hundreds of Indians and black slaves to wash for gold—all the while raising a family.

Incredibly, she decided to mount an expedition of her own to search for her husband and his men. She left her home in Bayamo and for nine months took up residence in the port of Santiago de Cuba. She purchased two brigantines, assembled a crew, and secured supplies and munitions. Her determination was unshakable. The only thing she could not do was lead the expedition herself. So María de Valenzuela relied on one of Narváez's associates in Spain, a man named Hernando de Ceballos. The indefatigable María must have instructed Ceballos to purchase provisions in Seville and take passage to Cuba, where he would take charge of the fleet. He promptly left Cuba with the two brigantines, and probably retraced Narváez's passage to Florida, but he had no more luck finding the overland explorers than had their own shipmates. Within months, he too abandoned the search and sailed to New Spain, where he sold the brigantines and pocketed the proceeds.[33]

Perhaps Ceballos misjudged María's character. This woman may have lost a husband and a small fortune looking for him, but her tenacity remained intact. She initiated proceedings against Ceballos to recover her money. The case reached all the way to the Council of the Indies and the Emperor. Ceballos claimed that he had spent more money searching for Narváez than what he received by selling the brigantines. Unimpressed, the judges ordered Ceballos to be held in chains. The message was clear: no one was about to take advantage of the indomitable María de Valenzuela.

María's legal victory, however, must have been a small consolation. That stubborn husband of hers, who had needlessly risked it all by going to Florida, was lost forever.[34]

CHAPTER 5

On Rafts

NARVÁEZ AND HIS MEN SET UP CAMP AT THE shallow estuary they had found and spent a month and a half there. They named it the Bay of Horses because every third day they would kill one horse to supplement their dwindling reserves of maize, beans, and squash. It is easy to imagine the grim ritual: the decision as to which horse would be sacrificed, the killing, the river of blood that washed over the sand as the men removed the animal's skin, the bonfire in which the flesh was roasted, the desperate starving men who devoured it. The carcasses were tossed aside; eleven years later another Spanish expedition found Narváez's camp and recognized it by the "horse skulls" and "the mortars that they had used to grind corn and the crosses cut into the trees."[1]

Stirrups, spurs, and crossbows—they all burned as well. In an extraordinary step, the men threw them into a hot fire and attempted to recast the hot clumps of metal into tools, mainly axes and saws. To produce enough heat to melt the metal, someone had devised a crude forge by jury-rigging a bellows out of deer hides; the pipes that drove the air out of the bellows were fashioned from hollowed-out logs.

The process of melting the weapons would have been enormously difficult, but there was no other choice: the men were desperate to leave Florida. By eating their animals and melting their weapons they were putting in place an extraordinary plan. They intended to construct five makeshift rafts to glide over the oyster reefs and sandbars and out into the Gulf of Mexico. Once in the open sea, they would either be spotted by the ships or they could sail to Pánuco, which they hoped and prayed would not be too far.

It had not been easy to agree on this bold scheme. Narváez had already faced a full-scale insurrection. Sometime after arriving at the Bay of Horses, the horsemen had secretly agreed to strike out on their own. They realized that they stood a much better chance of survival if they could just push ahead without being held back by the sick and the dying. Among the conspirators, however, there were "many hidalgos and men of good breeding," and they could not carry out their plans without first informing Narváez and other royal officials. As Cabeza de Vaca explains, the faction loyal to Narváez made the conspirators understand that they would be committing a grave crime by "abandoning their captain and those who were sick and without strength, and above all else removing themselves from the service of Your Majesty." Ultimately, the horsemen agreed to stay with their less-fortunate companions.[2]

The raft-building plan at the Bay of Horses was based on this pledge of unity. By killing the horses, all the men would be on the same footing and none would be able to abandon the group. This plan had one immediate reward: access to a steady supply of meat for some weeks. But it also amounted to a formidable gamble. The Spaniards were trading their most effective weapons against the Indians—horses and firearms—for five improvised vessels that might or might not be capable of carrying them to safety.

Horses and firearms had conferred upon sixteenth-century Spaniards an overwhelming superiority over the peoples of the

New World, something the conquistadors never forgot. When Narváez and his men disembarked in Florida, they had no idea how many Indians they would encounter or whether these natives harbored hostile or friendly intentions. In spite of this uncertainty, Narváez was confident that his men would prevail in just about any confrontation because of their firearms and animals.

Indeed, superior weapons had enabled Spanish expedition leaders to vanquish large numbers of indigenous opponents. When Hernán Cortés first reached the coast of Mexico, he had his ships grounded to prevent his men from going back and would go on to bring down Mexico-Tenochtitlán, a city of 250,000 inhabitants, with a little more than 1,000 soldiers. Similarly, in 1536–1537, Francisco Pizarro and some 180 Spaniards held off perhaps 100,000 indigenous attackers for more than a year in the heart of the Inca Empire. Thousands of Indians perished, but only one Spaniard died, a man who had failed to wear his helmet.[3]

Protected by their breastplates, fierce animals, and lethal weapons, conquistadors learned early on that they did not need to negotiate with the natives—in most cases, they could simply impose their will. Nor did Spaniards have to make an effort to understand the social world of the natives or, for that matter, conceive of them as anything other than potential subjects, captives, porters, guides, or slaves. Thus far, Narváez's men had run roughshod over the natives of Florida. Expedition members had taken the Indians' food and occupied their houses with little concern for effective retaliation. Technology underpinned a sense of supreme confidence and superiority.

However, such feelings began to ebb at the Bay of Horses. As the men killed their horses and melted down their crossbows, they must have been keenly aware that they were giving up their military advantages over the North American natives. From now on, they would have to face the New World fully exposed to its perils. Surviving because of superior military technology was one thing. It would be quite another to do so by wits alone.

IN THE LATE summer of 1528, the beach area overlooking the Bay of Horses must have resembled a chaotic campground. Some of the men operated the forge, while others cut down trees, and yet others went on raiding expeditions to get maize. The men had occasion to prove their enormous self-reliance and astonishing ingenuity. Not for nothing had they signed up to establish European settlements in the New World. Among them there were artisans, craftsmen, and talented builders, and their collective skills were being put to the test. Even if they had had all the necessary tools and materials, manufacturing five large, seaworthy rafts would have been a challenge. But the stranded explorers had to build their vessels from whatever items they had happened to carry with them or could procure in the marshes of Florida. Moreover, the men at the Bay of Horses possessed only the most rudimentary knowledge of shipbuilding; all of the men with shipboard experience had stayed behind with the maritime contingent. It was probably a Portuguese carpenter named Álvaro Fernández who led the construction effort. The expedition's last hope of survival rested on his shoulders.[4]

The first challenge was to design a raft that would actually float when fully loaded. Even though some of the men had perished in Indian attacks and many more had succumbed to illness, there were still 250 expeditioners alive out of the 300 who had started out from Tampa Bay. Each of the five rafts would have to carry 50 men, enough water for them, a heap of corn, trinkets, clothing, and the few remaining weapons. Assuming that each passenger weighed 150 pounds on average and allowing for a modest cargo of 1.5 tons per vessel, it turns out that each raft would need to transport a minimum of 5 tons.

To bear such loads, modern rafts are often made out of extremely buoyant materials such as Styrofoam or polyurethane. They are also designed with air compartments or inner tubes for additional flotation. The raft builders at the Bay of Horses could not even begin to dream of such conveniences. They had to depend solely on the upward lift provided by the wood itself. Therefore, choosing the right kind of tree was crucial, as different kinds of wood provide varying levels of flotation. Some hardwoods, such as teakwood and ebony, are actually so dense that they sink in water. Narváez and his men may have considered using the hardwood trees that grow in the Apalachee-Apalachicola area, such as gums, oaks, and willows. Such woods would have floated, but they would have been very difficult to cut and drag to the water's edge, and because of their high density they would have been unable to carry much freight. Far more viable was the abundant supply of conifers, such as cypresses, pines, and cedars, that grow in the region. Any of these species would have yielded timber of an intermediate density quite suitable for raft building.[5]

Chopping down the wood for the rafts was a truly gargantuan undertaking. According to Cabeza de Vaca, each raft was 22 elbows in length—perhaps 33 feet. In another passage he reveals that the rafts floated one *xeme* (from the thumb to the outstretched index finger), or about 7 inches above the water, when fully loaded. Assuming that each raft was made of wood of an intermediate density such as pine or cedar, that it measured 33 feet per side, and that the raft protruded 7 inches above the waterline when loaded with 5 tons, it can be deduced by Archimedes's principle that each raft must have weighed a little over 15 tons. We don't know the particulars of the design. But it can best be visualized as a large platform made up of twenty-nine logs lashed together, each of them measuring somewhat more than a foot in

These were the working materials available to Narváez and his men. In the Florida panhandle the pine flatwoods reach right up to the water's edge, thus facilitating the task of hauling the wood. Below the pines there is an understory of palmettos still quite characteristic. This picture was taken by the author at the St. Marks National Wildlife Refuge south of present-day Tallahassee.

diameter and 33 feet in length. To build five such rafts, the famished trekkers would have had to cut down about 150 mature pine trees or the equivalent amount in other species. Selecting the most appropriate trees, clearing the area around them, delivering hundreds of ax blows to each trunk, and running away from the falling giants must have been hard enough. And yet felling the trees was merely the beginning of the process. They still had to remove all the limbs, cut the trunks to the desired length, and drag the logs to the launching area. Even with properly manufactured tools, these tasks would have been overwhelming. Narváez's men had to do all this with crude axes and saws, racing against time as they consumed their last few horses. In order to ensure that all the members of the expedition shared in this brutal and exhausting labor, the leaders proclaimed that only those who worked would have access to horse meat.[6]

Once the logs had been gathered at the water's edge, the raft builders needed to devise a system to fasten them together firmly. But the group had no rope with them, so they had to make it themselves. They improvised once again by using the tough hair of the dead horses. Some members of the expedition must have spent countless hours gathering all the tails and manes of the dead horses, braiding the strands together into short sections of rope, and then tying the sections to one another. Even with thirty horses or so, rope must have been at a premium since it was needed not only for lashing logs but also for rigging the sails.

To a group of landlubbers—for most of the men, the voyage across the Atlantic was probably their first shipboard experience—it must have been alarming to realize that an undulating carpet of logs would be the only thing between themselves and the swallowing sea. The water would be visible through the gaps between the logs. The expedition members—many of whom could not swim—were so troubled by this prospect that they set out to fill the gaps. They gathered a great quantity of palmetto leaves, mashing them into a fibrous paste that was used as oakum to wedge between the logs. A Greek Christian named Doroteo Teodoro took this procedure one step further by collecting "a certain pitch extracted from some pine trees" to use as caulking. Of course, sealing the bottom of a raft contributes nothing to its seaworthiness—if anything, these materials added more weight. But for some of the men, at least, it must have been reassuring.[7]

A more relevant problem was how to make these 15-ton platforms navigate without spinning capriciously and drifting out of control. Narváez's men carved oars out of cypress wood and re-signed themselves to doing a lot of rowing. But they also hoped to marshal the power of the wind to make their way out of Florida. Masts rose out of the wooden platform, flying square sails. They must have been attached to the masts and spars in such a way that they could be trimmed and adjusted. Made of shirts sewn together, those sails must have been a wonder to behold.[8]

Lastly, the resourceful men at the Bay of Horses turned to matters of provisions. With no way of preserving horse meat or shellfish, they would have to depend largely on corn and perhaps some beans and squash that had been raided from nearby Indian communities. At departure, each raft must have carried a considerable amount of corn. Even so, the men probably intended to mount additional food raids along the way.[9]

Carrying an adequate supply of fresh water posed the greatest challenge for the men at the Bay of Horses. In our age of plastic bottles, it is easy to forget how hard it is to make waterproof containers. Making pots out of clay would have been the simplest solution: such containers could have been made impermeable by baking them with fire. Historically, most agricultural societies around the world, including the native people of Apalachee, have stumbled upon this same basic solution, but it seems to have eluded the expedition members. Perhaps they found no suitable clay by the sandy coast. Instead, Narváez's men tried a different approach. They stripped the legs of the horses and cured the hides to make leather water bags.[10]

After five or six weeks of hard work, the rafts were ready, and only one horse remained alive. The men slaughtered it and devoured what they knew would be the last meat they would taste for quite some time. Then, after dragging the rafts into the water and loading them up, fifty men piled onto each one. There was so little space on board that the men could hardly move.

More alarmingly, the passengers found themselves floating barely a few inches above the waterline; the waves would wash over the men as they traveled.

Narváez commanded the "lead raft." He was sailing with his inner circle and some of the strongest and healthiest men. A second raft was given to Royal Comptroller Alonso Enríquez and Fray Juan Suárez. It would carry the religious personnel. The third and fourth rafts were entrusted to two pairs of captains. One was assigned to Captains Téllez and Peñaloza, and the other one to Captains Alonso del Castillo and Andrés Dorantes. Presumably these four captains would be sailing with their respective companies. The Castillo-Dorantes raft must have included Estebanico, the African slave. The fifth and final raft was to be jointly commanded by Cabeza de Vaca and the Royal Inspector Alonso de Solís.

On September 22, 1528, the Spaniards set sail. "And so greatly can necessity prevail," a somewhat philosophical Cabeza de Vaca writes, "that it made us risk going in this manner and placing ourselves in a sea so treacherous, and without any one of us who went having any knowledge of the art of navigation."[11]

FOR THE FIRST seven days of their voyage, the Spaniards were forced to negotiate a labyrinthine series of inlets and sandbars before reaching the open sea. During this time, the water was never more than waist deep. At the end of this initial passage, the men arrived at an island (possibly present-day St. Vincent Island) that was so close to the continent that the two landmasses formed a strait. Beyond it lay the Gulf of Mexico. As the fleet neared the island, Cabeza de Vaca's raft drifted ahead, "and from it we saw five canoes of Indians approaching, which they abandoned and left in our hands, seeing that we were headed for them." The Spaniards immediately appropriated the

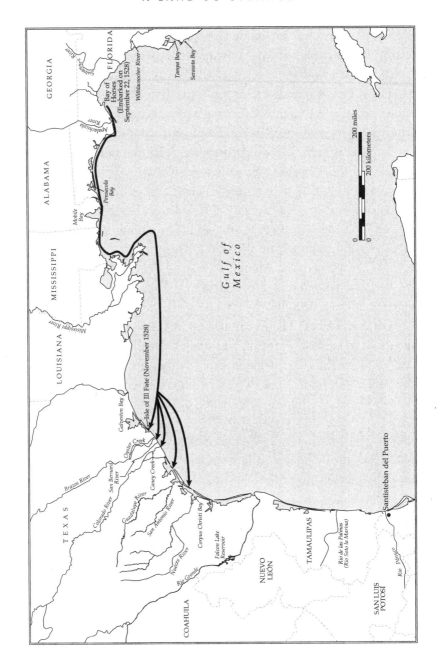

abandoned canoes; they used them as timber to add gunwales to the rafts. The rafts now had two spans of freeboard, and at least some of the water would be kept out.[12]

The men also spotted some Indian houses along the shore; this small fishing community must have seemed like an ideal target to the expeditioners. They went ashore and were delighted to find many mullets and dried roe, an unexpected delicacy. It was "a great help for the necessity in which we found ourselves," writes Cabeza de Vaca.[13]

Once in the open sea, the improvised flotilla sailed west for a month. The rafts were making headway, perhaps faring better than anyone had expected, and for the first time since the beginning of the expedition, things appeared to be going well. The rafts hugged the coast, entering inlets and bays that were dangerously shallow. Sometimes they would run into Indian fishermen whom Cabeza de Vaca describes as "poor and wretched."[14]

After one month of uneventful sailing, the problems returned. The rations started to dwindle, but the raftsmen were especially tormented by their lack of fresh water. The water bags that the castaways had fashioned out of horse legs had rotted completely and were unable to hold the precious liquid. As the men floated on open rafts, exposed to the sun's full heat and drying power, they must have regretted a thousand times their decision to carry their water in hides.

Finding fresh drinking water soon became the Spaniards' overriding concern. They steered the rafts close to the coast in hopes of spotting a stream or a lake, but to no avail. Then they saw a small island that seemed empty and decided to go there. It seemed like a prudent course of action. The men anchored their rafts and reached the island just in time because a storm overtook the castaways there. The storm was so powerful that it prevented the men from leaving the island. Within the first day ashore, the expeditioners finished what little water they still had. The men must have fanned out scouting for even the most miserly brook or the muddiest spring. But the island was bone dry, and the storm, which must have carried little rain, gave no sign of abating.[15]

As dehydration overtook them, Narváez and his men must have progressed from dryness in the mouth and a mild sense of discomfort to more dangerous symptoms: lightheadedness, inability to sweat, shrinking of the skin, and an irrepressible urge to drink a liquid of any kind. Not surprisingly, after five days they made the worst possible choice: they succumbed to the urge to drink water from the sea. "And some were so careless in doing so," says Cabeza de Vaca, "that suddenly five men died on us." Saltwater actually accelerates the dehydration process; the ingested sodium binds with any surrounding water molecules, forcing the cells to give up their moisture. A sudden jolt of salt can induce seizures and brain damage. Cabeza de Vaca glosses over those dark moments: "I do not think there is need to tell in detail the miseries and hardships in which we found ourselves, since considering the place where we were and the little hope we had of survival, each one can imagine a great deal of what would happen there."[16]

The Spaniards' situation could not have been bleaker. They were caught between extreme dehydration and an enraged sea. Unable to resist any longer and with the storm still raging, the unfortunate raftsmen took to the sea, entrusting their fate to God and choosing to defy the elements rather than perish from thirst.[17]

That entire day in late October or early November 1528, as the men attempted to cross the open water to the continent, their rafts were buried by the waves only to reemerge instants later. In some respects the travelers were better able to withstand the storm on rafts than they would have been in regular boats, for no amount of water thrown aboveboard would have sunk them. Their main concern was the physical integrity of the vessels. The raft crews, weakened by the effects of severe dehydration, must have been barely able to steer. They were saved by a miraculous apparition. At sunset the rafts finally rounded a part of the coast that entered far into the sea, and the men found great calm and refuge on the other side. Many canoes came to meet the voyagers. "And the Indians who came in the canoes," Cabeza de Vaca recalls, "spoke to us and without wanting to wait for us, turned back. They were large people and well proportioned, and they did not carry bows or arrows."[18]

The battered fleet followed the canoes until they reached some houses by the shore. Amazingly, the Indians greeted them with cooked fish and many pots of water. The castaways must have been unable to believe their good fortune. The chief of this settlement warmly invited Narváez into his house. In exchange, the Spaniards gave out some of the maize that they still possessed, as well as some beads and bells.

But the cordial relationship quickly went sour. That night, the hosts attacked their guests, assaulting the sick men who were lying on the shore. They succeeded in killing three expedition members. The Indians also attempted to break into the chief's house where Narváez was sleeping, and the Governor sustained a rock wound but was not taken. Cabeza de Vaca offers no explanation for this assault.[19]

The visitors were barely able to retreat to their rafts. In the course of that eventful night, the Indians attacked three times, throwing rocks and other objects. They possessed very few arrows. But even so, they forced the visitors to retreat toward the shore and wounded many of them. Even Cabeza de Vaca suffered a cut in the face. The natives would have continued on the offensive had they not been surprised by a small group of Spaniards who hid behind some bushes and charged the Indians from the rear, disbanding them.[20]

The next morning a *norther* began to blow, preventing the castaways from leaving this hostile environment for at least one more day. To keep warm, they made fires. Cabeza de Vaca broke up more than thirty Indian canoes for kindling and firewood. As they waited for the weather to clear up, the Spaniards must have gathered all the clay pots lying around and filled them with water, but even thus provisioned, they would not be able to travel far.[21]

After three or four days at sea, the raftsmen had run out of fresh water once again. They were forced to enter an estuary and risk another confrontation. A canoe came within sight; the Indians aboard fearlessly approached the lead raft. Narváez asked for water. The Indians agreed to bring it to them, but only if they were given the pots to carry it. For the Europeans, it must have been a dramatic predicament. They were desperate for drinking water, but the pots were indispensable too. Losing them would be a serious setback. Negotiations must have dragged on, the tension heightened by the parties' inability to communicate except through signs. In the end Doroteo Teodoro, the Greek Christian who had collected the pitch at the Bay of Horses, volunteered to go with the Indians in the canoe. He would take along an African slave. In return, the natives consented to leaving two of their own men with the Spaniards.

That night, the Indians returned. The pots were still empty, and there was no sign of the Christians. From afar, the natives encouraged the men they had left with the Spaniards to throw themselves into the water. The Spaniards held the men to prevent them from escaping, and the Indians in the canoe quickly turned and rowed away. The parched Spaniards, now without their pots, remained on the rafts, brooding over the fate of the Greek man and the slave.

In the morning several canoes approached the rafts. The Indians were ill-disposed and demanded the release of their two companions. The Governor retorted that he would release the hostages only if they brought back the two Christians they had carried off. The canoes surrounded the rafts and attempted to close off the mouth of the estuary, but the rafts were able to reach the open sea. "And since they refused to return the Christians to us, and for this reason we would not give them the Indian hostages," Cabeza de Vaca writes, "they began to hurl stones at us with slings and throw spears, feigning to shoot arrows at us, although among all of them we saw no more than three or four bows. Being in this dispute the wind came up, and they turned back and left us."[22]

The Spaniards had to leave behind an African slave and the courageous Greek man who had gathered the pitch at the Bay of Horses to seal the bottom of the rafts. A later Spanish expedition learned that these two men were taken inland and subsequently killed. There is no record of what the Spanish did to their two Indian hostages.[23]

The next day the castaways found all the fresh water they could ever want. They came upon the delta of a very large river. It entered the gulf like a broad, majestic avenue, carrying so much water that the raft crews were able to drink straight from the sea. They had reached the Mississippi River. Since leaving the Bay of Horses they had navigated perhaps 370 miles. Unfortunately, Pánuco still lay 620 miles away.

Being able to drink water from the safety of the rafts was an unexpected blessing, but crossing the mighty river posed a formidable challenge. Its discharge was so massive that it forced the rafts away from the shore. The problem was compounded by the wind, which was at the time blowing from the land toward the sea, further pushing the makeshift vessels into the open water. The fleet was driven half a league (1.5 miles) away from the land. The raftsmen were powerless to counter these forces. It was imperative that they keep within sight of the continent; if they were pushed into the open water with no bearings to guide them, they would be lost forever. This drama lasted for two more days until the men were able to pull their rafts back in toward the coast.

Along the distant shore, the survivalists saw many spires of smoke but were unable to learn anything else since it was getting dark. The prudent men decided to wait until morning before getting any closer. Even though the water was shallow, they could not anchor the barges properly because they only had stones tied with ropes. That night, the rafts became separated. The wind must have picked up, blowing two of them into the open sea once again.

When morning came, all Cabeza de Vaca could see was two rafts on the horizon. His oarsmen rowed in the direction of the closest one, which turned out to be Narváez's. When the two vessels came within shouting distance, the Governor asked the Royal Treasurer his opinion about what should be done. Cabeza de Vaca suggested that they should all try to sail in the direction of the third raft and keep together. Narváez replied that it could not be done "because the raft was very far out to sea and he wished to return to land." By way of explanation, one of Narváez's companions added that their main goal was to reach land because if they didn't, the people aboard would start dying of starvation.[24]

It was just a matter of time before all the rafts became separated. Cabeza de Vaca's men tried to follow the Governor, rowing desperately, trying to defy currents and winds to make landfall, but the crew was exhausted. For three days they had been subjected to a daily ration that consisted of one handful of raw corn. In contrast, Narváez's craft was somewhat lighter and carried the strongest and healthiest men, so it naturally kept running ahead. Unable to keep up the pace, Cabeza de Vaca finally asked the Governor to throw him a line. He refused, saying that the men on his raft were determined to reach land that very night and could not spare their effort or time helping those on the other rafts. After hearing that, Cabeza de Vaca answered that he didn't think they would be able to keep up with the Governor's raft and asked Narváez to tell him his orders. The reply was decisive. Narváez said that "it was no longer time for some men to rule over others, but that each one should do whatever seemed best to save his life." Bent on saving himself, Narváez had abandoned his command over the other four rafts. Each vessel would have to fend for itself.[25]

Cabeza de Vaca ordered his men to sail toward the third raft which, amazingly, was still visible. This vessel was the one commanded by Captains Téllez and Peñaloza. The two crews traveled together for four more days. They must have carried some fresh water with them; their provisions, however, were nearly exhausted. The rations had to be cut to only half a handful of raw maize per day. By this point, the men had almost certainly lost the strength to row. Their only hope of survival was pinned on the capricious wind, and yet the elements did not cooperate. A sudden storm caught up with the two rafts, separating them and threatening to break them apart.

Somehow Cabeza de Vaca's raft made it through another day. Tormented by extreme hunger and drenched from the splashing of the waves, the men were all on the brink of death. Even the usually reserved Cabeza de Vaca paints a dismal picture: "The people began to faint in such a manner that when the sun set all those who came in my raft were fallen on top of one another in it, so close to death that few were conscious." Only the helmsman and Cabeza de Vaca took turns steering the raft. But the helmsman too began to falter. "Two hours into the night," Cabeza de Vaca says, "the helmsman told me that I should take charge of the raft, because he was in such condition that he thought he would die that very night." Cabeza de Vaca grabbed the tiller for some hours and after midnight went to check on the helmsman to see if he had died. To his surprise, he was feeling better and offered to steer until daybreak.[26]

Near dawn, Cabeza de Vaca heard the surf. The helmsman believed that land was near. The two men mustered enough energy to cast a lead line in the dark. The bottom was not more than seven fathoms deep. As dawn rose, they saw land not more than 3 miles away. Cabeza de Vaca picked up an oar and began to row. Most of the men remained lying while a handful rowed frantically toward salvation. In their desperation, the conscious men must have sailed past the wave break. By the time they tried to stop the raft, it must have been too late to save the raft from breaking apart on the beach. A large wave tossed the makeshift vessel squarely onto the sand, waking the sleeping men on impact. As Cabeza de Vaca recounts, "They began to leave the raft half walking, half crawling. And as they came on land to some bluffs, we made a fire and toasted some of the maize that we carried. And we found rainwater, and with the heat of the fire the men revived and began to regain strength." The Royal Treasurer and his men had reached an island off of what is now Texas.[27]

MIRACULOUSLY, ALL FIVE rafts reached different parts of that same coast. The raft that sailed the farthest was the one led by Captains Téllez and Peñaloza. When Cabeza de Vaca last saw this vessel somewhere west of the Mississippi River, its crew had

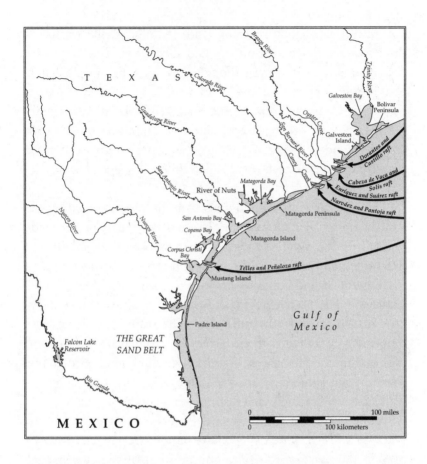

consumed nearly all its food and was headed into a storm. They must have been unable to land for several days, drifting in the high seas and facing the very real prospect of starvation. When these men finally reached Texas, perhaps as far south as present-day Mustang or Padre Islands, they must have been a sorry lot. Quite possibly, some of them had already died. It is hard to imagine how this raft crew was able to navigate some 155 miles more than Cabeza de Vaca's; perhaps they had resorted to cannibalism to stay alive. Yet they would not perish from starvation, at least not all of them. Upon reaching land, an Indian tribe known as the Camones descended on the famished crew. The castaways "were so skinny that even though they were being killed they could not defend themselves." Not a single man survived the attack. The Camones took all the Spaniards' objects, eventually selling them to other groups. The raft remained on the spot where it landed. It lay at the shore as a final testimony of the tenacity of its crew, who had sailed 750 miles since leaving the Bay of Horses.[28]

The raft carrying the religious men and commanded by the Royal Comptroller Alonso Enríquez and Fray Juan Suárez made landfall by the mouth of the San Bernard River. Their raft had overturned and must have been beyond repair. The men decided to abandon it and continue on foot toward Spanish-controlled territory. It had been a great loss, for they had arrived at a marshy area traversed by rivers and inlets. The raft would have been tremendously useful; without it, they had to expend precious energy and time building new vessels, quite small in all probability. Even though some men drowned along the way, they doggedly walked south for many miles, surviving on crabs and kelp.[29]

While marching south toward Pánuco, this group ran into Narváez's crew, which must have landed in the environs of present-day Matagorda Bay. The reunion of the two parties must have been joyous. Although temporarily separated, the two raft crews had already shared an unbelievable adventure and must have been avid to exchange tales of their ordeals. Above all, doubling their number and seeing familiar faces must have been immensely comforting in the midst of a completely alien land. But the chance encounter also raised troubling questions. Together, the two groups must have numbered eighty, but Narváez's raft could only carry half as many. Also, there appears to have been some tension between the leaders of the two groups. After all, Narváez had renounced his authority over the other barges in a most public way; the two contingents had acted independently for some time. The Governor now wanted to shore up his control. He felt threatened enough by the Royal Comptroller Alonso Enríquez to revoke his title as lieutenant governor and appoint one of his associates instead.

Narváez's arrogance proved to be his undoing. Fearful of an Indian attack, he granted himself the privilege of sleeping on his raft while the men camped on the shore. The Governor was accompanied by a minimal crew: a helmsman and a page. In the event of an ambush, these three fortunate men would at least have a chance to escape. In the middle of the night the wind picked up and became so strong that it blew the raft out to sea without anyone realizing what was happening. It must have been a cruel awakening for the three men. From the raft they must have been able to catch a final glimpse of the immense and hostile land that Narváez nominally ruled.[30]

The vessel carried no food or water, so the three men could not have lasted long. But there must have been some time for reflection. Against all odds, Narváez would not die of an Indian attack or a debilitating illness. Instead, in a supreme final irony, he spent his last hours confined to a small platform floating on the Gulf of Mexico and surrounded by the enormous *adelantamiento* that he had failed to conquer.

The rest of the men from the two rafts continued their journey to the south under new leadership. But it was already getting too cold. After some more days of painstaking travel, they stopped and decided to spend the winter on this strange coast. Pánuco would have to wait until the spring. The band of survivalists was large enough that it could not be easily attacked. They set up camp in a wooded area with abundant water and firewood and some crabs and shellfish and braced for the harsh weather.[31]

The winter was harrowing. After depleting their meager food supply, these wretched castaways were brought face to face with death. As they struggled to stave off starvation, they resorted to the ultimate solution. The living cut the bodies of the dead into strips, possibly drying the meat in the sun to preserve it from spoilage: "They were people beyond hope and all died that winter of hunger and cold, eating one another." By March 1, 1529, only one man remained alive. His name was Hernando de Esquivel, a native of Badajoz. An Indian found him still feeding on the body of Sotomayor, the former leader of this most unfortunate group.[32]

North of where this drama was unfolding, the last two rafts had also reached dry land. One was Cabeza de Vaca's. The other was the one led by Captains Andrés Dorantes and Alonso del Castillo. These groups of men had not seen each other since right after crossing the Mississippi River some 300 miles back. Following parallel trajectories, propelled by the same winds and buffeted by the same storms and currents, and by an incredible coincidence, they would come to land on opposite sides of the same island.

CHAPTER 6

Enslaved

AFTER BEING HURLED ONTO THE BEACH, CABEZA de Vaca and his emaciated crew spent some time regaining their strength. They built fires and roasted some of their remaining corn. A man named Lope de Oviedo, who was evidently healthier and stronger than the others, climbed up a tree to survey the land. "He discovered that we were on an island," Cabeza de Vaca writes, "and he saw that the land was rutted in the way that it usually is where cattle roam, and it seemed to him for this reason that it must be land inhabited by Christians, and thus he reported it to us." The news must have been electrifying.[1]

The men had reached an elongated island which was only 1.5 miles wide but 15 miles long. It must have been either Galveston Island or, more likely, the island immediately to the south.[2]

Cabeza de Vaca ordered Lope de Oviedo to explore further without straying too far. He found a trail and followed it for a little over 1 mile to a small Indian village. As the huts were abandoned, the Spaniard took a pot and filled it with mullet and started to make his way back to the beach. A small dog followed him. Once on the trail, he also noticed three Indians with bows and arrows behind him. They called out to him. The castaway managed to rejoin his group before being overtaken, and the three natives prudently stopped at a distance. But within half an hour, 100 Indian men, all fully armed, had surrounded the Spaniards. Cabeza de Vaca makes only one dry but telling observation: "Whether or not they were of great stature, our fear made them seem like giants."[3]

Resistance was completely out of the question. Of the forty men in Cabeza de Vaca's contingent, not six would have been able to stand. The famished outsiders would either die on the spot or reach a compromise with the native islanders. The two Spanish leaders, Cabeza de Vaca and the Royal Inspector Alonso de Solís, decided to approach the indigenous fighters and call out to them. The Indians came forward. The two royal officials gave out bells and beads, and the Indians gave the two strangers arrows in return, which is a sign of friendship. And through gestures the Indians made the castaways understand that they would be back the next morning with food. The Spaniards must have spent a night filled with foreboding. The idea of making preparations to resist an attack must have crossed their minds.[4]

The next day at sunrise, the Indians returned. As promised, they brought with them fish and some curious roots unknown to the foreigners—quite likely cattail roots—that were about the size of chestnuts and that the Indians dug out from under water with great difficulty. In the afternoon the natives brought some more food. They had grown so confident that this time they came accompanied by women and children. The stranded men, so strikingly different, must have been for the Indians fascinating to observe. The natives kept visiting the castaways' camp for some days, always delivering fish and roots.[5]

As the Spaniards regained some strength, they thought about resuming their journey to Pánuco. They dug the raft out of the sand and dragged it to the edge of the water. The weakened but resourceful men must have gathered some water and probably saved some of the roots that they had been given. When everything seemed ready, the men removed their clothes so as to keep them dry, and then waded into the cold water to push the raft off from the shore. After they leapt aboard and had traveled some distance, a huge wave hit them, and, as Cabeza de Vaca explains, "Since we went naked and the cold was very great, we dropped the oars from our hands." The raft drifted just a little longer before another large wave overturned it. The Royal Inspector Alonso de Solís and two other men clung to the barge so tenaciously that they became trapped underwater and drowned. All of the other men were plunged into the cold and tempestuous ocean; they were half-drowned and shivering when they made it back to the beach.[6]

The Spaniards lost all their remaining possessions in that failed attempt to leave the island. They had been shedding baggage throughout Florida and the Gulf Coast, and now the process was complete. The castaways now faced the New World quite literally naked. "It was November," writes Cabeza de Vaca, "and the cold was very great; and we were so thin that with little difficulty our bones could be counted, and we appeared like the very image of death."[7]

At the time of the Florida expedition, North America was colder than it is today. From the 1300s thru the 1800s, the world experienced a prolonged period of cooling, and the evidence suggests that the years from 1527 to 1529 were especially harsh. Cabeza de Vaca had complained about the cold in the middle of the Florida summer; the winter must have been daunting indeed.[8]

Already hypothermic from their spell in the water, the men returned to their camp, where mercifully they found some last embers to rekindle a fire. They spent the next few hours huddled and commiserating: "And thus we were beseeching our Lord for mercy and the pardon of our sins, shedding many tears, each one having pity not only for himself but for all the others whom they saw in the same state." As their situation became more desperate, the stranded men sought strength and consolation in their religious beliefs.[9]

When the Indians returned at sunset to bring food as usual, they were shocked to see the Christians so changed. They withdrew immediately, and Cabeza de Vaca had to run after them to try to explain what had happened. Gradually, the natives came to understand the disaster that had befallen their guests. They also saw the bodies of two of the drowned Europeans. At last, they sat down among the castaways. "And with the great grief and pity they felt on seeing us in such a state," Cabeza de Vaca writes, "they all began to weep loudly and so sincerely that they could be heard a great distance away." The weeping lasted for more than half an hour. "And truly," the Royal Treasurer marvels, "to see that these men, so lacking in reason and so crude in the manner of brutes, grieved so much for us, increased in me and in others of our company even more the magnitude of our suffering and the estimation of our misfortune."[10]

Once the weeping ended, Cabeza de Vaca resolutely asked the islanders to take them to their homes. There was no alternative that he could see, as the stranded men would otherwise die of exposure and hunger. And the Indians seemed willing to oblige. But even in these desperate circumstances, there were some expeditioners who opposed the plan, especially those who had been to Mexico and had seen or heard about Aztec practices of human sacrifice and ritual cannibalism. "We should not even speak of it"—they had objected—"because if they took us to their houses, they would sacrifice us to their idols."[11]

The Indians went away to make some preparations. They returned that night, having kindled four or five great bonfires between the coast and their hamlet. They feared that without such a precaution some of the foreigners might fall unconscious and die from exposure during the short journey from the beach to the village. When everything was ready, the Indians started carrying the castaways, taking them to the first fire, "and when they saw that we had regained some strength and warmth, they carried us to the next one, so rapidly that they almost did not let our feet touch the ground." Not all the Spaniards consented to go with the islanders. At least five men chose to stay by the beach on their own, a decision they would soon come to regret.[12]

When Cabeza de Vaca and his companions arrived at the village, they saw that the Indians had prepared a large house with many fires inside. The dancing began barely an hour after the outsiders had arrived, and the celebration lasted all night long. "For us there was neither rejoicing nor sleep"—Cabeza de Vaca recalled—"as we were awaiting the moment when they would sacrifice us." But the men survived through the night, and the next morning the Indians gave them more food and continued to treat them kindly, allaying their fears.[13]

The Indians' generosity was astonishing. They had taken food to the Europeans twice a day for some time and had gone to great lengths to transport them to their camp and give them shelter. Potentially they would have to sustain this helpless crew through the winter. For a small community of not more than a few dozen families, feeding forty additional adults would constitute a significant drain on their food supplies.

That same day Cabeza de Vaca spotted a native man carrying some European objects that had not come from his raft. The Royal Treasurer anxiously asked the native where he had procured the items. Amazingly, he responded to Cabeza de Vaca through signs that he had received these objects from other men like himself, and that this second group was farther away but also on the island.[14]

This revelation must have caused great commotion among the stranded men. Cabeza de Vaca immediately sent two of his men to look for these other Europeans, but the scouting party did not have to travel far. The other group of castaways was already on its way to the village, having been alerted about Cabeza de Vaca's crew by other Indians who lived on that side of the island. They turned out to be the contingent under the command of Captains Andrés Dorantes and Alonso del Castillo, which must have also included Estebanico. "Upon encountering us," Cabeza de Vaca recalls, "they received a great fright to see us in the condition we were in."[15]

The reunion must have seemed to all like a miracle. They had last seen each other at the crossing of the Mississippi River and had faced so many dangers in the intervening weeks that each group must have assumed that the other had perished.

Tantalizingly, the members of the Dorantes-Castillo party were still in possession of their raft. At least some of the men would have a chance of going forward to Pánuco. The eighty men set to work immediately. They decided that the strongest among them would continue; the rest would remain on the island to recover and perhaps would attempt to reach Spanish-controlled territory by land in the spring.

But the raft was unable to support the castaways' hopes. When they launched it a few days after their reunion, it immediately broke apart and sank to the bottom. The men were now without crafts or provisions. Moreover, winter was looming and many of the men were naked, so swimming across rivers and bays was impossible. Pánuco would have to wait until the spring.[16]

But even without the raft, the castaways decided to send an advance party to the south. Four men would make a last-ditch effort to reach Pánuco over the winter. They must have been given clothing and provisions. Perhaps a small raft was built for them. These four men were among the strongest survivors and were all good swimmers. Unfortunately, even they were unable to reach Christian lands; all four died in the attempt.

After this disaster, the remaining Spaniards, emaciated and destitute as they were, must have come to count themselves as fortunate. At least they had washed up among friendly Indians.

THE SURVIVORS OF the Pánfilo de Narváez expedition were the first outsiders to have lived in the immense territories north of Mexico and to come in contact with many peoples across North America. It was an experience that neither the Spaniards nor their Amerindian hosts would forget.

At contact, both groups appeared strikingly different. The contrasts were so patent that many Europeans openly discussed whether the natives were human at all and vice versa. Two large contingents of the human species had reestablished contact after a very long time. The peoples of the New World were descended from a small group of men and women who had crossed the Bering Strait some 12,000 years ago and migrated to America, the last great land mass of the world that had remained unpopulated. Shortly after this migration episode, both worlds lost touch once again.[17]

Over the millennia, these true pioneers of the New World explored the entire continent and multiplied until reaching some 60 or 70 million by the fifteenth century (comparable to Europe's population at the time). They built monumental ceremonial centers, established impressive trading networks, and waged war on one another. It was a world unto itself, unconnected to and unconcerned with the rest of the planet. Recent DNA evidence confirms that all Native American lineages can ultimately be traced back to Asia, but that for thousands of years they evolved completely independently from all other humans. It was not until

1492, when Columbus reached the Caribbean, that these two huge fragments of the human family were finally reunited.[18]

Despite their long separation, the Old and the New World had undergone remarkably parallel developments. The peoples of both worlds had domesticated plants and animals; organized themselves in chiefdoms, principalities, monarchies, and empires; and developed forms of writing and mathematics. Most early European explorers were initially drawn to the stark differences between themselves and the natives they encountered. Cabeza de Vaca and his men, unlike other explorers, had the luxury of direct and patient observation. Moreover, their lives depended on the commonalities.

The island where the two rafts had landed harbored two small indigenous groups: the Capoques and the Hans. The sheer appearance of these two groups was daunting. They were tall, not infrequently reaching 6 feet, easily towering over the Spaniards. The natives went about completely naked, and their physique was robust and flexible. They were fond of piercing one nipple, sometimes both, and inserting through the holes large reeds that could be as thick as two fingers and two and a half palms in length. They also pierced their lower lip, inserting yet another reed, although this one *only* half a finger in thickness. Only the women covered part of their bodies, making garments out of a tree fiber, while the maidens wore deerskins.[19]

Cabeza de Vaca and his crew lived with one of the two bands, though he fails to mention which one. The Dorantes-Castillo contingent resided with the other. It appears that the two groups of survivors were allowed to visit each other freely at first, for relations between Capoques and Hans were cordial. Even though they spoke mutually unintelligible languages, the two bands had no qualms about sharing their commodious island. Each group must have numbered perhaps 400 or 500 individuals.[20]

Caranca*bueses*

Even in the nineteenth century the Karankawa Indians were regarded as indomitable and representative of a primitive way of life. Watercolor by Lino Sánchez y Tapia in Jean Louis Berlandier, *The Indians of Texas in 1830.* Courtesy of the Gilcrease Museum.

Nothing could have prepared the castaways for the lifestyle they would have to adopt to survive. The Capoques and Hans were fully nomadic peoples. They led a roving life, seldom spending more than a few weeks in any given site. They had but few possessions and lived in simple, semicircular tents that were easily constructed and that provided only minimal protection from the elements. Their simple dwellings, however, belied their extraordinarily sophisticated use of their environment. Their knowledge of the coastal flora and fauna was simply un-matched. They were expert foragers. The Capoques and Hans moved in seasonal, deliberate patterns meant to take advantage of specific food items in a range that was not confined to their is-land but also extended into the flat, low-lying coastal prairie on the mainland. Their hunting skills were formidable as well. In Cabeza de Vaca's estimation, their hearing and eyesight were so sharp and attuned to even the slightest movement so as to rank among the best in the world.

When the two rafts made landfall in November, the Capoques and Hans must have just arrived at the island to spend the winter there. They typically subsisted on fish and roots, which were plentiful at first, but the natives knew well that things would deteriorate steadily, reaching a low point in February when the starchy tubers begin to sprout and are no longer edible.[21]

The winter of 1528–1529 was extraordinarily harsh. The cold and a series of great storms prevented the Indians from wading into the water to dig up the roots. Fishing became extremely difficult and generally yielded nothing. The houses may have been portable, but they afforded little protection against the inclement weather. Many castaways were unable to survive. "In a short time, of us eighty men who arrived there from both ends [of the island], only fifteen remained alive." With these few words, Cabeza de Vaca glosses over what must have been two months of unabated horror. Men must have been dying almost daily.[22]

The miserable winter conditions may have seemed apocalyptic to the last survivors, but the natives understood this hungry spell as part of an annual cycle. As winter eased into spring, and the roots began to sprout and were no longer edible, the Capoques and Hans began making preparations to go to the mainland in search of the one food item that was available all year round: oysters. Ordinarily they subsisted on these mollusks for three or four months of the year and, as some of the survivors pointedly observed, "in fact eat nothing else." Around April the Indians also combed the shore, "eating blackberries the entire month, during which time they do not cease to perform their *areitos* [feasts] and celebrations." In the summer it was time to hunt deer and bison, though without overlooking other food sources, including spiders, lizards, snakes, and rats. In the fall the Capoques and the Hans went back to their island to catch fish and harvest the aquatic roots, recommencing the yearly cycle.[23]

Living on the coast of Texas was not easy. The survivors of two rafts of the Narváez expedition had tried to spend the winter on their own and wound up cannibalizing each other. Yet for centuries, these coastal natives had survived and even thrived in the same environment. Even though other indigenous groups both to the south and to the north cultivated corn, the Capoques and Hans and their descendants relied solely on the bounty of the land.[24]

WHAT HAD BEGUN as a guest-host relationship between the natives and the Spaniards eventually degenerated into a relationship between masters and slaves. The transition was gradual but unmistakable. No doubt, the castaways did not take long to outlive their initial welcome. The Capoques and Hans had been extraordinarily generous to the marooned explorers, but with the onset of winter, the strangers must have been expected to pull their own weight. The Indians were surely shocked at how useless the foreigners were. The castaways must have been laughably incapable of hunting with bows and arrows, and their fishing skills could not have been much better, as their knowledge of local traps, weirs, and edible fish was minimal. Since the strangers could not be entrusted with manly occupations, they were given women's work. They had to dig for roots, carry firewood, and fetch water.[25]

One incident in particular strained their relationship. Not all of the Spaniards had taken up residence with the Indians. Five raftsmen had chosen to spend the winter by the beach; their fear of being sacrificed and eaten by the natives must have been overpowering. It had been a grave mistake. And the very thing that they dreaded the most—cannibalism—came to pass, albeit not in the way that they had expected it. Finding themselves without any food and in great necessity, they ate one another. And as Cabeza de Vaca notes with disarming logic, "Only one remained because he was alone and had no one to eat him."[26]

When the Indians learned what had happened, they became very upset. "The scandal among them was such that they would have killed the men had they seen them at the start; and all of us would have been in grave danger." Ironically, in later centuries Europeans accused the native peoples of coastal Texas of cannibalism. Little did they know that in the sixteenth century the Europeans themselves had been the cannibals, and the Indians the ones appalled by such behavior.[27]

The castaways' situation became even more precarious when the native islanders began dying from an "illness of the bowels," perhaps dysentery spread by the decomposing bodies of the Europeans. About *half* of all the Indians on the island died. It was an astonishing calamity and a terrible foreboding of the demographic disaster that would soon engulf the entire continent due to the introduction of new pathogens to the New World. Perhaps with good reason, the strangers were held responsible. "And taking this to be very true," Cabeza de Vaca writes, "the Indians agreed among themselves to kill those of us who remained."[28]

As the natives prepared to carry out their intentions, the Indian man who had come to own Cabeza de Vaca intervened. He forcefully defended the castaways by reasoning that if they had the power to cause illness among the natives, then they surely would have prevented the deaths of so many of their own kind. This Indian man, who must have been sufficiently influential to hold slaves and go against general opinion, noted that none of the foreigners did any harm or ill and concluded that the best thing to do was to let them be. Somehow his point of view carried the day, and the lives of the strangers were spared.[29] The men would remain on the island as slaves to the natives. Life became so harsh for the survivors that they took the habit of calling the island *Malhado*, the "Isle of Ill fate." For the next six years or so the castaways' lives revolved around unceasing work. Their chores were deceptively trivial: carrying wood, digging for roots, or fetching water. There was nothing insidious or cruel about these activities, but they were constant as well as physically challenging and often painful. The heavy stumps chafed directly against their bare backs, and the bearers' feet were hurt from walking over summer-hot sand and amidst fierce spiny plants. Cabeza de Vaca's fingers bled constantly from digging roots; and he was forced to venture completely naked through thickets of cattails and other plants.[30]

By this time, the survivors were entirely at the mercy of their masters. The native children mocked the Christians almost daily. According to Cabeza de Vaca, "Any child would give them a good hair pulling, and for them this was great fun, the greatest pleasure in the world." That was merely juvenile humor; the adults did not hesitate to use violence to obtain compliance. The captives reported being beaten with sticks, slapped in the face, and having their thick beards jerked out. A minor omission, delay, or infraction could bring about severe punishment, even death. Cabeza de Vaca recounts how three Christians were killed "only for daring to go from one house to another . . . and another three who remained alive expected to meet the same end." The castaways' daily anxiety over being punished or killed must have taken a dramatic toll. None of them could depend on staying alive from one day to the next. One Spaniard who had committed no infraction at all was killed simply because one Indian woman had a dream "of I don't know what nonsense," the castaways recall, "because in those parts they believe in dreams and kill their own children because of dreams."[31]

Undoubtedly, the castaways had become slaves. Yet it is also important to note that societies like the Capoques and Hans were not "slaving societies," in the sense that they did not actively procure and exploit slave labor. They certainly possessed slaves, which were a byproduct of their continuous warfare with neighboring groups or came about when wandering strangers like the castaways "joined" these bands to escape starvation. However, this system was a far cry from that employed by more centralized and hierarchical societies like Portugal and Spain, for instance, or other indigenous societies in the American continent. For the coastal peoples of Texas, slaves were decidedly marginal to their survival and well-being. For one thing, a slave may have represented one more pair of arms but also an additional mouth to feed. Rather than systematically procuring and exploiting slaves, they were tolerated like stray dogs and permitted to stay as long as they made themselves useful. Indeed, as the castaways would discover, some of the natives of Texas flatly refused to take them, even as slaves. But once the castaways had gained admittance, their lives depended entirely on the will of their masters. This peculiar context did not lessen the sufferings of Cabeza de Vaca and his companions. But it helps us understand why the castaways were enslaved only gradually, why they had to seek out unwilling masters who often abused them, and why during their six-year stay along the Texas coast they were able to flee from one indigenous clan to another.[32]

The once-mighty conquistadors had endured a precipitous fall. Life as an abused slave must have been indescribably bitter for the likes of Cabeza de Vaca and Captains Dorantes and Castillo. Castillo could have enjoyed the life of a judge or a municipal officer, had he only chosen to stay in Europe. What fool-

ish impulse had compelled him to join the Narváez expedition
and forsake a lifetime of comfort and happiness? Captain Dorantes may have been more of a man of action, perhaps more ac-
cepting of reversals of fortune and violence. After all, he already
bore a scar on his face from military action. But surely he never
imagined spending his last days on earth enslaved by a bizarre,
naked people halfway around the world.

And what to say of the Royal Treasurer? Generations of
Cabeza de Vacas had worked to further the imperial aims of Spain.
His grandfather had been the famous captain who had conquered
Gran Canaria. With the history of his ancestors in mind, Álvar
Núñez Cabeza de Vaca must have also dreamed of great acts of
conquest and bravery when the Florida expedition got underway.
Yet his ambitions had been shattered in the whirlwind of a hurri-
cane, a colossal navigational mistake, a difficult march through
Florida, a harrowing raft passage, and a sordid enslavement.
Surely this nobleman suffered greatly as he tried to reconcile himself to spending the balance of his life digging for roots until his
fingers bled and stoically withstanding beatings at the hands of natives who would never understand what he was meant to be.

The man best able to cope psychologically with the adverse
conditions was in all likelihood the African Estebanico. He was
no stranger to the life of bondage, as he had already once been
captured, taken away from his homeland, and sold in Europe.
His sufferings certainly increased in the New World as the expedition foundered, but his social standing had changed but little.
He had been Dorantes's slave; but now his master had himself
become enslaved, an odd twist of fate that probably gave Estebanico a certain unspeakable satisfaction. Although it is possible
that his subordination to Dorantes and the other Spaniards persisted in some fashion, the fact that the white Europeans were
also enslaved must have reduced the disparities. Indians, not

Spaniards, exercised the ultimate authority now, a fact that must have complicated immensely Dorantes's ability to enforce his authority over the African. With the passing of time, Estebanico became just another slave largely undistinguishable from his former masters.

Estebanico's sheer survival is miraculous. All the other castaways were elite Spaniards who were likely to outlast Africans, simply because they were better nourished and their bodies had been less exposed to the ravages of punishing physical labor. Moreover, Europeans in commanding positions were able to use their authority in ways that shielded them from danger and maximized their chances of survival. And yet, Estebanico managed to outlive dozens of Spaniards who could have reasonably expected to be among the last men standing. By all accounts, he was the ultimate survivor. He had experienced the life of bondage on three different continents and had been forced to face incredible perils and adventures. Against astonishing odds, he had survived through it all.

THE LAST REMAINING castaways endured as slaves on the coast of Texas for six years. By the spring of 1529, after that first brutal winter, only eighteen or so castaways remained alive. They became dispersed among the Capoques and Hans as they followed their respective masters.

Cabeza de Vaca's experience was especially trying because all of the European and African castaways hosted by his particular band of Indians (we don't know which of the two) died over the winter. By the spring he was the only remaining castaway within this band. In the spring Cabeza de Vaca's masters took him to the mainland. The Royal Treasurer's sense of loneliness and abandonment was compounded by a severe and prolonged illness that came to afflict him at this time.

It was also a time of despair. During his lengthy convalescence, Cabeza de Vaca learned that the majority of the castaways, still living on the island of Malhado with the other band, had agreed to resume their quest to Pánuco. This sizable contingent of twelve men—which included Dorantes, Castillo, and Estebanico—crossed to the mainland, not far from where Cabeza de Vaca was struggling to regain his health, and started journeying south.

The Royal Treasurer knew about his companions' intentions through his indigenous masters. Dorantes and Castillo even tried to contact Cabeza de Vaca, but were unable to see him. In any case, he could not travel. His companions' departure must have been a crushing blow for the Royal Treasurer.[33]

Cabeza de Vaca had little choice but to entrust himself to the mercy of God. His religious convictions constituted his last refuge. In the summer or fall of 1529, his captors took him back to Malhado. There the Royal Treasurer found out that not all the explorers had left for Pánuco, but that two very frail castaways had stayed behind at the island. Like Cabeza de Vaca, these two men had been unable to follow the Dorantes-Castillo contingent. There must have been a great deal of comfort in this news. These two men were Lope de Oviedo, the tree climber who had first explored Malhado, and another Spaniards by the name of Jerónimo de Alaniz.

Cabeza de Vaca remained with the same band of Indians for more than a year, traveling between Malhado and the mainland. But they treated the Royal Treasurer harshly and forced him to do a great deal of work. Cabeza de Vaca resolved to flee the island and join another band that lived in a forest on the mainland. These Indians were called the Charrucos. He must have come in contact with them during his travels with the native islanders.[34]

Thus began a new phase in Cabeza de Vaca's life. The Charrucos were at war with other groups surrounding them. They needed a neutral broker able to trade even in the midst of hostilities, and an outsider like Cabeza de Vaca was the perfect conduit. With the encouragement of the Charrucos, the former Royal Treasurer became an itinerant merchant carving for himself an extraordinary role among the Indians of the region. We can only imagine Cabeza de Vaca's trepidation as he ventured into new lands wholly exposed and carrying valuable wares, but the Charrucos urged him to go from one place to another to procure the things that they needed. Thus, for two years the resourceful castaway plied the trade.[35]

Cabeza de Vaca started his remarkable trading journeys by collecting among the Charrucos objects that were coveted by the peoples of the interior. Such coastal items included pieces of sea snail shells and the hearts of the animals themselves. He also took "sea beads"—a decidedly poetic if somewhat vague description that may refer to pearls—as well as a certain kind of shell that was used in the interior to cut a fruit that resembled a bean. (The natives used this fruit in their curing ceremonies and it was therefore greatly prized.) Armed with these goods, Cabeza de Vaca then ventured through the interior for weeks at a time, covering great distances of 120 miles or more. He must have been fed along the way and allowed to wander through the territories of various peoples, apparently without conflict.

In exchange for his coastal goods, Cabeza de Vaca received hides, which were always in great demand among the Charrucos. He also brought back red ocher, "with which they smear themselves and dye their faces and hair," as well as flints, glue, and hard canes to make arrows. "And this occupation served me well"—Cabeza de Vaca explains—"because practicing it, I had the freedom to go wherever I wanted, and I was not constrained in any way nor enslaved, and wherever I went they treated me well and gave me food out of want for my wares, and most importantly because doing that, I was able to seek out the ways by which I would go forward."[36]

Only the two fellow castaways who had remained on Malhado prevented Cabeza de Vaca from attempting to set out toward Pánuco. Jerónimo de Alaniz died some time later. But Lope de Oviedo endured on the island. Thus every year Cabeza de Vaca made his way across the bay to visit Lope de Oviedo and talk him into escaping together. Cabeza de Vaca's visits to Malhado are remarkable, for it means that his former masters no longer sought retribution for his escape, but perhaps were now more interested in gaining access to the Royal Treasurer's wares.

Despite Cabeza de Vaca's efforts to convince him, Lope de Oviedo was reluctant to leave the island, and kept postponing the date of their escape. He preferred to cling to his life in Malhado, however precarious and tormented, rather than risk death in unknown lands and amongst even more violent and unpredictable peoples.[37]

After three years, however, Cabeza de Vaca finally prevailed. In the spring or summer of 1532, the two survivors made their escape toward Pánuco. Lope de Oviedo did not know how to swim, so Cabeza de Vaca had to help him get across the bay to the mainland. They must have followed the same route that the Dorantes-Castillo party had taken years earlier, painstakingly moving through a region of four rivers until they fell in with a group of Indians known as the Quevenes. These Indians conveyed startling information to the two fugitives. The Quevenes first said that farther south there were three other Christians who were still alive. Cabeza de Vaca and Lope de Oviedo then asked about all the others, and the Quevenes responded that they had all died of cold and hunger. More ominously, the Quevenes said that the Christians were treated badly in that area and remarked that some neighboring Indians had even killed three Christians for their own amusement. By way of demonstration, the Quevenes proceeded to take Lope de Oviedo and hit him with a stick and slap him, "and I did not lack my share," Cabeza de Vaca writes, "and they threw mud balls at us, and each day placed arrows aimed at our hearts, saying that they wanted to kill us as they had killed our other companions."[38]

Lope de Oviedo, hard to convince in the first place, became discouraged and decided to return to the island. The Royal Treasurer tried to reassure his companion, talking to him for a long time. But he could not prevent Lope de Oviedo from going back to Malhado. His fate is unknown.

The Royal Treasurer proceeded alone with the Quevenes; there would be no turning back for him. They took Cabeza de Vaca to a lush, twisting river where various groups had gathered to eat nuts. When Cabeza de Vaca approached a dwelling where the Indians had taken him, Andrés Dorantes came out. The captain was greatly astonished to see a fellow Spaniard whom he had given up for dead so long ago. "We gave many thanks to God upon finding ourselves reunited," Cabeza de Vaca recalls, "and this day was one of the days of greatest pleasure that we have had in our lives." It was the fall of 1532; the two Spaniards had not seen each other for three and a half years.[39]

Cabeza de Vaca and Dorantes then went together to see Castillo and Estebanico, who were also encamped at what they called the "river of nuts." All four must have been able to spend some time talking and sharing their remarkable stories of endurance. Only then did Cabeza de Vaca learn of what had happened to these fellow castaways.

After that first disastrous winter of 1528–1529, Dorantes and Castillo had led most of the survivors out of the island of Malhado in the spring. The first step had been to persuade the people of Malhado to get them across to the mainland on canoes, as many of the castaways could not swim. Somehow these men were still in possession of some objects salvaged from their raft that they used as trade goods and gifts. To get to the mainland, the outsiders had to part a the valuable cloak of sable skins that they had pilfered during the raft voyage. The cloak was deemed to be "the finest to be found anywhere in the world," its scent was said to resemble that of "ambergris and musk, and it was so strong that it could be detected at a great distance."[40] The natives must have been sufficiently impressed, for they consented to letting this group of survivors go and even agreed to transport them to the other shore.

Once on the mainland, the members of the Dorantes-Castillo party had occasion to demonstrate their dogged tenacity. For weeks they walked along the shore, heading south. The terrain could hardly be more difficult: in fact, no other portion of the coast between the Mississippi River and the Rio de las Palmas is more intricately crisscrossed by water than the section they were now trying to traverse south of present-day Galveston Bay. They had to negotiate no fewer than four large rivers and at least three straits or bays. In each instance they were forced either to build makeshift rafts, repair abandoned canoes, or beg for the assistance from local Indians.[41]

The passage took a heavy toll. Some of the men drowned along the way, while others were killed by Indians. The party dwindled from twelve to ten to six and at last to only three: Dorantes, Castillo, and Estebanico. These three survivors were forced to "join" the local Indians to save themselves from starvation. They

were enslaved and reduced to following their respective masters, thus becoming separated. Still they somehow were able to keep sporadic contact with one another, and even at times to work side by side.

The reunion of these three castaways with Cabeza de Vaca in the fall of 1532 was momentous. It was a time of renewed hope and enlarged possibilities. The four men broached the subject of escape. "I told [them]"—Cabeza de Vaca recalls—"that my purpose was to go to the land of Christians and that on this path and pursuit I was embarked." Dorantes responded that he too had been urging his two companions to flee for years, but that neither Castillo nor Estebanico had wanted to go. These last two men were at a crushing disadvantage: they did not know how to swim. The costal environment amounted to the most extravagant prison that God could have devised for them.[42]

Now there might be a way out. The miraculous reunion had changed the castaways' possibilities of escape in one crucial respect: there were now two swimmers to help the nonswimmers. All four were hardy survivors well acquainted with the Indians and with the coastal environment. They hatched a plan. After a long hiatus, the foursome would resume their quest to regain Christian lands.

CHAPTER 7

Into the Heart of the Continent

THE CASTAWAYS DID NOT MEET BY CHANCE. Dorantes, Castillo, Estebanico, Cabeza de Vaca, and their respective Indian masters and guides had all been attracted to the river by the same reason: pecan nuts. For centuries large groves of pecan trees have grown on the lower Guadalupe River. Measuring as much as 30 or 40 yards, these majestic pecan trees spread their canopies along the valley floor all the way to San Antonio Bay. Pecans only bear their nuts every other year; in the fall of 1532 the trees were loaded with them. Like manna from heaven, the shiny nuts rained down on the ground. They were so plentiful, so easily harvested, and so nutritious (the golden kernels contain protein, fiber, and plenty of oily fats) that Indians found them irresistible. Bands came from as far away as 60 or even 90 miles to harvest the pecans. Among those who gathered at the river of nuts were the Yguases, who held Castillo and Estebanico; the Mariames, who had Dorantes; and the Quevenes, who had been traveling with Cabeza de Vaca. It is easy to imagine the four survivors talking while cracking pecans, picking up the edible pieces with spidery fingers, and munching with relish. Their meetings had to be inconspicuous and could not have

This is a nineteenth-century drawing of the life-sustaining prickly pears. After William H. Emory, *Report on the United States and Mexican Boundary Survey.* Washington, D.C., 1857.

lasted too long, but they knew what they were doing. Since winter was already looming, they would have to wait at least six months to put their plan of escape into effect.[1]

The four wanderers intended to take advantage of the seasonal movements of their indigenous masters to effect their escape. Dorantes had lived long enough with the Mariames and Castillo and Estebanico with the Yguases to know that every summer both bands headed south. From the river of nuts they traveled in the direction of Pánuco for about 75 to 100 miles, reaching the southernmost portion of their range in what is now the lower Nueces River, west of Corpus Christi Bay. They went there to harvest another type of food: prickly pears (*tunas*). The area was completely covered with the cacti that bore these fruits. The plants could grow higher than a man on horseback, and their thickets were massive and wholly impassable. Yet they were studded with enough of this colorful fruit that they could sustain several indigenous groups for two or three months over the summer.[2]

The castaways' plan was simple. They would follow their respective masters to the large *tunal*, which was, after all, on their way to Pánuco. Like everyone else, they would gorge themselves with prickly pears for some weeks. When the season was coming to an end around September, and just as the Indians were preparing to return to their winter range in the north, the foursome would sneak away from their captors and attempt to join other Indian bands who had come to the great *tunal* from farther south.

Having agreed to this plan, the survivors separated once more, following their respective bands to adjacent areas by the Guadalupe River valley. Castillo and Estebanico left with the Yguases. The Mariames kept Dorantes, but the Spanish captain would have familiar company now. The very family that held Dorantes also took Cabeza de Vaca as a slave.

Dorantes was very familiar with the Mariames, as he had already lived alone with them for ten months. Having learned the Mariame language, Dorantes must have been an excellent mentor for Cabeza de Vaca, who would also go on to master the language. The Mariames were a nomadic band of perhaps 200 individuals. One can imagine a camp of some forty movable houses. For nine months of the year, they ranged in the lower Guadalupe River valley. They moved constantly, every two or three days, and spent the days catching fish, digging roots, running down deer, and, of course, eating pecans whenever they were available. Only during the summer months would they leave this stable base and venture far to the south to the *tuna* ground.

During their time with the Mariames, Cabeza de Vaca and Dorantes came to appreciate the raw beauty of their surroundings. They describe the shimmering Texas coast and the flat grazing lands and good pastures that extended as far as the eye could see. Cabeza de Vaca even speculated that cattle would do well in such lands, thus anticipating—by 200 years or more— the world of ranches, cowboys, and massive cattle drives that one day would characterize this corner of the New World.[3]

Hunger must have focused the survivors' attention on the large animals that roamed the prairies along the San Antonio Bay. Dorantes recalled the herds of deer by the shore. To hunt them, native men ran after them for hours, exhausting the animals and even catching them alive sometimes. They also set encircling fires or approached the animals slowly, forming a line of sixty men to drive the deer into the water until they drowned. For men and women living at the brink of starvation, such daylong hunts must have been epic; the stakes were enormous. A few men could kill 500 deer, or sixty, or one, or as often happened, none at all.[4]

The castaways were also the first outsiders to spot those large "cows" with small horns and very long fur: the American bison or buffalo. In the early sixteenth century, their range reached into southern Texas. The largest mammal in North America, the bison can stand more than 6 feet from hoof to shoulder and can weigh up to 1 ton. A single animal would have been enough to feed an entire band. But hunting the bison was extremely difficult. It had to be done on foot and with only bows and arrows. On three different occasions Cabeza de Vaca was able to gaze at these imposing animals and taste their meat, which he pronounced better than beef.[5]

In spite of this natural bounty, the Mariames and their two European slaves went hungry at times. On such occasions they were reduced to eating two or three types of roots that were bitter in taste, had to be cooked for two days before they were edible, and even then caused bloating of the stomach. They also

The castaways were the first to describe the North American buffalo. Here is a seventeenth-century representation of an animal that would become synonymous with the vast interior of America. After Francisco Hernández, *Nova plantarvm, animalivm et mineralivm Mexicanorvm* . . . Rome, 1651.

ate spiders, ant eggs, worms, salamanders, lizards, and snakes and even resorted to eating earth, wood, deer excrement, and "other things that I refrain from mentioning," Cabeza de Vaca says, "and I believe assuredly that if in that land there were stones they would eat them."[6]

Notwithstanding these spells of hunger, the Mariames were a happy people. According to Cabeza de Vaca, most of them were great drunkards and liars and thieves who never failed to dance or make their celebrations and *areitos*. Evidently, the Mariames had a playful side. In the dead of winter, when the *tuna* season was still many months away, they teased Cabeza de Vaca and Dorantes by telling them not to be sad because "soon" there would be prickly pears. They conjured for their captives images of idle days spent eating *tunas* and drinking their sweet juice while watching their bellies swell.[7]

Cabeza de Vaca and Dorantes belonged to a family consisting of a man and a woman, their son, and another adult who lived with them. Curiously, the entire household was afflicted by an illness that had caused them to go blind in one eye. Cabeza de Vaca was particularly intrigued by the relations between Mariame men and women. Mariame males procured their women by purchasing them from their enemies. The cost of each bride was one bow and two arrows or, in the absence of these objects, a large fishing net. In return for this investment, a Mariame male obtained a very hardworking partner. On any given day a woman barely got six hours of rest, between firing her oven to dry the bitter roots, gathering firewood and water, caring for the children, and looking after the household belongings "because the men do not burden themselves nor carry anything of weight." And yet, for all their work, women were among the least appreciated members of the community (along with the elderly).[8]

The Mariames' disdain for women extended even to their own baby girls, who were often left outside and allowed to be eaten by dogs. According to Cabeza de Vaca, the Mariames engaged in female infanticide to deny potential wives to the surrounding groups who were their sworn enemies. "And if by chance," Cabeza de Vaca says, "they should marry off their daughters, their enemies would multiply so much that the Mariames would wind up captured and enslaved by them."[9]

But while the social and natural world they now inhabited may have been fascinating, Dorantes and Cabeza de Vaca nonetheless suffered due to their enslavement. The adjustment had been especially sudden for Cabeza de Vaca. He had been forced to give up his extraordinary life as an itinerant merchant among the Charruco, reverting to the status of a lowly captive of the Mariames. The heaviest work occurred in the summer, when Dorantes and Cabeza de Vaca became the first line of defense against the clouds of mosquitoes, a dangerous and omnipresent threat during the warm seasons. To this day the coast of Texas has the dubious distinction of harboring one of the most diverse and largest concentrations of mosquitoes anywhere in North America. The swampy coastal environment by San Antonio Bay provided an ideal habitat for these relentless insects, which were at best annoying and at worst lethal. It was quite possible to sustain hundreds or even thousands of mosquito bites in this infested environment; in aggregate, they could easily sap a person's vitality, leading to a generalized weakening of the body and possibly death.[10]

Dorantes and Cabeza de Vaca were charged with keeping smoky bonfires lit throughout the night at the camp to drive the mosquitoes away. Hauling the wood and feeding the fires during the warm season was exhausting. But if they fell asleep, the Mariames would wake up their captives by beating them with sticks and forcing them back to work. Combined with their arduous daytime labors, the chronic sleep deprivation must have been enormously taxing.[11]

Cabeza de Vaca and Dorantes spent the winter and spring of 1533 with the Mariames, biding their time. The sources tell us very little about Castillo and Estebanico's experience, but their lives with the neighboring Yguases must have been similar. In any case, winter and spring must have been seasons of anticipation as the four castaways waited to put their plan of escape into effect.

In the early summer of 1533 the Mariames and Yguases traveled south to the prickly-pear grounds, and the four castaways came together once more. Everything seemed to be going according to plan. Cabeza de Vaca, Dorantes, Castillo, and Estebanico would spend the summer with the Mariames and Yguases, but toward the end of the *tuna* season they would try to attach themselves to other Indians to travel farther south with them. But as the four survivors prepared to flee, a curious incident complicated things. The Indians who held the castaways quarreled among themselves over a woman, and the conflict escalated to the point that the Indians punched and hit each other with branches, inflicting head wounds on each other. The consequences of the disagreement were disastrous for the four survivors: "And with the great rage they felt"—Cabeza de Vaca writes—"each one collected his possessions and went his own way; and we Christians were forced to part company, and there was no way for us to get together until the following year."[12]

The four castaways must have been crestfallen to see their plan collapse. Now they would have to endure another year of abuse, hunger, and unfulfilled hopes before they would be in a position to gather once again at the great *tunal*. They might die during the intervening year, and even if they survived, something else might come up the following summer that would prevent their escape yet again. But there was nothing they could do.

That year, between the summers of 1533 and 1534, was bleak. Castillo and Estebanico stayed with the Yguases and Dorantes remained with the Mariames, but Cabeza de Vaca found the work so overwhelming and the hunger so great that he fled three times from his masters. Each time they went looking for him, and "put forth great effort to find and kill me. And God our Lord in his mercy chose to preserve and protect me from them." The two accounts offer precious few details at this dramatic juncture, but it seems that the Royal Treasurer drifted from one group to another, complicating even more the castaways' plan to reconvene at the great *tunal* the following season.[13]

Incredibly, however, they were able to reassemble the following year during the prickly-pear season. Somehow the four castaways were able to gather on the first day of the new moon, which Cabeza de Vaca reckons to have been September 1, 1534.

They agreed to give themselves one more month at the *tunal*, and when the moon became full, they would all leave. The final countdown was underway.

This time, the men would take no chances. At that crucial meeting on September 1, 1534, Cabeza de Vaca told the others that he would leave for Pánuco *with or without them*. He was not about to wait another year. All four must have agreed. That very same day, the bands that held the four castaways went their own separate ways, "and thus we parted," Cabeza de Vaca recalls, "and each one went off with his Indians." Their anxiety set in as the moon began to grow.[14]

Dorantes was the first to flee his indigenous masters and thus turn himself into a fugitive. He joined another band known as the Anegados who had just arrived to the prickly-pear stands. Captain Dorantes had either been very savvy or very lucky. The Anegados were on bad terms with the Mariames, and Dorantes was permitted to remain with them. Estebanico and Castillo followed suit. Barely three or four days after Dorantes's arrival, they shuffled into camp.

Although the trio had succeeded in slipping away from their former captors, their situation remained extremely dangerous. They had merely drifted from one part of the great *tunal* to another. The Mariames and the Yguases could still track down the runaways and punish them or the Anegados might turn them over to their previous owners. The three runaways must have made themselves useful with the Anegados. They were beginning to forge a new relationship, but their situation remained uncertain. Even a small gesture could be the difference between life and death.[15]

Meanwhile, Cabeza de Vaca had stayed with his Indian masters, waiting nervously for one month hoping that his companions would join him at some point so everyone could escape together. For some reason the Indians who held Cabeza de Vaca were not even on the *tuna* ground but had already traveled some distance in a southerly direction. The prickly-pear season was at an end, and this group must have started back to its winter range. Cabeza de Vaca would wait for his companions until the moon became full.

In the meantime, the three castaways who had remained at the *tunal* with the Anegados were running out of time. Moreover, they could not be sure where Cabeza de Vaca was. One day Dorantes, Castillo, and Estebanico saw a column of smoke rising over the prairie at some distance, indicating that an Indian group was encamped there. They became convinced that Cabeza de Vaca was with them. The three survivors must have considered their options. If all three were to leave the Anegados, they would become fugitives. Instead, the three castaways agreed that Dorantes and Estebanico would go forward to try to find Cabeza de Vaca and Castillo would stay behind. The latter's presence would serve to "reassure the Indians that the other two would be back and were not leaving . . . [and the Indians] were satisfied with this."[16]

For an entire day and part of the night, Dorantes and Estebanico walked in the direction of the column of smoke. In the wee hours they finally ran into an Indian who took them to the camp, where Cabeza de Vaca was indeed waiting. It was the thirteenth day of the moon, or around the middle of September 1534.

Dorantes, Estebanico, and Cabeza de Vaca now needed to find a way to retrieve Castillo, who was more than a day's walk away. Happily, the Indians at the camp unwittingly assisted them by deciding to move closer to the prickly-pear collecting ground. All four castaways were reunited again.

At last, almost two years after the foursome had first come together at the river of nuts and vowed to leave, they were able to escape. The brushland lay ahead, and they wasted no time.

Within days, only long enough to get their bearings and ask their Indian hosts about the landscape and peoples that lived there, the four stranded men quietly fled. Although these Indians had served the three Spaniards and the African well, they are never given a name in the surviving accounts.

CABEZA DE VACA and his companions pushed south, leaving behind almost six years of enslavement. But as the survivors drifted toward Pánuco, they underwent an even more profound transformation. The seeds had been planted years earlier, with the native islanders of Malhado, when the castaways had occasionally performed curing ceremonies. At the insistence of the Capoques and Hans, Cabeza de Vaca and some of the others had made the sign of the cross, said a Pater Noster or an Ave Maria, and begged God to restore the health of their patients. The ceremonies had been simple and infrequent, but as the survivors ventured south of the great *tunal*, they discovered that their fame as faith healers preceded them wherever they went. The natives kept bringing their sick to the castaways.[17]

As the survivors continued their passage toward Pánuco, they refashioned themselves as medicine men. In time, all four castaways would receive patients, and all four would cure. The healing was not merely a cynical ploy on the part of the castaways to get access to food and respect from the Indians. The four castaways were surely aware of the material advantages of their new occupation. But they also regarded their curing abilities as something spiritual and deeper. They came to see their incredible odyssey and their sufferings in North America as a kind of test to which God had subjected them before revealing the true purpose of their existence. As one of the castaways put it, "In this way Jesus Christ guided us, and his infinite mercy was with us, opening roads where there were none. And the hearts of men so savage and untamed, God moved to humility and obedience, as will be seen further on."[18]

Two very different religious cultures came in contact in the course of the healing ceremonies performed by the castaways. In the minds of sixteenth-century Spaniards, God and the Devil mingled freely with mortals. Their world was one in which mystics and seers held unprecedented influence and miracles were not uncommon. In fact, the years leading up to the Narváez expedition were unusually eventful in this regard. In 1513 the Virgin Mary was said to have revealed herself to a shepherd on the outskirts of the city of León, requesting that a shrine be built on that spot. A year later, a man from Cuenca named Juan de Rabe reportedly went into a trance and saw God in paradise along with saints, angels, and archangels. In 1523 the Virgin appeared once again to a certain Francisca la Brava of El Quintanar and this time even left some objects behind.[19]

Ordinary Christians constantly attempted to summon the power of God (or the Devil) for their own ends. Sorcery and witchcraft proliferated in Spain and elsewhere in Europe in the sixteenth century. In the 1520s a sect known as the *alumbrados* (or illuminati in Italy) sought novel ways to communicate with God. The *alumbrados* advocated mystic contemplation and obedience to one's emotional impulses, especially those pertaining to love. By allowing love to flourish, *alumbrados* claimed that they could establish direct contact with God and attain such a degree of perfection that they could even indulge their carnal desires without committing sin or staining their souls. While the castaways struggled to survive in the New World, a girl from Avila was able to establish regular contact with God and began her ascent into sainthood and the most exalted stage of mysticism. Known to the world as St. Teresa of Avila, her turbulent and extraordinary life included such signs of divine favor as a vision of the place reserved for her in hell had she decided to stray from the path of virtue, the transverberation of her heart (her heart was pierced with a dart of love thrown by an angel), and a mystical, rapturous marriage to Christ. St. Teresa's story left no doubt in the minds of devout Christians that ordinary human beings could aspire to see, hear, and even touch God. [20]

Early explorers and conquistadors were part of this culture. They were often devout Christians who believed in apparitions and miracles and lived in fear of God's wrath. Although motivated by material considerations and at times engaged in distinctly unchristian activities such as killing Indians, these pioneers were nonetheless persuaded that their exploits served to further God's aims. After all, hadn't Spain's spectacular discoveries in the New World opened a vast new field for religious conversion? Weren't such discoveries part of God's grandiose and mysterious plan to spread the good word? Certainly Pánfilo de Narváez had argued as much in his campaign to obtain a charter for the conquest of Florida.

There was more than opportunism to these expressions of religious fervor. As the Narváez expedition unraveled, its survivors clung ever-more desperately to their cherished faith. Indeed, the last three Spaniards (we don't know about Estebanico) came to think of their ordeal as a mighty test to expiate their sins, and as a martyrdom of sorts. When Cabeza de Vaca and his companions first became stranded on the island of Malhado after their raft was overturned by the large waves, the wretched, naked men spent hours crying around a fire and as Cabeza de Vaca pointedly remarks, "we beseeched our Lord for mercy and the pardon of our sins." In the same vein, Dorantes declared that "God gave them the strength and patience to atone for their sins, for they deserved an even worse fate."[21]

Whenever Cabeza de Vaca shed blood while hauling wood for the Hans, Capoques, Mariames, and other peoples, he found some consolation in thinking about Jesus Christ and his Passion, and in "considering that the torment he had suffered from the thorns had been so much greater than the one I endured at that time." Clearly, the Spaniards came to view their sufferings as mortification of the flesh, their beatings and extreme hunger akin to that of the flagellants who inflicted pain on their own bodies, or the monks who engaged in prolonged fasting.[22]

Their own survival was evidence of a supernatural design. For Cabeza de Vaca, Dorantes, Castillo, and possibly Estebanico, the fact that only four remained alive out of 300 men could not have been mere coincidence. Death on such a scale and survival against such overwhelming odds must have been inconceivable without divine intervention. The survivors had faced so many dangers and had seen so many of their fellow expeditioners pierced by Indian arrows, consumed by illness, lost in the wilderness, and brought down by starvation that they could not help but wonder just *why* they themselves were still standing.[23]

Indeed, the castaways' many near-death experiences must have persuaded them that God was guarding their lives. On one occasion, Cabeza de Vaca became separated from the others and was lost in the woods, unable to return to camp. Cabeza de Vaca was naked, and winter was already arriving, and he knew that the temperature would drop precipitously at night. Death from exposure seemed inevitable. "But it pleased God," Cabeza de Vaca explains with strikingly biblical imagery, "that I found a tree aflame, and warmed by its fire I endured the cold that night."[24]

For five days Cabeza de Vaca nursed the fire. It was his only lifeline. He kept a torch alight and carried a load of firewood while looking for his companions. At sunset, before going to sleep, he would dig a large pit and fill it with enough fuel to last for some hours, "and around that pit I placed four fires like the points of a cross." The burning cross on the ground, he must have believed, would allow God to see from above where Cabeza de Vaca was sleeping. Cabeza de Vaca did not eat a mouthful during this entire time. His feet bled. "And God took pity upon me," he remarks gratefully, "that in all this time the north wind did not blow, because otherwise it would have been impossible for me to survive."[25]

After five days of increasingly frantic searches, Cabeza de Vaca was at last able to rejoin his group. They had already taken him for dead, believing that he had been bitten by a venomous snake.

Was God merely conducting a cruel experiment, or did he have some larger plan for the castaways? The survivors' unlikely transformation into sacred healers left little room for doubt in their minds. A mysterious design was unfolding; how else could anyone interpret such an incredible turn of events? Indeed, they had become intermediaries between God and the natives. Their inescapable conclusion was that they had a special connection with God.

It was not the castaways who first suggested that they possessed the power to cure. The foreigners may have believed in miracles, but Indians were the ones who first compelled them to heal. Cabeza de Vaca recounts the story, half in jest: "On that island about which I have spoken [Malhado], they tried to make us physicians without examining us or asking us for our titles." In marked contrast to Spain's elaborate examination system to license physicians, the natives of Texas simply demanded that the castaways cure the sick by blowing on the afflicted. The outsiders took things lightly at first. "We laughed at this and said that it was a mockery and that we did not know how to cure." But it was hardly a laughing matter for the Indians. They stopped feeding the outsiders until they did as they were told. An Indian man patiently explained to the uncomprehending foreigners that "even the stones and other things that exist in the wild possess power, and that he used a hot stone rubbed on the abdomen to heal and remove the pain, and that we [the survivors] who were humans had even more virtue and power."[26]

The natives of Malhado were merely one example of a broader and far more encompassing belief system. For as far back as we can peer in the archaeological record, the natives of America have relied on shamans or medicine men (and medicine women) to seek health. They believed that certain extraordinary individuals were capable of curing by administering natural remedies like herbs or baths, or by establishing contact with supernatural forces. But these shamans were not easy to find. Many were monitored since childhood for their special talents or powers and spent years of apprenticeship with established practitioners. Once they were recognized as shamans in their own right, they acquired inordinate influence within their communities. They could cure, but they could also curse or kill *anyone*. Their dreams and visions were taken very seriously and could lead to peace or war with a neighboring group or could bring death to a member of the band.

The exalted stage occupied by native shamans impressed foreign observers from the time of contact all the way through the nineteenth and twentieth centuries. "The 'medicine men' wield an amount of influence which cannot be understood by civilized people who have not been brought into intimate relations with the aborigines in a wild state," wrote a bombastic Captain John G. Bourke after having traveled through the Southwest in the 1870s and 1880s. "Nothing has been so neglected by the Americans as an examination into the mental processes by which an Indian arrives at his conclusions, the omens, auguries, hopes and fears by which he is controlled and led to one extreme or the other in all he does."[27]

Of the four survivors, Castillo was at first the most sought-after healer. He had a quiet demeanor and was the least likely to engage in the kind of dramatic displays that could sway patients and onlookers. Castillo's healings were subdued affairs involving pious prayer and gentle blowing of breath. Yet he was the most obvious candidate to become a medicine man, as he was the best acquainted with Spain's medical world. Castillo's father had been a physician in the university town of Salamanca, and like most practitioners at the time, he must have kept a room at home where he received and treated his patients. Thus, Castillo must have grown up rummaging through his father's medical equipment, hearing his elders discuss remedies and surgical procedures, and witnessing the range of illnesses afflicting humans. Castillo's sudden induction into the field of New World medicine must have struck him as unmerited but nonetheless highly advantageous. Even though Cabeza de Vaca performed some healings as well, Castillo's profile as a medicine man was far greater initially. As the castaways fled south of the prickly-pear grounds, the various Indians they encountered continued to demand access to Castillo's healing powers.

In October 1534 the foursome fell in with a group known as the Avavares. Like the other groups with whom the castaways had lived, the Avavares were a small nomadic band. Their range was to the northwest of present-day Corpus Christi Bay. Cabeza de Vaca says that the Avavares already knew of the castaways' reputation and "about the wonders that our Lord was working through us." Since Avavares and Mariames spoke intelligible languages, the survivors made themselves understood in Mariame. The new hosts treated the four drifters with respect. They told them how delighted they were by their arrival, lodged them with their own healers, and fed them the last prickly pears of the season.[28]

Their healings began the very night of their arrival, when a group of Indians who suffered from head pains came looking for

Castillo. The physician's son did his part. He made the sign of the cross over them and begged God to give health to the Indians, "and the Indians said that all the sickness had left them. And they went to their houses and brought many prickly pears and a piece of venison, which at the time we didn't recognize." News of Castillo's abilities drew more patients and prompted dancing and a celebration that lasted three days.[29]

The survivors' newfound position was a far cry from their past lives as captives. Natives who were treated by a medicine man were accustomed to giving everything that they possessed to him and even sought additional gifts from their relatives. Over the course of a few days with the Avavares, the four outsiders received so many pieces of venison that they didn't know what to do with all the meat. Both because of this generosity and because the cold season was already upon them, the travelers decided to remain among the Avavares. They would end up spending eight months with this group.[30]

As the castaways' reputation as effective healers rose, so did their religious zeal. While among the Avavares, the castaways found what they considered to be many disturbing signs of the Devil's presence. Most poignantly, the Christians learned from the Avavares that fifteen or sixteen years earlier, a strange creature had visited them. The Spaniards called him Mala Cosa or Evil Thing. He was "small in body" and, although nobody had seen his face clearly, wore a beard like the Europeans. Mala Cosa carried a sharp flint. Whenever he appeared, the natives trembled and their hair stood on end "and he took whichever one of them he wanted, and he gave them three large incisions in the sides," Cabeza de Vaca was told, "and he placed his hands into those wounds and pulled out their entrails, and cut off a piece, more or less a span long, and threw the part that he cut off into the fire." Mala Cosa also dislocated arms and then set them back in place, and lifted huts high in the air and let them drop to the ground. The strangers were skeptical of these tales at first. But some Avavares came forth, showing the scars that they still bore from the cuts made years earlier by Mala Cosa. In many ways Mala Cosa was a mirror image of the four medicine men. "And we gave them to understand that, if they believed in God our Lord and become Christians like us, they would not be afraid of him, nor would he dare to come and do those things to them."[31]

It was during their time with the Avavares that the explorers performed their single greatest healing feat. One day a group of Susolas came into the camp of the Avavares asking to see Castillo, whose reputation had already spread to the neighboring Indians. The Susolas were at war with other groups in the area, and therefore their warriors often sustained arrow wounds. The Susola delegation begged Castillo to travel to their camp to see a wounded man and some other individuals who were ill. They were especially concerned about one man, who appeared to be at the very doorstep of death. Castillo was already an experienced healer, but he was also selective. "[He] was a very cautious physician," Cabeza de Vaca notes, "particularly when the cures were threatening and dangerous. And he believed that his sins would prevent the cures from turning out well every time." There is no evidence to suggest that Castillo's self-doubt was anything but sincere, for he was a genuinely pious and God-fearing Christian. In the end, Castillo's worries caused him to refuse to accompany the Susolas, and so the task fell upon Cabeza de Vaca. The Susolas had already met the former Royal Treasurer at the river of nuts and although they may have preferred Castillo's services, there was little they could do.[32]

By the time Cabeza de Vaca, Dorantes, and Estebanico reached the Susola camp, the man in question appeared to be dead. His body was surrounded by many weeping people, and his house was dismantled, "which is the sign that the owner is dead." His eyes were turned up and blank, and no pulse could be detected. The situation seemed hopeless. Still, Cabeza de Vaca decided to go through the motions of a healing. He removed the mat that had been placed over the man's body and prayed to God fervently. He would be merely the instrument; God would do the rest. Cabeza de Vaca made the sign of the cross and blew on the corpse several times as the Indians did. The crowd surrounding the body may have harbored some hopes, but the undertaking was extremely risky, even foolish, at a time when Cabeza de Vaca's fame was only just being cemented.

After the rituals were over, the two Spaniards and the African spent the rest of the day tending to other Susolas with less serious afflictions. "[At] nighttime"—Cabeza de Vaca writes—"they returned to their houses and said that the man who had been dead and whom I had cured in their presence had arisen in good health and had strolled around and eaten and spoken with them, and that all of those that I had cured had become well and were without fever and very happy."[33]

Cabeza de Vaca's work with the Susolas caused a sensation among the Indians of the region. These Indians were both admiring and alarmed, for, if the former Royal Treasurer had the power to revive his patients, then it stood to reason that he could just as easily turn the living into the dead. "In all the land they spoke of nothing else," Cabeza de Vaca reports. The natives were convinced that the four strangers were "children of the sun," having come from the east, where the sun rises beyond the great ocean. They had so much confidence in the power of the strangers that they came to believe that no Indian would die so long as the castaways would remain with them.[34]

Explaining these extraordinary healings posed no problems for either the healers or the healed, although the two groups offered very different interpretations. The Europeans had become convinced that their preternatural interventions reflected God's divine plan for North America. They would have been unable to cure by themselves, but they had been turned into God's intermediaries and thus derived the power to heal. For their part, the natives had always believed that certain individuals were capable of manipulating the natural and supernatural orders. It is easy to see how the Avavares and their neighbors may have reached the conclusion that the four strangers possessed special healing abilities. The three Spaniards and the African looked decidedly different, claimed to have come from a land beyond the ocean, spoke unintelligible languages, and therefore perhaps, just perhaps, possessed the power to cure.[35]

The mystery of the healings has deepened over time. Can we take Cabeza de Vaca at face value when he reports that he and his companions "never cured anyone who did not say that he was better"? Were the healings mere coincidence? Was their success due to the power of suggestion, the victory of mind over body? Were they in fact miracles?

Cabeza de Vaca himself studiously avoided the use of the word "miracle" in his *Relación*, for a very good reason. He first published his book at a time when the Spanish Inquisition exercised complete control over the publication of books. The Inquisition closely scrutinized all manuscripts for their religious content and issued licenses only to those texts deemed compatible with established dogma. The mere mention of miracles would bring about suspicion and perhaps condemnation, for no individual could claim to have performed a miracle without the backing of the church and only after a period of rigorous investigation. So in spite of Cabeza de Vaca's belief in his extraordinary powers to cure, he always portrayed himself and his fellow castaways as God's humble servants. God was acting through the castaways, who were themselves little more than bystanders.[36]

Later writers would gloss over such subtleties. Francisco López de Gómara, a near contemporary, was one of the first to actually apply to the word "miracle" to Cabeza de Vaca's activities during the episode with the Susolas: "Álvar Núñez [Cabeza de Vaca] made the sign of the cross and blew three times, and the man came back to life, and it was a miracle." One generation later, in 1605, el Inca Garcilaso de la Vega went several steps further, stating that through "miracles" and "prodigies" the castaways had "attained such respect and fame among the Indians that they were adored as gods." By the 1640s, the Jesuit Andrés Pérez de Ribas had rendered the castaways' adventure into something of a biblical tale: They "walked in the midst of innumerable barbarous nations, performing prodigies and miracles among them, through virtue and divine will, and with the sign of the cross." With the passage of time, the number of reported miracles performed by the survivors increased dramatically. By 1723, almost 200 years after the expedition, the Spanish chronicler Gabriel de Cárdenas Cano credits Cabeza de Vaca and his companions with performing "infinite miracles and dispensing health in God's name and prodigiously to the Indians who were sick."[37]

Today we live in a more skeptical age. We seek out alternative explanations for these healings, such as the power of suggestion, exaggeration on the part of Spaniards' accounts, or even deceit by the Indians. But there is no more evidence to support those explanations than there is to support the faith of both the castaways and the natives in supernatural intervention. All we can say with confidence is that this gift of curing, whether real or imagined, allowed the castaways to move toward their deliverance.

AFTER SPENDING EIGHT lunar months with the Avavares, the foursome left their camp and headed in the direction of Pánuco. This time the survivors started their travels in the late spring or early summer of 1535, intending to make headway during the warm months.

From the first prickly-pear ground, the castaways had already journeyed with the Avavares to a second *tunal*, located five days away in a southerly direction. From this second prickly-pear collecting ground, the healers continued to move south but chose to follow an inland route to avoid two dangers. First, they wanted to steer clear of the coast to prevent further contact with shoreline Indians. Through the Indians, the castaways had learned that some of the coastal bands were hostile to outsiders. Among them were the dreaded Camones, who had mercilessly massacred all members of one of the rafts of the Narváez expedition, subsequently selling off their possessions. Additionally, by traveling parallel to the coast but through an inland route, Cabeza de Vaca and his companions hoped to skirt a forbidding tongue of desert that extends south from Baffin Bay, Texas, to the Rio Grande delta and is known today as the coastal sand plain.[38]

Their inland route south took the castaways through the *monte* of south Texas, a lush tapestry of brushlands and prairies, graced with thickets of mesquite, prickly pear, and creosote. Their progress was slow and indirect. "The land is so rugged and impassable," Cabeza de Vaca writes, "that many times when we gathered firewood in the dense thickets, when we finished taking it out we were bleeding in many places from the thorns and brambles that we encountered, for wherever they ensnarled us they broke our skin." Having lost sight of the coast, they were also forced to rely on the sun for direction.[39]

The trekkers left the Avavares two weeks or so *before* the start of the prickly-pear season. Their timing meant that procuring

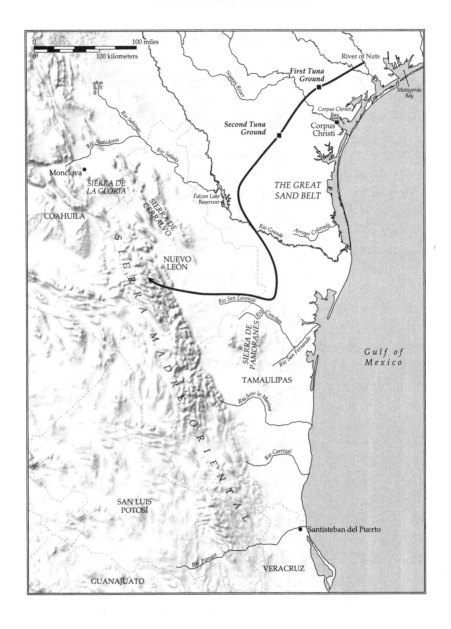

food along the way would be enormously challenging and would require a great deal of knowledge of the animals and plants of the region. Water would be even more difficult to obtain. The *monte* is almost devoid of running streams, so they would only be able to collect water in naturally occurring gathering places known as *tinajas* or by digging in arroyo beds. Both would have required a deep understanding of the terrain of south Texas. Almost certainly, the four outsiders could not have traveled far on their own.[40]

Fortunately, they soon found help. They had scarcely ventured for one day through the *monte* when they ran into a band known as the Maliacones. The Maliacones were subsisting on a tree fruit that was very bitter (possibly the fruit of ebony trees known today as *maguacates* or perhaps mesquite beans). After spending three days with the Maliacones, the castaways moved on with another group called the Arbadaos, with whom they endured more days before the *tunas* became ripe: "All day long we ate no more than two handfuls of that fruit, which was green. It had so much milk that it burned our mouths and while we lacked water, it made everyone who ate it thirsty." In addition to the bitter fruit, the Indians relied on boiled leaves of the prickly-pear cactus (*nopales*), which are still widely consumed in Mexico and parts of the Southwest. Yet such staples of southwestern cuisine were not enough to satisfy the castaways' hunger. Their torment was so great that they parted with some nets and skins that they had been carrying in exchange for two dogs, which the famished survivors promptly devoured. Thus fortified, Cabeza de Vaca, Dorantes, Castillo, and Estebanico continued their journey and were able to subsist until the prickly pears became ripe.[41]

The four voyagers must have spent about a month negotiating the *monte*. They moved slowly from one Indian group to the next, pausing for two weeks at a sizable settlement of forty or fifty dwellings. Their observations constitute fleeting anthropological glimpses of a region that seems to have been very heavily populated. For instance, Cabeza de Vaca documents instances of effeminacy among the Indians of southern Texas: "And they are effeminate, impotent men. And they go about covered like women, and they perform the tasks of women, and they do not use a bow, and they carry very great loads. And we saw many of them, thus unmanly as I say, and they are more muscular than other men and taller; they suffer very large loads."[42]

Cabeza de Vaca also noted how these Indians made war on one another, constantly engaging in elaborate ambushes. "These are the people most fit for war of all I have seen in the world." Whenever they were in danger of being attacked, they would set up their houses in a dense part of the wood and pretend to be sleeping there, even lighting fires throughout the night to lure their enemies. In reality they were hiding in trenches nearby, where all the warriors would be covered in light brush. They were so cunning that they behaved "as if they had been raised in Italy." (Cabeza de Vaca had first-hand experience of the Italians. He had taken part in the battle of Ravenna of April 11, 1512, and had also seen action in Bologna.)[43]

At last the four wanderers came upon a river that they estimated to be "wider than the Guadalquivir in Seville" and that almost certainly must have been the Rio Grande. They probably crossed near the Falcón Reservoir basin, about 120 miles from the river's mouth. Just a few days later, Cabeza de Vaca and his fellow travelers began to see mountains in the distance, quite likely the Sierra de Pamoranes of northern Tamaulipas.[44]

Since leaving the Avavares, the castaways had been welcomed wherever they went. The natives here were no exception. They rejoiced at the arrival of the strangers, fed them, and presented their ill for healing. They treated the three Spaniards and the

African with a respect that bordered on reverence. Once, as the four survivors approached a village, the Indians rushed out to receive them "with so much shouting that it was a fright and vigorously slapping their thighs," Cabeza de Vaca would later write, and "they crowded us so much that they nearly could have killed us. And without letting our feet touch the ground, they carried us to their houses." In fact, the survivors' progress was hindered by the commotion they caused everywhere they went: "Along this entire road we had very great difficulty because of the many people who followed us," Cabeza de Vaca says, "and we could not flee from them, although we tried, because the quickness with which they came to touch us was very great. And so great were their demands about this, that for three hours we could not finish with them so that they would leave us alone."[45]

Women also rushed to touch the four healers. Their perceived power must have been alluring in many respects, not least of which was sexual. Undoubtedly, the castaways had opportunities to satisfy their desires, perhaps long suppressed. Right before crossing the river, for instance, the survivors found themselves followed by a group of women. These women ended up leading the four men to the river, though not before they spent some days and nights together. Of course, none of the accounts contain even a single word about romantic or sexual encounters: understandably, the survivors did not want to have problems with the church or with their families back in Spain.[46]

The trekkers continued to move south toward the mountains for some days. The Sierra de Pamoranes is an interior range that runs parallel to the Gulf of Mexico at a distance of about 40 miles inland. The four survivors had to decide whether to flank the sierra on the eastern side, facing the sea, or on the continental side to the west. As they began their ascent, they came upon a river moving from west to east. It must have been the river system formed by the present-day San Fernando and Conchos. The survivors began following that river upstream toward the west, veering away from the coast.[47]

They were already quite close to their final goal. Although the travelers may not have realized it, the Rio de las Palmas, the river that they had sought since disembarking in Tampa Bay, was only about 75 to 90 miles away to the south. A maximum of two weeks of purposeful marches would get them there. Beyond the Rio de las Palmas, 120 miles farther south, lay Santiesteban del Puerto, the northernmost Spanish outpost along the Gulf of Mexico coast. After having rounded the Gulf of Mexico coast for perhaps 1,200 miles, their deliverance was well within reach.

But then the survivors did something extraordinary: they suddenly and inexplicably shifted course to the west and north, away from the coast and the promise of salvation. There is no record of what led them to one of the most mysterious and stunning decisions of their entire voyage—the decision to abandon their quest for Pánuco, and instead venture deep into the heart of the unknown continent.

Perhaps their urge to explore was reasserting itself; perhaps they wished to see more of this strange and beautiful land in which they found themselves. But a psychological transformation must have also occurred for the men to make such a dramatic decision: they must have been convinced that they would survive such a journey across the continent. For months, the Indians had been treating the four men like demigods and surely on some level the men had begun to believe it themselves. Cabeza de Vaca, Castillo, Dorantes, and Estebanico must have become persuaded that they were destined to survive; that nothing could harm them; that God himself was looking after them.[48]

CHAPTER 8

Following the Corn Trail

IN THE SUMMER OF 1535, WHEN THE FOUR CASTAWAYS walked south of the Rio Grande, it became clear to them that they had entered a new exchange zone. The four survivors had stumbled on an east-west trade route connecting Tamaulipas with cultural centers deep in what is now the American Southwest. For at least 1,000 years, indigenous merchants had made the journey from the Huasteca region on the Gulf Coast through northern Tamaulipas and into the interior deserts of North America. They carried such luxury goods as live scarlet macaws.[1]

The four survivors never mention in their accounts that they had chanced upon an indigenous thoroughfare, yet their observations leave few doubts. Immediately after shifting course to the west, away from Pánuco, the trekkers came across two Indian women bearing loads. "Upon seeing us"—Cabeza de Vaca recalls—"[they] stopped and put down their loads and brought us some of what they were carrying, which was maize flour, and they told us that farther ahead on that river we would find houses and many prickly pears and more of that flour." The sight of maize must have been immensely encouraging. The four men had not seen the New World staple during the entire time they had lived in captivity in Texas, nor had they found any sign

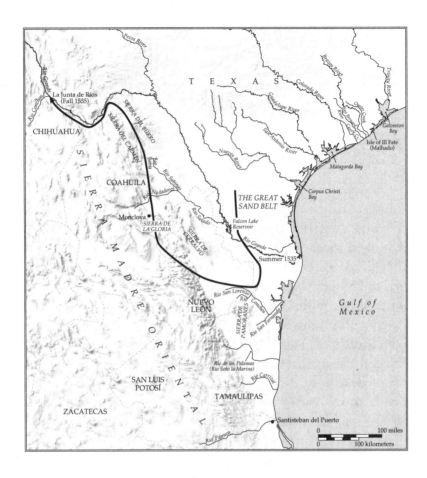

of it south of the Rio Grande prior to this encounter. The corn flour must have come from far away, but it was still possible to carry it into northern Tamaulipas. Maize presaged the existence of a sedentary, agricultural people, the kind of society that had sustained the Spanish presence in the Caribbean and Mexico. The castaways were uncertain of what they would find, but at least they seemed to be headed in the direction of advanced cultural centers.[2]

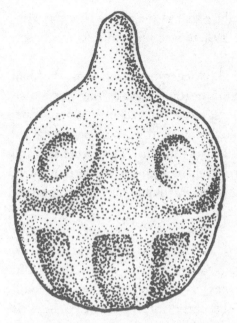

The copper bell with a face mentioned by Cabeza de Vaca matches only one type of bell found by modern archaeologists. This one was found in Paquimé, not far from where the castaways passed, and overlaps chronologically with the Florida expedition. The face etched on it represents the Mesoamerican divinity Tlaloc. Courtesy of the Amerind Foundation, Inc., Dragoon, Arizona.

As they moved through the sierra foothills farther west, the three Spaniards and the African found more objects that they had not encountered before. One day they met a troupe "from another nation and language who said that they had come from farther inland." It was a trading party of respectable size, whose camp consisted of about forty huts able to shelter up to 100 people or more. These merchants gave the castaways a large and thick copper bell with a face etched on it and some cotton blankets. The gift-givers said that these objects had come "from the North and across the land toward the South Sea [the Pacific Ocean]." The healers must have been stunned at the sight of these items. The Narváez expedition had not found copper *any-where* throughout Florida, the northern rim of the Gulf of Mexico coast, Texas, or Tamaulipas. The implication of wealthy Indian settlements was inescapable. As the survivors put it,

"From this fact one can deduce that in the area where these objects had come from, even if there was no gold, there were settlements and smelting."[3]

The four wanderers were no longer mere castaways; they had become explorers once again, heading west to find the settled peoples who knew how to cast metals. But theirs was a most peculiar expedition. Four naked and unarmed outsiders were led by hundreds, even thousands, of Indians. They were fed and protected and passed off from one indigenous group to the next, as if they were prized possessions moving along an ancient trading route across the continent.

THE EXPLORERS' PROGRESS inland was rapid. The two sources refer to the landscape along the way only sporadically, providing just enough clues to keep generations of road-interpreters arguing over the party's precise route. Cabeza de Vaca reports, for instance, that he and his companions passed through "a sierra of seven leagues and the rocks in it were of iron slag" before reaching an Indian village set on the bank of a very beautiful river. All around the area there were small pine trees with cones "like small eggs," and pine nuts that were better than those of Castile "because they have very thin shells." Remarkably, in this instance the shards of available evidence do point to a specific location. In the present-day state of Coahuila there is a sierra about 21 miles long, containing rocks made of iron. It is known as the Sierra de la Gloria. At about a day's walk from the Sierra de la Gloria, there is indeed a delightful river flanked by groves of cypress and pecans called the Rio Nadadores. Most persuasively, botanists have recently identified a pine-nut species with extraordinarily thin seed shells. This small pine tree, *Pinus remota*, is appropriately called "paper-shell piñón," and is especially common at low elevations in central and northern Coahuila. It is quite likely that Cabeza de Vaca passed through the Sierra de la Gloria. In many other cases, however, the clues scattered in the sources do not lead to definite conclusions.[4]

The four healers moved rapidly. West of the Sierra de la Gloria, they began to make out the imposing Sierra Madre Oriental. It must have appeared to them like a huge crumpled wall, bisecting the continent from the southeast to the northwest. The Spaniards and the African wished to go west toward the setting sun and the copper-smelting settlements that lay in that direction. However, the mountain range forced them to bear north toward the Rio Grande yet again. They walked through so many Indian communities and heard so many different languages that their memories failed to recall them all.[5]

As they traveled, the castaways continued to burnish their reputation as healers. Cabeza de Vaca in particular became more confident in his skills. He became bolder in his interventions; he was no longer content merely to pray and blow. The medical procedures he employed may go some way toward explaining his success. Not far from the Rio Nadadores, he treated a man who had been struck by an arrow below the shoulder. "I touched him and felt the point of the arrow, and I saw that it had passed through the cartilage," Cabeza de Vaca writes with the precision of a surgeon, "and with a knife that I had, I opened his chest to that place. And I saw that the point had passed through and was very difficult to remove. I again cut deeper, and I inserted the knife point, and with great difficulty, at last I pulled it out. It was very long. And with a deer bone, plying my trade as a physician, I gave him two stitches, and after that he bled a great deal and with scraps of hide I stopped the bleeding." After the surgery, the patient claimed that he no longer felt pain. The arrowhead was passed around throughout the land, and everyone was amazed by the miraculous cure that Cabeza de

Cabeza de Vaca is still remembered in some quarters for his daring medical procedures. Painting by Tom Lea. Courtesy of the Moody Medical Library, University of Texas Medical Branch at Galveston.

Vaca had bestowed. The travelers' authority over the peoples of central Coahuila became great indeed.[6]

They never traveled alone. Since crossing into northern Tamaulipas, they, and their string of indigenous hosts, had worked out a system that was part processional, part doctor's visit, and part plunder. It must have been a marvel to behold. When the strangers arrived in each new Indian community, it set an elaborate series of rituals in motion. The natives would offer shelter, food, and gifts to the four men in exchange for access to their healing powers. Festivities would follow, sometimes for days. Then, reluctant to see the medicine men go, the Indian hosts would insist on traveling with them to the next settlement.

The four survivors had set ideas about where they wanted to go: first due south toward Pánuco, and then due west toward the metal-working peoples. They could not, however, simply dictate their route. Their Indian sponsors had their own notions and constantly tried to steer the drifters toward their friends and away from their enemies. The route actually taken by Cabeza de Vaca and his companions was often the result of complicated negotiations, and occasionally of deception. A native group by the Sierra de Pamoranes, for instance, tried to dissuade the four men from going inland by falsely claiming that there was neither food nor people in the direction the healers wished to travel. In that case the wanderers paid little attention and pursued their inland course. Yet in general they were not immune to such subtle manipulation, as they depended entirely upon their indigenous followers for information and knowledge about the terrain and geography of the region.[7]

Each time the explorers approached the next indigenous settlement on their journey, a curious exchange would ensue. Those who had accompanied the medicine men would pillage the new hosts, entering their huts and plundering whatever possessions or food they could carry back to their own encampment. In return, they left the medicine men. A certain sense of reciprocity undergirded the entire transaction, yet the details were unsettling for the explorers. They were initially taken aback by this custom when they first witnessed it in northern Tamaulipas. They were distressed by how badly the new hosts were treated and feared that the widespread sacking would lead to serious altercations. Yet their fears turned out to be unfounded as the plundered Indians offered reassurance. "On seeing our sadness," Cabeza de Vaca writes, "[they] consoled us by saying that we should not be grieved by that because they were so content to have seen us that they considered that their possessions had been well employed, and that farther ahead they would be compensated by others who were very rich." And indeed, a few days later the erstwhile victims would plunder the villagers that followed, "and the ones always sacked the others, and thus those who lost, like those who gained, were very content."[8]

Precise instructions about how to deal with the healers were also passed down from group to group. The hosts were told to lead the foreigners onward, always treating them "with great respect and being careful not to anger us in anything," Cabeza de Vaca writes, "and to give us everything they had, and to take us where there were many people, and that wherever we arrived to steal and loot what the others had because such was the custom." Soon the "new custom" became so entrenched and so well known that native villages on the way began to take precautions like hiding their most valuable possessions in advance of the procession's arrival. Reverence and intimidation were closely intertwined. An approaching band bent on plunder could easily cower villagers into surrendering their possessions and venerating the four outsiders.[9]

Life on the move was exhilarating but tiring for the survivors. They found themselves at the head of moving crowds that could reach as many as 3,000 or 4,000 people. They were veritable armies, capable of foraging along the way. In one instance, when the group went through a dry area, the women actually carried water, and the authority of the foursome was so great that no one dared to drink without their permission. Other followers gathered prickly pears and spiders and worms on the march. Many of the natives carried wooden clubs, and when a hare came out of its nest, they immediately surrounded it and threw themselves on it, swinging their clubs in a rain of blows. And these hunts were a wonder to see because the hare jumped from one place to another and sometimes, not knowing what else to do, came to rest in the hands of one of the hunters. The deer hunters went away to the sierras during the day and came back at night, carrying five or six animals for each of the four healers and also bringing quail and other game. "And everything, finally, that the people killed, they put before us without daring to take one single thing without our first making the sign of the cross over it, even though they might be dying of hunger." Every day the four medicine men spent hours blessing and blowing on every scrap of food and drink. And after the blessings were concluded, the healers ordered the Indians to roast the hares and the deer and the quail and the other animals in ovens that they made for this purpose. Cabeza de Vaca, Dorantes, Castillo, and Estebanico took whatever food they wanted and left the rest for their followers.[10]

Although the outsiders appeared to lead the procession, real power remained in the hands of Indian lords who chose to stay in the background. The healers themselves would have been unable to coordinate the imposing machine of exchange and pillage with which they were traveling. After all, much of the work of organization had to be conducted in languages that they could scarcely understand, and deciding on the procession's precise route required an understanding of the geography and human landscape of North America that the four men did not possess. Indigenous leaders were the only ones capable of organizing and directing the movements of the group. Cabeza de Vaca reveals only in passing that one indigenous man—"the principal man of these people who had come with us"—was the one who distributed the food after the healers had eaten. It is almost certain that this mysterious figure oversaw other aspects of the venture, including the division of goods after each looting spree. Cabeza de Vaca also mentions that either this lord or others cultivated the healers' reputation, shrewdly claiming that the four men were the "children of the sun" and spreading the word that they could either heal or kill, and "said even greater lies since these Indians know well how to do it when it suits them." Unfortunately, the sources do not give us more information about this principal man or the others. But clearly the four men had become complicit in a system of pillage that they did not control, a system that nonetheless permitted their safe passage across the continent. [11]

From the Rio Nadadores in central Coahuila, the trekkers followed a northwesterly course, traversing some 90 miles of prairies and more than 150 miles of desert and rugged terrain that caused them great hardship. The group must have been moving parallel to the Sierra Madre Oriental, skirting the narrow ranges of northwest Coahuila and ascending into plateaus at ever-higher elevations. The landscape grew more and more barren as they approached eastern Chihuahua. The land was uninhabited and so devoid of game that the hunters and foragers could not get enough food for everyone. The travelers suffered greatly from hunger, and some fell ill. At last, they crossed "a very great river in which the water came up to our chests," probably a reference to the Rio Grande. After this crossing, they walked onto a plain where the traveling procession encountered a new group of Indians. These new hosts had come from very far away and carried many things with them. The usual plundering exchange took place. But this time the loot was so great that the departing Indians could only take half of it, leaving the rest lying on the ground. The four wanderers told their new hosts to take the remaining objects with them, but they refused, saying that once they had made an offering, it was not their custom to take it back. And thus, Cabeza de Vaca says, "holding it in low estimation, they let all of it be lost." [12]

To their new hosts, the explorers expressed their intention to go west. But the Indians demurred. They said that in that direction the people were very distant and unfriendly to them. Their refusal angered the castaways. One night Cabeza de Vaca separated himself from camp, intending to spend the night alone to show his displeasure. But the Indians went looking after him and remained awake the whole night trying to please the healers and telling them how terrified they were. The four men pretended to be angry while they continued to haggle over which route to take. And during this time, the Royal Treasurer reports a strange occurrence: some of the Indians fell suddenly ill, and the next day eight of them died. The fear among the natives became overpowering. The castaways too were taken aback by these deaths. They must have felt responsible for bringing about this tragic event and also feared that, if the Indians continued to die, all the others would abandon the healers. The four men prayed to God fervently and begged him to restore the health of the Indians. Cabeza de Vaca and the others believed that they could summon God's power and were now beginning to learn the alarming consequences of their extraordinary gift.[13]

For fifteen days the Indians went completely quiet. No laughs or cries were heard, even from children or babies at breast. Some Indians were evidently grieving their spouses or children or other relatives who had succumbed to the mysterious illness, but they too remained silent and showed no emotion, as if nothing at all had happened. Whenever they stood in front of the four mighty men, they did not dare to speak or lift their stare from the ground. One little girl, who dared to cry before Cabeza de Vaca, was immediately taken far away, and with the sharp tooth of a rat, had her body slashed from the shoulders to the legs. "And seeing this cruelty and angered by it, I asked them why they did it. And they responded that it was to punish her because she had wept in front of me."[14]

The natives understood that they had no choice but to take the travelers wherever they wished to go, even into enemy territory.

Since Indian men could not venture west for fear of being killed, two women were sent as guides. Women were able to move about unencumbered, even in periods of internecine hostilities. Moreover, one of the two women guides was a captive who hailed from the place where the four men wanted to go; she would know the way and be able to communicate with her kin. Castillo, Estebanico, and the two indigenous guides went on ahead. The two hidalgos, Cabeza de Vaca and Dorantes, followed behind with a modest entourage of twenty or thirty Indians. The captive woman led the party to a river that ran through the sierras, finally arriving at a village where her father lived. The travelers caught a glimpse of a sizable settlement and of the first dwellings that had the appearance of being permanent houses. It was the first real settlement the wanderers had encountered since leaving Florida.[15]

THE CASTAWAYS HAD reached an agricultural oasis in the midst of a sea of nomads. The captive's village turned out to be part of a cluster of settlements located at the confluence of the Rio Grande and the Rio Conchos, an area aptly known today as La Junta de los Rios ("The Juncture of the Rivers"), between Presidio, Texas, and Ojinaga, Chihuahua. Almost fifty years after Cabeza de Vaca's visit, another Spanish expedition headed by a Mexico City merchant named Antonio de Espejo went through La Junta area and counted five pueblos and more than 10,000 inhabitants living in flat-roofed houses. Espejo learned another interesting fact. The residents told him that "three Christians and a negro had passed through there." Espejo immediately concluded that such visitors could only have been "Alonso [sic] Núñez Cabeza de Vaca, Dorantes, Castillo Maldonado, and a negro, who had all escaped from the fleet with which Pánfilo Narváez entered Florida."[16]

A nineteenth-century drawing of the old Rio Grande encountered by the castaways. After William H. Emory, *Report on the United States and Mexican Boundary Survey.* Washington, D.C., 1857.

The Indians at La Junta de los Rios were farmers. The damp islands and bays formed by the rivers were propitious for the farming of corn, beans, and squash. Cabeza de Vaca and his companions quickly learned that these Indians possessed corn; "and this was the thing that gladdened us more than anything else in the world, and for this we gave infinite thanks to our Lord."[17]

By the time of the castaways' visit, these Indians had occupied the river juncture continuously for around three centuries. They would continue to cling tenaciously to the area until their final amalgamation into Spanish society in the eighteenth century. Their centuries-old history has been largely lost, but it is not too difficult to imagine the tribulations of an agricultural island and strategic crossroad of exchange, where hunter-gatherers of the southern Great Plains, merchants from the Southwest, and travelers from the Gulf of Mexico region converged. These people—known variously to the Spaniards as Jumanos, Patarabueyes, and *rayados*—had to adapt and shift to survive, at times aligning themselves closely with the centers of the Southwest and at other times strengthening their ties to the nomads of the Plains. Regardless of the dominant cultural elements, they always straddled the divide between the settled and the nomadic worlds.[18]

The material possessions of the Indians of La Junta revealed the extent to which they inhabited both worlds. On the one hand, Cabeza de Vaca and his companions were impressed by the obvious signs of village life, such as the sturdy houses that overlooked their cornfields. Unlike the portable skin tents that the castaways themselves had been using for years, the people at La Junta de los Rios lived in spacious square structures anchored with pillars as thick as a man's thigh and with walls plastered with mud. On the other hand, this same people seemed to lack such essentials as pots. To boil water, they resorted to filling gourds with water and throwing hot stones into them, "and then they would add the bean meal, and put more stones on top, until the pap or porridge was cooked, and then they would eat it." They were also astonishingly mobile, and periodically embarked on lengthy expeditions to trade and hunt buffalo. "And we called them the people of the cows," Cabeza de Vaca explains, "because the greatest number of those cows are killed near there. And upstream along that river for more than fifty leagues they go killing many of them."[19]

Cabeza de Vaca, Dorantes, Castillo, and Estebanico stayed in these settlements for some weeks, surely contemplating their achievements and wondering how their journey would end. Their breathtaking gamble of forsaking Pánuco and venturing inland seemed to have paid off. By letting go and allowing themselves to be driven along by throngs of Indians, they had traveled halfway across the continent. They had seen many peoples and had covered much ground that no other outsider had seen before, getting closer to the Indians with metallurgical knowledge.

The four men must have been humbled, however, by the enormous and eerie land ahead of them. They asked "the people of the cows" about the country to the west and were told that there was a great deal of corn there. In fact, for two years in a row the rains had not come to La Junta de los Rios. "The people of the cows" had lost their crops and had been forced to import corn from the land to the west. The wanderers must have been delighted to know that ahead of them lived peoples who were in possession of great stores of corn, but they also learned that this land of plenty was very distant and it would be difficult to get there. They would have to start by following the river (most likely the Rio Grande) upstream for seventeen days, where they would find nothing to eat except for a certain fruit that grew in trees that the Indians called *masarrones* and that had to be crushed with rocks. Even then, they were told, it was "very bad stuff, not even fit for animals."[20]

After pondering their options for two more days, the foursome decided to follow the trail of the maize, "and the fear they put into us about the great hunger that we were to endure, which, in truth, we suffered all the seventeen days' journey about which they had told us, was not sufficient to stop us from doing this." The trekkers ascended the river. They did not eat the unpalatable *masarrones* but subsisted instead on daily rations of deer fat. They needed the calories badly, and there was nothing else to be had. As they proceeded up river, the explorers found empty Indian camps; most of the regular occupants had gone north to hunt bison. But the few Indians who stayed behind were friendly, allowing the expeditioners to sleep in the empty huts and giving them bison robes and other things.[21]

On the seventeenth day, Cabeza de Vaca and his companions stopped following the river and veered west. They were traveling with some natives who told them where to go. The medicine men walked another seventeen or twenty days through a high plain. The vast landscape was broken only by stands of creosote, yucca, and mesquite. In the distance the majestic Sierra Madre Occidental loomed interminably from south to north, completely blocking their way. They reached the foothills of the massive range, and their Indian hosts steered them through passes that gave way to even higher and more desert-like tablelands. Somehow—the sources provide precious few clues—the group was able to negotiate the continental divide, eventually reaching the Pacific slopes of the mighty sierra. The entire area was fringed by mountains crowned with pine trees. The cold must have been unbearable at night as the dreaded winter approached once again.[22]

The castaways must have passed very near the ancient city of Paquimé (Casas Grandes or "Big Houses"), once a cultural center of the first magnitude. Between 1250 and 1450, Paquimé had dominated a vast realm, controlling outposts stretching as far away as La Junta de los Rios to the east and the Pacific coast to the west. The people of Paquimé were consummate merchants. They had been the preeminent importers of live scarlet macaws, copper bells, and shells, and the greatest exporters of turquoise into central Mexico. The city itself—first described by a European party of exploration in the 1550s—appeared compact but extremely dense. It boasted structures that were as high as six or seven stories. According to an account of this expedition, Paquimé could well have been constructed by the ancient Ro-

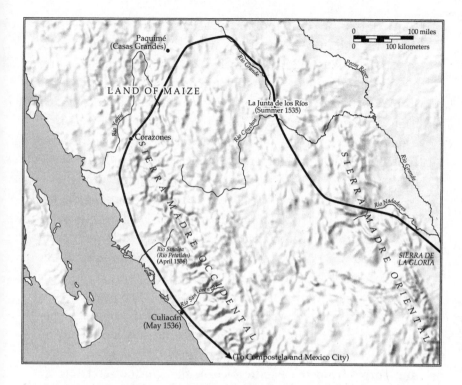

mans. It possessed "towers and walls like fortresses" and "magnificent patios paved with enormous and beautiful stones resembling jasper." Yet, Paquimé became depopulated and was finally destroyed and burned to the ground sometime around 1450 or 1500, only two or three generations before the passage of Cabeza de Vaca's party. The great city and its surroundings were by then inhabited by recent arrivals, nomads who did not so much live in the ruined stone houses as camp in them. The erstwhile residents of Paquimé had scattered in all directions, moving into a constellation of modest villages that, in all likelihood, were some of the settlements that the castaways encountered "every two or three days," and where they rested as they made their way to the Pacific coast.[23]

After two or three months of arduous marches, the three Spaniards and the African at last arrived at the "land of maize," sometime in late 1535 or early 1536. They ventured into a region of many villages boasting permanent houses and large stores of maize. The four healers were given corn flour and beans and squash, "and we loaded those who brought us there," Cabeza de Vaca says, "and with this they went home the most contented people in the world." The castaways walked for 300 miles or more without ever leaving the maize country.[24]

The four wanderers must have been traveling through the fertile valleys of northern Sonora, already on the Pacific slopes of the Sierra Madre Occidental. The Indians there lived in permanent houses and wore shoes, and the women wore cotton shirts all the way to their knees and long deerskin skirts that touched the ground. They appeared to the four men to be "the most decently clad women we had ever seen in any part of the Indies." They continued to cure and in return received many rich presents, including cotton mantles "better than those of New Spain," beads and corals from the Pacific Ocean, fine turquoises from the north, and what was described as "emeralds made into arrowheads." But the most extravagant gift that they received was a bundle of more than 600 hearts of deer, split-open through the middle and dried. For that reason, the adventurers called that village *Corazones*, or "Hearts."[25]

Throughout the "land of maize," the people had flocked to the strangers, asking to be touched and to have the sign of the cross made over them. The ill and the healthy alike approached the healers, and even the women who had just given birth took their babies to be blessed. The Indians following the four men numbered 1,500 and could reach up to 3,000 or more. The four medicine men sought to enhance their authority by speaking as little as possible, communicating mostly through the African Estebanico, an arrangement that must have seemed impressive to the Indians. While the three Spaniards remained aloof and forbidding, Estebanico was gregarious and easygoing. He was the one who informed himself about the roads and villages ahead. His gift for languages and communication through signs was tested to the limit. Even though the healers were now able to speak six indigenous languages among them, they were of little use in a land where so many tongues were heard. "And among all these peoples, it was taken for certain that we came from the sky," Cabeza de Vaca writes, "because all the things that they do not have or do not know the origin of, they say come from the sky." The Indians would come out at sunrise, raising their hands to the sky and then running them over the strangers' bodies.[26]

The four wanderers' ascendancy over the natives was so great that they could not help but think about how to use it to advance Spain's imperial aims. Instead of bringing the Indians into the Christian fold through violence, the healers dreamed of accomplishing this grandiose project peacefully and humanely. Since Narváez was dead, Cabeza de Vaca and the others may have considered the possibility of going back to Spain to obtain his *adelantamiento*. For the moment they did what they could, as Cabeza de Vaca says, "And we told them by signs, because they understood us, that in heaven there was a man whom we called God, who had created the heaven and the earth, and that we adored him and served him as Lord, and that we did whatever he commanded us, and that from his hand came all good things, and if thus they were to do it, it would go very well for them."[27]

The healers may have been humane, but they were also sixteenth-century Christians. They believed that the throngs of Indians that showed so much reverence and devotion toward them would be infinitely better off as Catholics under Spanish rule. The castaways thus intended to forge a Christian kingdom out of these untamed lands. Unfortunately, their dreams would soon collide with a different kind of kingdom—one of brutality and greed.

Around Christmas of 1535, Castillo spotted a Spanish buckle and a horseshoe nail tied around the neck of an Indian in the manner of jewels. It was a small detail that he could easily have overlooked, but once he spotted the necklace he must have been overcome with excitement. He took the buckle and the nail and asked the man where they had come from. The Indian responded that they had belonged to "some men who wore beards like us, who had come from the sky and arrived at that river, and who brought horses and lances and swords, and who had lanced two of them." Trying not to appear too eager, the medicine men inquired further about the activities of these Europeans. They were told that the foreigners had been seen by the coast.[28]

The survivors had decidedly mixed feelings upon hearing the news that there were conquistadors not far from where they were. On the one hand, they were grateful to God because they appeared at last to be at the very doorstep of deliverance. Almost a decade of hardship, privation, and uncertainty seemed to be coming to an end. But on the other, they felt greatly disturbed and saddened that other Christians had already reached these remote lands and were causing so much harm to the natives. These conquistadors had destroyed towns throughout the area and had captured men, women, and children. The medicine men promised their Indian hosts that they would look for these men and try to get them to stop killing and enslaving the natives. The Indians of the maize were greatly pleased at hearing this promise.[29]

CHAPTER 9

Contact

E VEN BY THE DISMAL STANDARDS OF SPAIN'S early involvement in the New World, the bearded conquistadors who had left Mexico City and made their way up through the Pacific coast were notorious. Nuño de Guzmán and his men exercised a level of violence that has few equivalents in the dark annals of conquest.

By 1536 Guzmán's grim reputation was quite well known. For nearly a decade he had been the master of Pánuco, amassing a fortune through the enslavement of natives and their sale in the Caribbean. The scope of his slaving activities had been momentarily threatened by Pánfilo de Narváez's projected occupation of the large area north of Pánuco. Of course, Narváez's arrival never materialized, leaving the field wide open to the enterprising Guzmán.[1]

After securing his hold over Pánuco, Nuño de Guzmán moved to Mexico City. The Crown intended to make out of this audacious nobleman an effective counterweight to the headstrong Hernán Cortés. In 1528 Guzmán received an appointment as president of the first *audiencia* of Mexico, the second-highest ranking official in the land. His backers were not disappointed, as Guzmán used every opportunity to loosen Cortés's grip and wage a bureaucratic war on his allies. But his

Nuño de Guzmán as depicted by indigenous artists of the mid-sixteenth century. The Spanish gloss accompanying this codex reads as follows: "In the year 11 house of 1529 Nuño de Guzmán left [Mexico City] for Jalisco which he went to conquer"... Codex Telleriano-Remensis, folio 44r.

tenure was tumultuous, with allegations of mismanagement, widespread slaving, and extortion prompting his excommunication by the bishop-elect of Mexico.[2]

Just prior to Christmas of 1529, under a cloud of ruthless maneuvering and illegality, Nuño de Guzmán left Mexico City at the head of 400 Spaniards and as many as 12,000 Indian porters and auxiliaries. They were bound for the unexplored lands to the north and west, where they hoped to find even greater kingdoms than those of central Mexico. Guzmán, not unlike his archrival Cortés, intended to redeem himself by fiat.[3]

Guzmán's expedition left a trail of desolation wherever it went. On its way to the Pacific coast, it passed through the great kingdom of Michoacán. There Nuño de Guzmán and his men tortured and executed Cazonci, the native ruler, for failing to deliver enough tribute. This powerful lord—deemed to be "as great as Moctezuma and even richer in gold and silver"—was

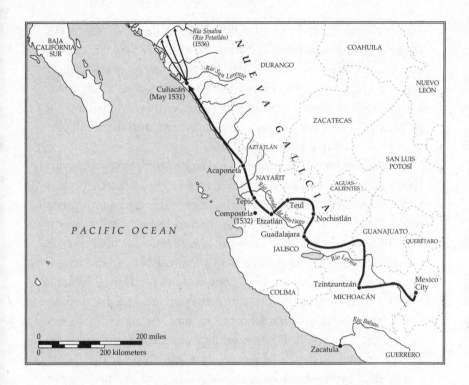

dragged by a horse, strangled with a *garrote*, and burned at the stake. It was an outrage that Cazonci's subjects could scarcely begin to comprehend. Before leaving Michoacán, Guzmán demanded an additional 8,000 Indians for the expedition. Many of them were put in chains or wore collars around their necks.[4]

By the summer of 1530, Guzmán's party had reached the indigenous province of Aztatlán, a thin strip of hot country along the Pacific coast between the Santiago and Culiacán Rivers in northwest Mexico. The onset of the rainy season finally halted its advance. The showers would soon become so torrential that the Indians were forced to leave their huts and climb up in trees. From their high perches, they could not see land but only an ocean of mud; toads jumped through the camp. Most expedition members fell ill, and out of 8,000 Indians there were not 200 who remained standing. The natives who were strong enough attempted to flee this watery hell, but many were instead caught and tortured. Guzmán ordered the construction of a large pen. Inside, Indian men were held in place with steel collars, the women were tied with ropes in groups of ten, and the small children were confined in groups of five.[5]

At the center of this brutal activity was the contradictory Guzmán. In his own way he was a very religious man who professed a special devotion to the Holy Spirit. He had a puritanical streak, evident in his intolerance toward those Spaniards who kept Indian concubines or uttered blasphemies in his presence, practices that must have been nearly impossible to eradicate in the rough-and-tumble world of conquistadors. His megalomania reached such immense proportions that he insisted that Indians sweep the streets and roads ahead of him. At times he seemed downright delusional. He was among the most enthusiastic believers in the existence of Amazons farther up on the Pacific coast, of a land where women only tolerated the presence of men at certain times of the year.

His rigid and perhaps even pathological personality aside, Nuño de Guzmán was a bold strategist bent on uniting his holdings on the Gulf of Mexico and the Pacific coast, and a shrewd businessman who knew how to keep his men loyal by lavishing authority and slaves on them. Most importantly, the Crown's strong backing enabled Guzmán to continue to dream about Amazons and vast new kingdoms.[6]

In the early 1530s Guzmán's haphazard conquests hardened into a permanent new province called Nueva Galicia. The Empress herself sent Guzmán a congratulatory letter naming him governor. With the passage of time, Guzmán's drab military camps became cities and ports ruled by his associates. Nueva

Galicia comprised a large coastal region from the present-day states of Jalisco all the way to Sonora.

At the far end of this province, cavalry detachments continued to explore further into the north. Captain Diego de Alcaraz led one of these units. His efforts were chiefly devoted to finding and enslaving Indians. These mounted Spaniards faced an entire continent teeming with Indians who could not move faster than their own legs would carry them. Even half a dozen European horsemen could turn into an extremely efficient enslaving machine. And they did. Small detachments fanned out, actively burning villages and ruining crops and carrying off men, women, and children.

At first, perhaps out of natural curiosity, Indians would approach the slavers. But they learned quickly, and by the mid-1530s they had abandoned their cornfields and dwellings on the more accessible coastal locations to take refuge in the myriad crevices of the Sierra Madre Occidental. The slavers were thus forced into ever-more difficult and unsuccessful searches. This is the world that Cabeza de Vaca, Dorantes, Castillo, and Estebanico encountered as they descended the sierras and headed toward the coast.[7]

FROM THE VILLAGE of *Corazones*, the castaways traveled with an entourage to another town, where the heavy rains forced them to stop the march for two weeks. After another trek of 240 miles, they reached the Rio Sinaloa. In the vicinity of that river, the four men found a spot where Europeans had recently spent the night. The signs were unmistakable: the camp had stakes where the horses had been tied. Some Indian guides had actually seen how the Spanish slavers transported many Indians using chains. "And those who came with us," Cabeza de Vaca says, "were very disturbed by this." That very night the Royal Treasurer vowed to make contact with the horsemen. He asked one of his younger and stronger companions to rush ahead with a few Indians to overtake the Spaniards, but the man, probably Dorantes, excused himself, saying that it would be too difficult and tiresome. So the next morning, Cabeza de Vaca set out to do it himself. He took Estebanico and eleven Indians and began tracking the Christians. The men exerted themselves to the limit, covering almost 30 miles in a single day, and passing through no less than three abandoned Christian encampments. It must have been April 1536, almost nine years since the survivors had left Europe.[8]

The following morning, Cabeza de Vaca's party came within sight of four Christian horsemen. From a distance the thirteen men, walking barefoot and clad in skins, must have seemed rather ordinary, except for their boldness in moving straight toward the horsemen. At closer range the disconcerting details must have become visible: first Estebanico's skin color and then Cabeza de Vaca himself. His hair dropped down to his waist, and his beard reached to his chest. When the two parties came face to face and the white man spoke in perfect Andalusian Spanish, the slavers were dumbfounded. "They remained looking at me for a long time," Cabeza de Vaca writes, "so astonished that they neither spoke to me nor managed to ask me anything."[9]

The initial exchange must have been awkward, but the men agreed to walk together for another 1.5 miles to meet Captain Diego de Alcaraz, who was encamped with the rest of his men, altogether about twenty horsemen, by the Rio Sinaloa. Alcaraz was angry because his unit had been unable to take Indian captives—for two weeks the slavers hadn't even seen any Indians. The arrival of Cabeza de Vaca and Estebanico was shocking and impossible to explain, but at least they had brought some natives. What Cabeza de Vaca said next could not have failed to ignite Alcaraz's imagination. The Royal Treasurer explained that about 30 miles away two other Spaniards had stayed behind, and that they were waiting "with *many people* who had guided them." Alcaraz and his men must have struggled to conceal their anticipation at the thought of so many potential captives. The group then formulated a plan. Estebanico would go back to guide the two remaining castaways into Captain Alcaraz's camp. He was ordered to depart immediately with a posse of three Spanish horsemen and about fifty Indian porters.[10]

Estebanico must have sensed that his status was diminishing quickly. Through many hardships and adventures across North America, the African had emerged as a full partner of the three Europeans. Lately he had served as their principal scout and as an intermediary between the Indians of the "land of maize" and the three Spaniards. Unquestionably, Estebanico had been essential to the band's survival, but upon reaching Christian-dominated lands, whatever equality he had been able to achieve evaporated rapidly. The Spanish horsemen must not have given a second thought to his condition as a slave. Even his fellow castaways had started to reassert their authority. Cabeza de Vaca himself takes for granted the Moroccan's opinion when, after getting the first inklings of the presence of Christians, he writes coldly that he "took the black man" with him to search for them. Estebanico received orders from the white men, and he obeyed them. It must have been a difficult transformation for someone who had been so revered by the Indians.[11]

Five days later Estebanico returned leading Dorantes, Castillo, and more than 600 Indians who had been hiding from the slavers but now insisted on staying with the castaways. No longer angry about the dearth of natives, Captain Alcaraz now worried about his food stores. He begged Cabeza de Vaca to call on the Indians who had been hiding in the mountains to bring some corn, but "this was not necessary," Cabeza de Vaca says, "because they always took care to bring us all they could. And we then sent out our messengers to call them, and six hundred [additional] people came who brought us all the maize they could obtain." Even though the Indians had not been able to sow, they had placed their leftover corn in clay pots, sealed them, and buried them. The natives took these pots to the castaways, who ate what they wanted and gave the rest to the slavers. The Indians must have been perplexed by this behavior, but they remained confident in the four medicine men.[12]

With their bellies full, the survivors and the horsemen finally quarreled. Between the 600 Indians who had brought Estebanico and the other 600 who had brought the corn, there must have been more than 1,000 natives around the Spanish camp. The castaways had promised them that they would get the slavers to stop their depredations, and here was their chance. Cabeza de Vaca laid out his vision of prosperity for all. Never prone to wordiness or exaggeration, he curtly informed the horsemen that this coastal area was "without a doubt the best of any to be found in these Indies and the most fertile and abundant in foodstuffs." It was so rich, he claimed, that Indians sowed three times a year and gathered "many fruits" and there were "beautiful rivers and many other good waterways" and many indications of gold and silver mines, even if the Indians did not care for these metals. As for the people, Cabeza de Vaca said, they were "well disposed" and "of very good inclinations." In short, there was nothing lacking for Christians and Indians alike to prosper in such a privileged environment.[13]

Making use of all the authority he could muster as Royal Treasurer of the Florida expedition, Cabeza de Vaca must have indicated to the slavers that they had erred in having entered the land to wage indiscriminate war on the natives. The result was plain to see: the land had been abandoned, the fields were overgrown with vegetation, and the Indians had taken refuge in the

mountains, making life for the Spaniards themselves very difficult. But Cabeza de Vaca had a solution. The castaways had
given ample proof of their great influence over the Indians. Now
they offered to call out to the Indians to resettle the land and restore the lost Eden. Cabeza de Vaca had already broached the
subject with the Indians, and they had said that they would go
back to their old houses and fields, if the Christians would only
promise that all would live in peace.

The Spanish horsemen were unimpressed by Cabeza de
Vaca's vision. They saw a human cargo worth a fortune standing around them. They had not lived among the Indians like the
castaways had and could not begin to fathom the utopian project proposed by this Spaniard gone native, who believed in his
mysterious powers to cure. The conversation deteriorated. "And
we suffered greatly and had great disputes with them," Cabeza
de Vaca says, "because they wanted to enslave the Indians we
had brought with us."[14]

In a last-ditch effort to save them, Cabeza de Vaca commanded
the Indians to disperse. But they refused to go. The natives fully intended to turn the strangers over to another group, as was their
custom, and believed that they would die if they failed to do so. As
long as the castaways stayed with them, "they feared neither the
Christians nor their lances." The Spanish horsemen became very
annoyed, and through some interpreters they let the Indians know
that the four survivors were Christians like themselves. The Indians refused to believe it. Their eloquent rebuttal resonates today,
reminding us that not all Spanish expeditions were the same. They
said, Cabeza de Vaca remembers, that "we came from where the
sun rose, and they from where it set; that we cured the sick, and
they killed those who were well; that we came naked and barefoot,
and they went about dressed and on horses and with lances; and
that we did not covet anything but rather, everything they gave us

we later returned and remained with nothing, and that the others had no other objective but to steal everything they found and did not give anything to anyone."[15]

At last the castaways were taken away with some of the Indians in great haste, but they left behind many bows and leather pouches and the five emerald arrows, which must have fallen into the hands of Captain Alcaraz and his men. Under a Spanish guard, the Florida expeditioners headed toward Culiacán, the northernmost Spanish town, which was still 90 miles away. The irony of the situation was not lost on Cabeza de Vaca, "for we went to them [the Spaniards] seeking liberty and when we thought we had it, it turned out to be so much to the contrary." Cruelly, the Spanish guard took the castaways through overgrown and depopulated areas "to remove us from conversation with Indians along the way"—Cabeza de Vaca says. The thickets were dense and nearly impassable, and there were no roads. They found no water for two days, "and we all thought that we would perish from thirst, and seven men died from it, and many [Indian] friends."[16]

At Culiacán the four wanderers were presented to the *alcalde mayor* and captain of the province, Melchor Díaz. He must have been astonished to learn that his guests were the last survivors of the ill-fated expedition of Pánfilo de Narváez to Florida. "And he wept a great deal with us, praising God our Lord for having shown so much mercy to us"—Cabeza de Vaca writes—"and he spoke to us and treated us very well. And on behalf of the governor, Nuño de Guzmán, as well as his own, he offered us everything that he had and could." The *alcalde mayor* conveyed his sorrow at the bad treatment the four survivors had suffered at the hands of Captain Alcaraz and his men and wished he had been there to prevent it.[17]

The four healers spent some weeks at Culiacán, making contact with the Indians of the area and trying to persuade them to return to the coastal plains to plant corn. These efforts were consistent with the castaways' vision of a kingdom of cooperation, but such a realm depended on the promise that Spaniards would cease to make war on the Indians, a promise that neither Cabeza de Vaca nor the others could enforce. Unfortunately, they soon learned that the horsemen by the Rio Sinaloa had resumed their slaving raids, and that the newly resettled Indians had become their targets.

On May 16, 1536, the castaways began their march toward Compostela, the capital of Nueva Galicia, where Nuño de Guzmán awaited. The four healers were accompanied now by just a few dozen Indians. This group of about eighty was driven by a guard of twenty horsemen. All of them were trailed not by throngs of adoring Indians but by 500 Indian slaves who were probably in chains. On the way they witnessed the ravages of the Spanish *entrada* along the Pacific seaboard. In a stretch that extended for 300 miles or more, Cabeza de Vaca says, "the country is entirely depopulated and [so] filled with enemies, it was necessary that we should have protection."[18]

Still scantily clad in skins, the four survivors arrived in Compostela, where a circumspect Nuño de Guzmán greeted them. Their adjustment to European life had been halting. After years of living simply and in the open, such Spanish customs as donning a full complement of clothes with stockings, handkerchiefs, rosaries, and perhaps a shoulder cape appeared cumbersome to the survivors. The governor gave them clothes from his own wardrobe, a gesture that may have been prompted partly by his puritanical sensibilities. "I was unable to wear [the clothes] for many days," Cabeza de Vaca writes, "nor were we able to sleep but on the ground."[19]

The survivors were dismayed by the extensive slaving and human suffering and raised the subject with the prickly Guzmán, but the governor became displeased and promptly dispatched the castaways to Mexico City.[20]

Cabeza de Vaca and his companions stayed in Compostela for two weeks before departing for Mexico City with their small entourage of loyal Indians. When they arrived on Sunday, July 23, 1536, the citizens of the capital were in high spirits. It was the eve of the Day of Saint James, and the city residents were preparing for a series of bullfights and *juegos de caña* (jousting matches). The arrival of the four heroes contributed greatly to the expansive mood. Viceroy don Antonio de Mendoza and the Marqués del Valle Hernán Cortés warmly received the four wanderers, giving them food and clothes.

The survivors could not help but become pawns in a power struggle. The viceroy and the marquis were rivals, and the survivors' unexpected arrival would plunge them into a headlong competition over the exploration of the vast lands north from Mexico. The value of what the wanderers knew was incalculable. Mendoza did everything he could to attract them to his camp. He opened his house and kept them as honored guests. He also agreed to look after the few dozen Indians from the north that Cabeza de Vaca and his companions had brought. In return Viceroy Mendoza was able to question the four men in the comfort of his home, and even asked them to draw a map of all the lands they had visited.[21]

As the celebrations unfolded, Mexico City succumbed to a newfound fever to explore those marvelous regions of which the castaways spoke. Unwittingly, the castaways had ushered in yet another wave of conquests.

Epilogue

CABEZA DE VACA, CASTILLO, DORANTES, AND Estebanico had journeyed to the New World as settlers. As they set off from Spain, they must have imagined themselves leading simple lives in incipient communities in Florida, making do with whatever foods, building materials, and friendships their immediate surroundings afforded them. Certainly, they never expected to find themselves spending close to a year in Mexico City, subjected to constant scrutiny and attention. But the four survivors had become a sensation. They were feted and paraded around town. They had even appeared in one of the main city churches stark naked but for the deerskins covering their private parts, startling details that Mexico City residents would still remember a generation later. With all the pageantry and commotion that surrounded them, the travelers must have been hard-pressed at first to reflect on their odyssey and on their hopes for the future.[1]

Of the four, Cabeza de Vaca was the one who had found his calling. He intended to go back to Spain to submit a report to the Emperor; it was his duty as Royal Treasurer. But, since Narváez was dead, Cabeza de Vaca also hoped to use the occasion to petition for the vacant *adelantamiento*. The Royal Treasurer's plan was not outlandish: he was deserving and loyal, and his story would leave little doubt among court members that he had earned his reward with sweat and blood. But far more importantly, Cabeza de Vaca believed that his peaceful ascendancy over the Indians of North America would sway the members of the Spanish court into believing that a more humane kind of colonial occupation was achievable. Instead of enslaving Indians and torching villages as Nuño de Guzmán was doing, the Royal Treasurer would make a case for establishing a partnership with them.

Over the course of his journeys, Cabeza de Vaca had found that America's bounty consisted not only of gold and silver, but also of land and good people. Together, Europeans and Native Americans could make the New World yield spiritual as well as material wealth. Such a proposition would appear woefully idealistic and impracticable, but when coming from one of the "children of the sun," the Crown might find it worth considering. The Royal Treasurer understood the fears and hopes of the natives better than any other Spaniard, and perhaps had already talked to them about such a grandiose alliance.[2]

Cabeza de Vaca stayed in Mexico City for two months in order to regain strength and reacquaint himself with the affairs of the empire. The most intriguing news came out of Peru. In 1532 Francisco Pizarro had come in contact with the Inca and in short order had captured its leader and demanded a roomful of silver for his release. More recently, however, the situation had taken a turn for the worse. Over the summer of 1536, Pizarro frantically requested reinforcements from Guatemala and New Spain. Men of enterprise in Mexico City eagerly discussed whether there was any silver left in Peru, tantalizing talk of plunder and war that nonetheless must have been unsettling for someone advocating a peaceful colonization of America.

In the fall of 1536, Cabeza de Vaca went to Veracruz seeking passage to Europe. The natural elements continued to dog him.

He learned at the Mexican port that the ship that he intended to board had capsized in a storm. He could have waited for another ship, but it would be winter by the time it arrived, a dangerous time to be sailing across the Atlantic. Forced to spend the winter in Mexico City, Cabeza de Vaca made a second attempt to sail in February. That time he succeeded, but at great peril. Near the island of Bermuda, 600 miles from the coast of America, a powerful storm nearly sank his ship. To make matters worse, some days later French privateers caught up with the lone vessel as it negotiated the Azores. The ship carried gold and silver amounting to 300,000 pesos, a worthy prize. During an agonizing afternoon and an entire night of terrible forebodings, the French corsairs pursued their prey, cutting it off but postponing the final assault until the morning. Only the miraculous appearance of a Portuguese fleet prevented the final coup. Cabeza de Vaca gave thanks to God for having escaped "the hardships of the land and the perils of the sea."[3]

In August 1537, after an absence of a decade, the Royal Treasurer finally set foot on European soil. The ship arrived in Lisbon, from where Cabeza de Vaca traveled to Castile to settle his long-neglected affairs. By December he was at court in Valladolid delivering his report to the King.

Cabeza de Vaca was in for a terrible disappointment. In Valladolid, he learned that the Crown had already given away the commission for the conquest of Florida. In an instant his cherished plans, long harbored during his travels in North America and in the months that he had stayed in Mexico City, came to naught. The King had foreclosed the destiny that God had intended for the Royal Treasurer.

Cabeza de Vaca apparently had trouble letting go of his vision of peaceful colonization of the lands of North America. He sought out the man who had received the royal license for

Florida, Hernando de Soto, to discuss the possibility of a partnership, but ultimately they could not come to an agreement. Their differences had been ostensibly over money, but Cabeza de Vaca also admitted that he "did not wish to go under the banner of another." It must have been exceedingly difficult for the castaway to come to terms with his diminution in status from powerful healer to mere second-in-command of another grasping conquistador.[4]

It would take Cabeza de Vaca three more years of patient lobbying to secure an *adelantamiento* in his own right. He would be going to the Rio de la Plata, at the other end of the hemisphere in what are now portions of Argentina, Uruguay, and Paraguay. The brand new Governor must have experienced a sense of déjà vu as he sailed toward the coast of South America in 1540 to begin asserting his control. At last, he would put his plan for the New World into effect.[5]

His methods of conquest were decidedly unconventional. Instead of riding on horseback, Cabeza de Vaca went barefoot ahead of his men, calling out to the Indians of the region, the Guaraní, and trying to lure them gently. He gave out gifts to the Guaraní and ordered his men to pay scrupulously for all the goods received from them. To prevent any abuses, Cabeza de Vaca always set up his camp away from native villages and allowed his men to trade with the Indians only through a licensed agent.[6]

Cabeza de Vaca's men did not appreciate these methods. The European residents of the Rio de la Plata had their own ideas about how to treat Indians and profit at their expense. Having lived in the area before Cabeza de Vaca's arrival, most of them came to resent this curious leader, who behaved more like a missionary than a conquistador. There were rumblings of rebellion. Perhaps more jarringly for Cabeza de Vaca, the Guaraní Indians also became disaffected. They balked at his Christianizing program, which included such strictures as the eradication of cannibalism and the imposition of monogamous marriage.[7]

By the spring of 1544, Cabeza de Vaca's men had had enough. They seized the Governor and sent him back to Spain, accused of charges ranging from confiscating the property of dead European residents, to not bringing sufficient supplies to Paraguay, to forbidding Europeans to trade freely with the Indians and thus reducing them to poverty, to delivering twenty-five friendly Indians to the Guaranís to be killed and eaten.[8]

Cabeza de Vaca's forced return to Spain was a time of reckoning for him. His colonization project in South America had been a utopian dream. It was one thing to wield the power of an indigenous shaman, and quite another to act as the leader of a band of conquerors. His extraordinary experiences in North America had given him a false sense of what he could accomplish at the Rio de la Plata. At the very least, he had grossly overestimated his influence. Cabeza de Vaca had been unable to control his men and to persuade the Indians that they would be better off under Spain's tutelage. Gentle and well intentioned as he may have been, a conquest was still a conquest, after all.[9]

Cabeza de Vaca's subsequent legal ordeal lasted eight long years after his imprisonment in South America. He faced four different lawsuits and more than thirty criminal charges. In 1551 the Council of the Indies found Cabeza de Vaca guilty. He was banned in perpetuity from the Indies and stripped of all his titles. In addition, he was sentenced to five years in a penal colony in Oran (in present-day Algeria). It was a precipitous fall for someone who had once wielded the power to cure the Indians and had been treated like a demigod. Cabeza de Vaca fought back, appealing his sentence and calling witnesses who spoke in his favor. In 1552 the most onerous portions of his sentence were rescinded or reduced, and by 1555 he had come close to achieving complete vindication.

Cabeza de Vaca chose to spend the last years of his life in his ancestral village of Jerez de la Frontera, like his grandfather, the conqueror of Gran Canaria. In his ripe old age, the wanderer of North America and former governor of the Rio de la Plata became a larger-than-life figure and protector of his family. In 1559 the castaway signed a bond for a ransom payment on behalf of Hernán Ruiz Cabeza de Vaca, a relative who was being held captive by the king of Algiers.

But in the end, Cabeza de Vaca must have reflected on the fact that, unlike his grandfather, he had never attained the glitter of successful conquest. All along he had been a more tragic figure: an orphan, a self-man man, a visionary, a fervent Catholic, and a consummate survivor who had overcome the most adverse circumstances while holding fast to his ideals.[10]

ANDRÉS DORANTES AND Alonso del Castillo, the other two European castaways, had less difficulty readjusting to colonial life. They followed a markedly different trajectory than their former Royal Treasurer. They decided to stay in New Spain, continuing their dealings with Native Americans no longer as medicine men but as colonial officials and wealthy residents.

Their transformation from ragged shamans to men of means was the handiwork of don Antonio de Mendoza. As Dorantes's son would explain decades later, Viceroy Mendoza took Captains Dorantes and Castillo into his household, honoring them and marrying them to widows. Viceroy Mendoza proved to be a wily matchmaker. Within months of his arrival in Mexico City, he married Castillo to doña Isabel de Sanabria, the wealthy widow of a deceased conquistador. Castillo thus gained an instant stake in the wealth of New Spain and doña Isabel a trophy husband, part miracle man, from an illustrious Spanish family. Four years later, Castillo and his wife appeared as co-owners of an *encomienda*, comprising fully half of the town of Tehuacán located at the heart of a large valley of rolling hills about 100 miles to the southeast of Mexico City. The Indians who lived there were *entrusted* to the Spanish couple. They would continue to live in their own community but would also be obligated to give tribute to Captain Castillo and doña Isabel, who could then sell these agricultural products at a profit. In return, Castillo and his wife had to make sure that the Indians thus entrusted to them received proper religious instruction.[11]

Captain Dorantes took more time to settle down. Early in 1537 he made an unsuccessful attempt to go back to Spain. For much of that year, he also considered going back to the north as the leader of a swift exploratory expedition that would be sponsored by Viceroy Mendoza. But ultimately Dorantes followed in Castillo's footsteps and married a wealthy widow, doña María de la Torre. Dorantes held jointly with his wife an *encomienda* in Atzalán-Mexcalcingo, to the east of Mexico City. According to a 1560 estimate, the grant comprised 1,608 Indians and yielded a tribute in cotton, honey, beans, *ají* (chili peppers), chickens, fish, and maize.[12]

Perhaps the castaways' intimate knowledge of the Indians of the north influenced how they treated those entrusted to them in central Mexico. It is impossible to tell from the sources. Most likely, Castillo and Dorantes acted like typical *encomenderos*, neither more benevolently nor more cruelly than others. In any case, neither was involved in the day-to-day management of their Indian grants, as both became absentee owners.

Castillo and Dorantes adapted well to their new lives, alternating the management of their *encomiendas* with courtly life in Mexico City, the viceregal capital. Castillo received a one-year appointment as *alcalde ordinario* (ordinary mayor) of Mexico City. By 1547 Castillo felt sufficiently knowledgeable and meritorious to request a position as councilman of Mexico City, one of the most coveted offices in all of New Spain. His request was turned down.[13]

The peripatetic Dorantes accepted riskier assignments. According to his son, Captain Dorantes assisted in the settlement of areas inhabited by fierce Indians where no Spaniards lived. Interestingly, Dorantes had occasion to return to the province of Nueva Galicia, where the castaways had first encountered the Spanish slavers after their incredible adventures in the interior. Nueva Galicia experienced a massive Indian insurrection in 1541–1542 that nearly succeeded in dislodging the Spanish presence there. Viceroy Mendoza had to request thousands of volunteers from central Mexico and personally led these forces into this northwestern province to put down the movement. The viceroy must have greatly appreciated the services of Captain Dorantes, who was both familiar with the region and well acquainted with the Indians there. No sources shed light on whether Dorantes ever attempted to use his past influence over the Indians to bring about peace.[14]

Unlike Cabeza de Vaca's fitful re-immersion into the imperial world, Dorantes and Castillo throve in Mexico's colonial society. With the passage of time, these two Spaniards must have taken for granted their sense of belonging to the powerful *encomendero* class and their right to demand tribute and labor from the Indians. They became respectable heads of households, property owners, and esteemed leaders. Their dreams of carving a place for themselves in the New World had come true.

OF THE FOUR castaways, Estebanico was the only one who returned to the vast lands of North America. The furor caused by the arrival of the castaways in Mexico City prompted Viceroy Mendoza to enter the field of discovery. In 1537 he decided to send an expedition to the far north. Yet one by one, each of the survivors declined to join this new venture. Cabeza de Vaca may have been already too keen on returning to Spain. Castillo, yearning for a more stable existence, probably decided early on to stay in New Spain. Dorantes remained the viceroy's most promising prospect. "I spoke with him many times," Mendoza would later write to the Emperor, "because it seemed to me that it could be of much service to Your Majesty to send him with forty or fifty horsemen to learn the secret of those regions." The viceroy spent a great deal of money making the necessary arrangements. Yet something happened toward the end of 1537 or early in 1538 that changed Dorantes's mind.[15]

Viceroy Mendoza's last hope was Estebanico. He spoke to Dorantes about securing the services of the Moroccan, but the captain reportedly experienced deep grief at the thought of parting with Estebanico. Despite the vast social differences and the inequality of their relationship, a strong bond of comradeship must have united these two men. Don Antonio Mendoza sent 500 pesos on a silver plate, but Dorantes refused his generous offer. In the end Dorantes surrendered his dear slave to the viceroy without payment because of the potential benefits to Spain and to the Indians of North America.[16]

The North African did not have a choice in the matter, yet, considering his subsequent behavior, he may have actually welcomed the idea. Estebanico departed from Mexico City in 1538, guiding a reconnaissance party headed by a Franciscan friar named Marcos de Niza. After reaching Culiacán, they pushed farther north in early 1539, leaving behind the last European settlement. The Indians immediately recognized Estebanico (his skin color would have been unmistakable), and gave him turquoise and women.

Estebanico's insistence on keeping these presents, especially the women, caused some consternation among Fray Marcos de Niza and his fellow friars. But Estebanico must have felt sufficiently secure to persist. To keep the disapproving friars at arm's length, the Moroccan ventured ahead of them at a considerable distance.[17]

After crossing an unsettled land, or *despoblado*, with only the women and a few Indian auxiliaries, he ran into another group of Indians, possibly in what is now northern Sonora. Confident and unconcerned, Estebanico candidly explained to these Indians that he was the harbinger of a group of white men "sent by a great lord . . . and that they were coming to instruct them about things divine." Even more brazenly, Estebanico asked for more turquoise and women.[18]

The Indians had nothing to gain from Estebanico's embassy. They deliberated for three days about what to do and finally chose to kill him. According to a later description, he ended his days "full of arrows like a Saint Sebastian." Too late, he must have realized his monumental blunder. Only a set of extraordinary circumstances had preserved Estebanico's fragile existence up until that point, and what could have occurred at any moment of the last ten years at last came to pass. Estebanico had come far—farther than any of the other men on this journey: born in Morocco, enslaved in Europe, reenslaved in North America, worshipped as a "child of the sun," enslaved yet again in Mexico City, and at last given relative freedom to lead a band of Europeans into the strange lands where his remarkable life would come to an end.[19]

ACKNOWLEDGMENTS

The genesis of this book can be traced with precision to a phone conversation one afternoon in the fall of 2003. Chip Rossetti, then a senior editor at Basic Books, was on the line inquiring if I would write a book about Cabeza de Vaca. I was skeptical at first knowing that much ink had already been spilled over this saga. Thus my first debt of gratitude is with Chip who first understood the need to retell this story using all the scholarly insights that have accumulated over the years. Chip went beyond the call of duty by reading my early chapters even after having left Basic Books. I am similarly indebted to Susan Rabiner, my agent. Her clear thinking, vast experience, and no-nonsense style kept me going as I struggled to turn a plausible idea into a book project. Lara Heimert, my new editor at Basic Books, brought a fresh perspective to the project and conducted a most thorough, exacting, and useful read of the manuscript. I cannot thank her enough. In this regard I also want to acowledge my appreciation of Jake Cumsky-Whitlock who also tackled the whole manuscript, asking sound questions along the way. The University of California, Davis, has been a most propitious home. My colleagues and friends Arnold Bauer, Tom Holloway, Alan Taylor, Chuck Walker, and Louis Warren read chapters and dispensed their insight, encouragement, and good cheer. Help also came from other quarters; in particular I want to thank Donald E. Chipman, Jerald T. Milanich, Samuel Truett, and Nancy Marie White, all of whom read portions of the manuscript (or the entire draft) saving me from a number of errors, pointing me to new sources, and offering sound editorial suggestions. Stephen C. Cote helped me tackle the daunting task of procuring images. Kevin Bryant walked me through several technological hurdles. My dear friend

Samuel R. Martin read each and every chapter not once but several times; I am truly privileged to count on his formidable editorial talent. My mother, María Teresa Fuentes, remains a source of inspiration blossoming in yet new directions after her retirement. I am at a loss to express my gratitude to Jaana Remes, my wife, for her boundless enthusiasm and support ever since we first discussed this project while driving toward Baja California. Our two children, Vera (6) and Samuel (8), have taken it all in stride, tramping along the possible route of the survivors in the Florida panhandle, and discussing over dinner the critters that Cabeza de Vaca and his companions were forced to eat.

FURTHER READING

Anyone wishing to venture deeper into the Florida expedition can do no better than read the two eyewitness accounts of this tragic undertaking: the *Joint Report* and Cabeza de Vaca's *Narrative*. There are only a handful of English-language editions of the *Joint Report*. One is included as an appendix in Alex D. Krieger's *We Came Naked and Barefoot: The Journey of Cabeza de Vaca across North America*. Austin: University of Texas Press, 2002. Although harder to find, there is an excellent bilingual edition by Basil C. Hedrick and Carroll L. Riley entitled *The Account of the Narváez Expedition, 1528–1536, as Related by Gonzalo Fernández de Oviedo y Valdés*. Carbondale, IL: University Museum Southern Illinois University, 1974. The *Joint Report* is actually book 35 of the massive and endlessly informative *Historia general y natural de las Indias* by chronicler Gonzalo Fernández de Oviedo y Valdés. Oviedo got to know Narváez, Cabeza de Vaca, and the other protagonists of the expedition. There are many editions in Spanish and English of Cabeza de Vaca's *Narrative*. Easily the most ambitious and insightful is Rolena Adorno and Patrick C. Pautz's *Álvar Núñez Cabeza de Vaca: His Account, His Life, and the Expedition of Pánfilo de Narváez* 3 vols. Lincoln: University of Nebraska Press, 1999. This is a monumental bilingual edition of the *Narrative* plus two volumes of "notes" including information on many aspects of the expedition, the background of the voyagers, and blow-by-blow commentary of the adventure, the literary history of the *Narrative*, and many other subjects. This work has taken our understanding of Cabeza de Vaca's epic to a new level.

To learn more about Spain's occupation of the Caribbean and Pánfilo de Narváez's early career, readers can turn to Carl O. Sauer's classic *The Early*

Spanish Main. Berkeley: University of California Press, 1966 and the relevant sections in James Lockhart and Stuart B. Schwartz, *Early Latin America: A History of Colonial Spanish America and Brazil.* New York: Cambridge University Press, 1983. For a blow-by-blow account of Spain's activities by a well-informed contemporary see Pietro Martire d'Anghiera (or Pedro Mártir de Angelería), *Décadas del Nuevo Mundo* 2 vols. Mexico City: Porrúa e Hijos, 1964. Martire d'Anghiera was an Italian attached to the Spanish court and member of the powerful Council of the Indies. Kathleen Deagan and José María Cruxent provide valuable information about the material possessions of early Europeans in the Caribbean in *Columbus's Outpost among the Taínos: Spain and America at La Isabela, 1493–1498.* New Haven, CT: Yale University Press, 2002. Those interested in the occupation of Cuba should read the old but still unsurpassed Irene A. Wright, *The Early History of Cuba.* New York: MacMillan Company, 1916; and for the earliest phase of the conquest Hortensia Pichardo Viñals, *La fundación de las primeras villas de la isla de Cuba.* Havana: Editorial de Ciencias Sociales, 1986. For first-hand accounts of the conquest of Cuba there is nothing better than Bartolomé de las Casas, *Historia de las Indias.* Edited by Agustín Millares Carlo. Mexico City: Fondo de Cultura Económica, 1986; and to a lesser extent his *Devastation of the Indies: A Brief Account.* Johns Hopkins University Press, 1992. At least two letters of Diego Velázquez dated April 1, 1514, and August 10, 1515, have survived until today. Both can be consulted at the *Colección de documentos inéditos relativos al descubrimiento, conquista y organización de las antiguas posesiones españolas de América y Oceanía* ... 42 vols. Madrid, 1864–84, XI, 412–429. Much information is also contained in the *Cedulario Cubano* edited by José María Chacón y Calvo. Madrid: Compañía Ibero-americana de Publicaciones, S. A., 1929. Included here there are gems such as the provisión real sobre hacer guerra a los indios caribes y tomarlos por esclavos, Burgos, December 24, 1511, 411–414; a letter from King Ferdinand to Diego Columbus, Seville, June 6, 1511, 327; and a most interesting document entitled La pragmática sobre el vestir e gastar seda en las indias, Valladolid, November 12, 1509, 191–196, detailing the extravagant purchases of European residents of the Caribbean.

Leading an expedition was at once every conquistador's most cherished dream and his worst nightmare. It was the opportunity of a lifetime, the way to catapult one's self into a position of prestige and wealth far above what one could hope to achieve by any other means. But for all the potential rewards, expeditions of conquest also entailed colossal risks. Expedition captains had to spend with abandon to charter ships and buy arms, horses, and supplies. Those interested in the organization of early bands of conquistadors will find much material in Mario Góngora's *Los grupos de conquistadores en Tierra Firme* (1509–1530): fisonomía histórico-social de un tipo de conquista. Santiago: Universidad de Chile, 1962; Bernard Grunberg's *L'Univers des Conquistadores: Les hommes et leur conquête dans le Mexique du XVIe siècle.* Paris: L'Harmattan, 1993; and James Lockhart's *The Men of Cajamarca: A Social and Biographical Study of the First Conquerors of Peru.* Austin: University of Texas Press, 1972.

The indigenous Caribbean population and its tragic demographic demise have given rise to a vast literature. Irving Rouse's *The Tainos: Rise and Decline of the People Who Greeted Columbus.* New Haven, CT: Yale University Press, 1992; and William F. Keegan's *The People Who Discovered Columbus: The Prehistory of the Bahamas.* Gainesville: University Press of Florida, 1992, provide overviews of the precontact inhabitants of the area. The timing and severity of the demographic cataclysm constitute one of the most important and contentious topics of research. A good place to start is William M. Denevan's edited volume entitled *The Native Population of the Americas in 1492.* Madison: University of Wisconsin Press, 1976; especially Woodrow Borah's "The Historical Demography of Aboriginal and Colonial America: An Attempt at Perspective," 13–34; and Ángel Rosenblat's essay entitled "The Population of Hispaniola at the Time of Columbus," 43–66. Both of these essays are worth contrasting with Esteban Mira Caballos's fine study *El Indio Antillano: repartimiento, encomienda y esclavitud (1492–1542).* Seville: Muñoz Moya editor, 1997. The most recent round of discussion is being propelled by DNA evidence. Researchers have recently found that fully 53 percent of contemporary Puerto Ricans have indigenous ancestries through the maternal line. Similar results have been obtained for Aruba. Such high percentages of indigenous DNA markers do contradict the image of total annihilation, although they can be consistent with dramatic declines, especially if we consider that Europeans constituted small minorities in these islands. See Martínez-Cruzado, J. C. [et al.], "Mitochondrial DNA Analysis in Puerto Rico" *Human Biology* 73 (2001), 491–511; Carles Lalueza-Fox [et al.], "mtDNA from Extinct Tainos and the Peopling of the Caribbean" *Annals of Human*

Genetics 65 (2001), 137–151; and Gladis Toro-Labrador [et al.], "Mitochondrial DNA Analysis in Aruba: Strong Maternal Ancestry of Closely Related Amerindians and Implications for the Peopling of Northwestern Venezuela" *Caribbean Journal of Science* 38:1 (2003), 11–22. For the situation on the mainland see Henry F. Dobyns's provocative *Their Number Become Thinned: Native American Population Dynamics in Eastern North America.* Knoxville: University of Tennessee Press, 1983; and Ann F. Ramenofsky and Patricia Galloway, "Disease and the Soto Entrada" in *The Hernando de Soto Expedition History, Historiography, and "Discovery" in the Southeast.* Lincoln: University of Nebraska Press, 1997, 259–279. We may well be at the dawn of a new era in the study of the role of epidemics in the New World. See Ann F. Ramenofsky, Alicia K. Wilbur, and Anne C. Stone, "Native American disease history: past, present and future directions" *World Archaeology* 35:2 (2003), 241–257.

On the workings of the Spanish court, I have relied heavily on Antonio de Guevara's *Libro llamado aviso de privados y doctrina de cortesanos.* Antwerp: Martij, 1545. Guevara was a longtime courtier who wrote a book of advice for the benefit of those who contemplated joining. Manuel Giménez Fernández's masterful *Bartolomé de Las Casas: delegado de Cisneros para la reformación de las Indias, 1516–1517,* 2 vols. Seville: Escuela de Estudios Hispanoamericanos de Sevilla, 1953, not only sheds light on the involvement of Las Casas in the Spanish court but also provides biographical information of various figures and broaches a number of topics related to indigenous rights. Another unique source that contains much courtly gossip and scathing characterizations of grandees and courtiers is Francesillo de Zúñiga's *Crónica burlesca del emperador Carlos V.* Barcelona: Editorial Crítica, 1981. Francesillo was a jester in Charles V's court who was able to write a book about his experiences. Hayward Keniston's study of Charles V's powerful secretary, *Francisco de los Cobos, Secretario de Carlos V.* Madrid: Editorial Castalia, 1980, contains useful information, some of it relevant to the Florida expedition. Also valuable for additional context are M. J. Rodríguez-Salgado, "Charles V and the Dynasty" in Hugo Soly, ed., *Charles V 1500–1558 and His Time.* Antwerp: Mercatorfonds, 1999; and Bethany Aram, *Juana the Mad: Sovereignty and Dynasty in Renaissance Europe.* Baltimore: Johns Hopkins University Press, 2005. The text of Narváez's charter of conquest can be found at Milagros del Vas Mingo, *Las Capitulaciones de Indias en el siglo XVI.*

Madrid: Instituto de Cooperación Iberoamericana, 1986 along with other patents of conquest and a luminous introduction. Key documents pertaining to Narváez's experience at the Spanish court are available in the Colección de documentos inéditos relativos al descubrimiento, conquista y organización de las antiguas posesiones españolas de América y Oceanía. Madrid, 1864–1884. 42 Volumes. Such documents include the representación hecha al Rey por el clérigo Bartolomé de Las Casas, en que manifiesta los agravios que sufren los indios de la isla de Cuba de los españoles, 1516, VII, 5–7; informe de los procuradores de la isla de Cuba, Pánfilo de Narváez y Antonio Velázquez, 1516, VII, 8–13; a letter of Bernardino de Santa Clara to Secretary Francisco de los Cobos, October 20, 1517, CDI XI, 557; a letter of Diego Velázquez to King Charles I, October 12, 1519, XII, 248; a letter of Diego Veláquez to King Charles, Santiago of Cuba, October 12, 1519, XII, 247; the first petition of Pánfilo de Narváez to Emperor Charles V, Toledo, 1525, X, 40; the second petition of Pánfilo de Narváez, n.p., n.d., X, 41; and the third petition of Pánfilo de Narváez, n.p., n.d., X, 46.

As one would expect, there is a vast literature on the early exploration and conquest of Mexico. Easily the most detailed treatment of Narváez's involvement in this episode can be found in Hugh Thomas, *Conquest: Montezuma, Cortés, and the Fall of Old Mexico*. New York: Simon and Schuster, 1993. I also found useful information in Henry R. Wagner's *The Rise of Fernando Cortés*. New York: Kraus Reprint Co., 1969; and Richard Konetzke, "Hernán Cortés como poblador de la Nueva España" in *Lateinamerika: Entdekung, Eroberrung, Kolonisation*. Böhlau Verlag Köln Wien, 1983, 157–171. Chroniclers of the sixteenth century provide valuable information about Narváez's activities, most especially Bernal Díaz del Castillo, *Historia verdadera de la conquista de la Nueva España* 2 vols. Mexico City: Editorial Porrúa, S.A., 1977. Other relevant accounts by contemporaries or near contemporaries include Andrés de Tapia's "Chronicle" in *The Conquistadors: First-Person Accounts of the Conquest of Mexico*. Edited and translated by Patricia de Fuentes. New York: Orion Press, 1963, 17–48; and Francisco Cervantes de Salazar's *Crónica de la Nueva España*. Mexico City: Editorial Porrúa, 1982. Key documents are reproduced in the *Documentos cortesianos*, 4 volumes, edited by José Luis Martínez. Mexico City: UNAM/Fondo de Cultura Económica, 1990, including the instrucciones de Diego Velázquez a Hernán Cortés, Santiago,

October 23, 1518, I, 45–59; the Instrucciones de Hernán Cortés a los procuradores Francisco de Montejo y Alonso Hernández Portocarrero, enviados a España, Veracruz, early July 1519, I, 77–90; and a letter of Diego Velázquez to Bishop Juan Rodríguez de Fonseca, Santiago of Cuba, October 12, 1519, I, 91–94. The *Espistolario de Nueva España* edited by Francisco del Paso y Troncoso. Mexico City: Porrúa, 1939, 3 volumes, is another rich source containing such indispensable materials as the información que hizo la villa de Santiesteban del Puerto sobre la conveniencia de enviar esclavos a las islas para cambiarlos por caballos, yeguas y otros ganados, Santiesteban del Puerto, October 9, 1529, I, 153–166; a letter from King Charles to Diego Velázquez, Zaragoza, December 12, 1518, I, 38; the testimonies of Francisco de Montejo and Alonso Hernández Portocarrero in Información recibida en La Coruña sobre la armada que Diego Velázquez dispuso para el descubrimiento de Nueva España y nombramiento de capitán general de ella a Hernán Cortés, La Coruña Spain, April 29–30, I, 44–50; and Diego Velázquez's Testament, Santiago, Cuba, April 9, 1524, I, 67.

On Seville's maritime world I found two books particularly useful: Pablo E. Pérez Mallaína's *Spain's Men of the Sea: Daily Life on the Indies Fleets in the Sixteenth Century*. Baltimore: Johns Hopkins University Press; and María del Carmen Mena García's *Sevilla y Las Flotas de Indias: La Gran Armada de Castilla del Oro (1513–1514)*. Seville: Universidad de Sevilla-Fundación El Monte, 1998. Interesting demographic, social, and cultural information about Seville is available in Ruth Pike, *Aristocrats and Traders: Sevillian Society in the Sixteenth Century*. Ithaca: Cornell University Press, 1973. On the surprising prevalence of women in the early exploration and colonization of the New World see Richard Konetzke, "La emigración de mujeres españolas a América durante la época colonial" in *Lateinamerika: Entdeckung, Eroberung, Kolonisation*. Böhlau Verlag Köln Wien, 1983, 1–28. Spain was the beneficiary of a number of advances in navigation, cartography, cultural attitudes, warfare techniques, etc. For the broader context see Felipe Fernández-Armesto, *Before Columbus: Exploration and Colonization from the Mediterranean to the Atlantic, 1229–1492*. London: Macmillan, 1987; and Felipe Fernández-Armesto, *The Canary Islands after the Conquest*. Oxford: Oxford University Press, 1982. For a careful study of Spain's maritime activities around Cuba, Florida, and the coast of Mexico see Robert S. Weddle, *Spanish Sea: The*

Gulf of Mexico in North American Discovery, 1500–1685. College Station: Texas A&M University Press, 1985. The enterprising Antonio de Guevara once again wrote a how-to guide, this time aimed at would-be passengers. Guevara's book is entitled *Arte de marear y de los inventores della con muchos avisos para los que navegan en ellas*. Valladolid, 1539. My discussion of navigational techniques in the 1520s relies on Alison Sandman, "Cosmographers vs. Pilots: Navigation, Cosmography, and the State in Early Modern Spain" Ph.d. Dissertation, University of Wisconsin, Madison, 2001. Portolan charts constituted a major technological breakthrough. On portolan charts in general see Edward Luther Stevenson, *Portolan Charts: Their Origin and Characteristics with a Descriptive List of Those Belonging to the Hispanic Society of America*. New York: Knickerbocker Press, 1911. Portolan charts existed for the Caribbean and Gulf of Mexico regions by the time of Narváez's expedition. See Jerald T. Milanich and Nara B. Milanich, "Revisiting the Freducci Map: A Description of Juan Ponce De León's 1513 Florida Voyage?" *Florida Historical Quarterly* 74:3 (Winter 1996), 319–328; and Richard Uhden, "An Unpublished Portolan Chart of the New World, A.D. 1519" *Geographical Journal* 91:1 (January 1938), 44–50.

Biographical information of the four protagonists of the expedition can be found in Rolena Adorno and Patrick C. Pautz's encyclopedic *Álvar Núñez Cabeza de Vaca: His Account, His Life, and the Expedition of Pánfilo de Narváez* 3 vols. Lincoln: University of Nebraska Press, 1999. These volumes contain much data from a variety of published and unpublished sources and include a detailed genealogical study of Cabeza de Vaca's family. Although somewhat dated, some information can also be found in Morris Bishop's *The Odyssey of Cabeza de Vaca*. Westport, CT: Greenwood Press, Publishers, 1933. This book is a full biography of Cabeza de Vaca detailing his expeditions both to North and South America. David A. Howard's more recent *Conquistador in Chains: Cabeza de Vaca and the Indians of the Americas*. Tuscaloosa: University of Alabama Press, 1997 also looks at the entire span of Cabeza de Vaca's life with a particular emphasis on his attitudes toward Indians. First-hand information about the Royal Treasurer can be gleaned from Hipólito Sancho de Sopranis, "Datos para el estudio de Álvar Núñez Cabeza de Vaca" *Revista de Indias* 8 (1947), 69–102; and Hipólito Sancho de Sopranis, "Notas y documentos sobre Álvar Núñez Cabeza de Vaca" *Revista de Indias* 23 (1963),

207–241. A brief sketch of the expedition leader can be found in Frank Goodwyn, "Pánfilo de Narváez, a Carácter Study of the First Spanish Leader to Land an Expedition to Texas" *Hispanic American Historical Review* 29:1 (February 1949), 150–156. Baltasar Dorantes de Carranza—the son of Captain Andrés Dorantes—wrote an interesting chronicle that includes original information about his father. The chronicle is entitled *Sumaria relación de las cosas de la Nueva España*. Mexico City: Imprenta del Museo Nacional, 1902.

Scraps of information of other members of the expedition can be painstakingly extracted from the Archivo General de Indias in Seville, Spain. On slaveholding expeditioners see the real cédula a Pedro Lunel para que pueda pasar cuatro esclavos negros a la tierra de la gobernación de Pánfilo de Narváez. Valladolid, March 29, 1527. Indiferente 421, L. 12, F50v–51r; real cédula a Juan de Sámano para que deje pasar sin pagar derechos de almojarifazgo cuatro esclavos a Diego Solís, que va como veedor de fundiciones a la tierra que Pánfilo de Narváez ha de poblar, April 12, 1527. Indiferente 421, L. 12, f71v–72r. On special treatment accorded to a certain expedition member see the título de regidor del primer pueblo que descubriese y poblase Pánfilo de Narváez en la Florida para Juan Velázquez de Salazar, n.p., 1527. Patronato 19, R. 1/1/2–4; the real cédula a los oficiales de la casa de contratación de Sevilla para que paguen al Padre Fray Juan Suárez de la orden de San Francisco 8,000 ducados . . . , Granada, November 26, 1526. Indiferente 421, L. 11, F. 348v–349r; and the real cédula a Fray Juan Suárez de la orden de San Francisco y Obispo del Rio de las Palmas y Florida, Burgos, February 15, 1528. L. 13/1/131 (60r). On the losses due to the hurricane in Cuba and the wealth of Vasco Porcallo see the real cédula a Álvar Núñez Cabeza de Vaca, tesorero del Rio de las Palmas y la Florida, en respuesta a su carta escrita en el puerto de Jagua . . . Madrid, March 27, 1528. Indiferente 421, L. 13 /1/ 520; and the letter from Empress Isabel to Vasco Porcallo, Madrid, December 22, 1529. Santo Domingo 1121, L. 1 f. 13v. The only testimony that I know of by one of the women of the expedition is in the real cédula al virrey de la Nueva España que Mari Hernández, mujer que fue de Fco. de Quevedo, ha hecho relación que ella y el dicho marido fueron conquistadores de la Nueva España . . . y que luego se fueron a la conquista de la Florida con Pánfilo de Narváez donde murió el dicho Fco. de Quevedo . . . , Toledo, August 2, 1539. Mexico 1088, L. 3/1/256 r and v. Some information about the activities of Castillo and Dorantes in New Spain can be obtained in the traslado de una real cédula confiriendo la encomienda de la mitad del pueblo de Tehuacan en Alonso del Castillo Maldonado como marido de la viuda de Juan Ruiz de Alanís, Madrid, February 11, 1540. Patronato 275, R. 39/1/1; the real provisión a Alonso del Castillo Maldonado, dándole facultades para comprar heredades a los indios de Nueva España, Madrid, February 25, 1540. Patronato, 278, N. 2, R. 230/1/1; and the real provisión de la audiencia y chancillería de Nueva España para que el pueblo de indios que Andrés Dorantes, vecino de la ciudad de México, tiene encomendados, pasen como herencia a su mujer e hijos tras su muerte, Mexico City, November 2, 1540. Patronato 278, N.2, R. 30/1–5. The indefatigable María de Valenzuela, Narváez's wife, left a trail of information. In the Bancroft Library at the University of California, Berkeley, one can consult the información hecha en la Isla de Cuba a pedimento de María de Valenzuela, la muger de Pánfilo de Narváez, contra Hernando de Ceballos sobre dos bergantines, e bastimentos y municiones, Cuba, 1530, The Stetson Collection, reel 1. This document is a microfilmed edition of Justicia 972, 51–2/12 at the Archivo General de Indias. See also the deposition of Manuel Hojas, San Salvador, April 29, 1530. The Stetson Collection, reel 1. This file needs to be completed at the Archivo General de Indias with Hernando de Ceballos to the King of Spain, Cuba, March 16, 1531. Indiferente General 1203, No. 28, folios 1–11.

The route followed by Cabeza de Vaca's party has long fascinated scholars. For an excellent introduction to the various route interpretations since the nineteenth century see Donald E. Chipman, "In Search of Cabeza de Vaca's Route across Texas: An Historiographical Survey" *Southwestern Historical Quarterly* 91 (1987), 127–148. Brownie Ponton and Bates H. McFarland were among the first to attempt to pinpoint the landing sites of the rafts of the expedition on the Texas coast in "Álvar Núñez Cabeza de Vaca: A Preliminary Report on His Wanderings in Texas" *Southwestern Historical Quarterly* 1:3 (1898), 166–186. A string of articles followed including Bethel Coopwood, "The Route of Cabeza de Vaca" *Texas State Historical Association Quarterly* (October 1899), 108–140 (January 1900), 177–208 (April 1900), 229–264 (July 1900), 1–32; and James Newton Baskett, "A Study of the Route of Cabeza de Vaca" *Texas State Historical Association Quarterly* 10 (1907), 246–279. Harbert Davenport and Joseph K. Wells pioneered the so-called "southern route" of the expedition survivors in "The First Europeans in Texas, 1528–1536" *Southern Historical Quarterly* 22:2 (October 1918), 111–142 and 205–259. For the most detailed rendition of the "northern route" see Cleve Hallenbeck, *Álvar Núñez Cabeza de Vaca: The Journey and Route of the First European to Cross the Continent of North America 1534–1536*. Glendale, CA: The Arthur H. Clark Company, 1940. Alex D. Krieger spent many years considering the different alternatives and trying to solve this irresistible historical, geographic, and archeological puzzle. Krieger's work has been recently translated into English and published under the title of *We Came Naked and Barefoot: The Journey of Cabeza de Vaca across North America*. Austin: University of Texas Press, 2002. Adorno and Pautz offer extensive comments on the various route interpretations and provide their own views in *Álvar Núñez Cabeza de Vaca: His Account, His Life, and the Expedition of Pánfilo de Narváez*.

One of the unexpected pleasures of delving deeper into the Florida expedition is learning about plants and animals that become important at various stages of the journey. I was particularly influenced by Aldemaro Romero [et al.], "Cubagua's Pearl-Oyster Beds: The First Depletion of a Natural Resource Caused by Europeans in the American Continent" *Journal of Political Ecology* 6 (1999), 57–78; J. X. Corgan, "Cabeza de Vaca, Dealer in Shells" *American Malacological Union, Annual Reports for 1968* (1969), 13–14; Richard F. Darsie, Jr., and Ronald A. Ward, *Identification and Geographical Distribution of the Mosquitoes of North America, North of Mexico*. Fresno, CA: American Mosquito Control Association, 1981; Donald W. Olson [et al.], "Piñon Pines and the Route of Cabeza de Vaca" *Southwestern Historical Quarterly* 101 (October 1997), 174–186. William C. Foster persuasively argues that the route followed by the Florida survivors from northern Tamaulipas through La Junta de los Rios and into the Paquimé area had been pioneered centuries before by indigenous merchants carrying live scarlet macaws. Foster, "Introduction," in *The La Salle Expedition on the Mississippi River: A Lost Manuscript of Nicolas de La Salle, 1682*. Austin: Texas State Historical Association, 2003. I learned a great deal about the uses and trading routes of scarlet macaws in Lyndon L. Hargrave, *Mexican Macaws: Comparative Osteology and Survey of Remains from the Southwest*. Tucson: University of Arizona Press, 1970; Paul E. Minnis, Michael E. Whalen, Jane H. Kelley, Joe D. Stewart, "Prehistoric Macaw Breeding in the North American Southwest" *American Antiquity* 58:2 (1993), 270–276; Darrell Creel and Charmion McKusick, "Prehistoric Macaws and Parrots in the Mimbres Area, New Mexico" *American Antiquity* 59:3 (1994), 510–524; and Charmion R. McKusick, *Southwest Birds of Sacrifice*. Globe: Arizona Archaeological Society, 2001.

Slavery is a major theme underpinning the entire expedition. On the institution of slavery in southern Spain during the sixteenth century, I would turn first to Aurelia Martín Casares, *La Esclavitud en la Granada del siglo XVI: género, raza y religión*. Granada: Universidad de Granada y Diputación Provincial de Granada, 2000. Other useful works include Franco Silva, *La esclavitud en Andalucía 1450–1550*. Granada: Universidad de Granada, 1992; and José Luis Cortés López, *La esclavitud negra en la España peninsular del siglo XVI*. Salamanca: Ediciones Universidad de Salamanca, 1989. Once in America some African slaves became conquistadors in their own right. See Peter Gerhard, "A Black Conquistador in Mexico" in *Slavery and Beyond: The African Impact on Latin America and the Caribbean*. Wilmington: SR Books, 1995; and Matthew Restall, "Black Conquistadors: Armed Africans in Early Spanish America" *The Americas* 57:2 (October 2000), 171–205. Indigenous slavery is fascinating. Some of my thinking was shaped by Theda Perdue, *Slavery and the Evolution of Cherokee Society, 1540–1866*. Knoxville: University of Tennessee Press, 1979; and Leland Donald, *Aboriginal Slavery on the Northwest Coast of North America*. Berkeley: University of California Press, 1997. For a general assessment of the many faces of slavery, especially in the context of a subsistence economy, see David Turley, *Slavery*. Oxford: Blackwell Publishers, 2000. On how the imperial aims of various European powers transformed and expanded slaving practices in North America see James F. Brooks, *Captives and Cousins: Slavery, Kinship, and Community in the Southwest Borderlands*. Chapel Hill: University of North Carolina Press, 2002; and Alan Gallay, *The Indian Slave Trade: The Rise of the English Empire in the American South, 1670–1717*. New Haven, CT: Yale University Press, 2002.

The curing ceremonies performed by Cabeza de Vaca and the other survivors raise many interesting medical, cultural, religious, and literary questions. For a medical description of one of Cabeza de Vaca's most involved operations see Jesse E. Thompson, "Sagittectomy: Operation Performed in America in 1535 by Cabeza de Vaca" *New England Journal of Medicine*

289:26 (December 27, 1973), 1404–1407. This operation leaves no doubt that the survivors became skilled surgeons in the course of their adventures. But the survivors' influence stemmed chiefly from their perceived ability to manipulate the supernatural world. Unfortunately, it is impossible to know exactly what the indigenous hosts thought about Cabeza de Vaca and the others, but it is possible to contextualize their likely beliefs on the basis of other cases. On shamanism as it was practiced by a Comanche woman see David E. Jones, *Sanapia: Comanche Medicine Woman*. Prospect Heights, IL: Waveland Press, Inc., 1972. Sixteenth-century Spaniards believed in God's direct and constant involvement in human affairs in the form apparitions, miracles, etc. On Iberian religious and popular beliefs there are several good books, including Sara T. Nalle, *God in La Mancha: Religious Reform and the People of Cuenca, 1500–1650*. Baltimore: Johns Hopkins University Press, 1992; Sara T. Nalle, *Mad for God: Bartolomé Sánchez, The Secret Messiah of Cardenete*. Charlottesville: University Press of Virginia, 2001; Richard L. Kagan, *Lucrecia's Dreams: Politics and Prophecy in Sixteenth-Century Spain*. Berkeley: University of California Press, 1990; William A. Christian, Jr., *Apparitions in Late Medieval and Renaissance Spain*. Princeton: Princeton University Press, 1981; and William A. Christian, Jr., *Local Religion in Sixteenth-Century Spain*. Princeton: Princeton University Press, 1981. Jacques Lafaye studied how Cabeza de Vaca's curing ceremonies became "miracles" in the pages of later chroniclers and historians in an essay entitled "Los 'milagros' de Álvar Núñez Cabeza de Vaca (1527–1536)" in *Mesías, cruzadas, utopías: el judeo-cristianismo en las sociedades ibéricas*. Mexico City: Fondo de Cultura Económica, 1984, 65–84. Faced with these miracles, some scholars coming from the literary side have considered the veracity, purpose, and impact of Cabeza de Vaca's *Narrative*. Some of the works in this category include Rolena Adorno, "The Negotiation of Fear in Cabeza de Vaca's Naufragios" *Representations* 33 (Winter 1991), 163–199; Ralph Bauer, "Mythos and epos: Cabeza de Vaca's empire of peace" in *The Cultural Geography of Colonial American Literatures: Empire, Travel, Modernity*. Cambridge: Cambridge University Press, 2003, 30–76; and Aurelio de los Reyes, "*Naufragios* de Álvar Núñez Cabeza de Vaca. ¿Novela, crónica, historiografía?" in *Nómadas y Sedentarios en el Norte de México: Homenaje a Beatriz Braniff*. Mexico City: UNAM, 2000, 395–417 just to name a few. A number of essays in this venue appear in

Margo Glantz, ed., *Notas y comentarios sobre Álvar Núñez Cabeza de Vaca*. Mexico City: CNCA/Grijalbo, 1993.

The Pánfilo de Narváez expedition is the perfect vehicle to survey the archeology, geography, and early colonial history of a large swath of North America. For a general introduction to the administrative units of this entire area see Peter Gerhard, *The North Frontier of New Spain*. Princeton: Princeton University Press, 1982. For Spain's early attempts to colonize the coastal area north of Florida see Paul A. Hoffman, "A New Voyage of North American Discovery: Pedro de Salazar's Visit to the 'Island of Giants'" *Florida Historical Quarterly* 58:4 (April 1980), 415–426; and Paul A. Hoffman, *A New Andalucia and a Way to the Orient: The American Southwest during the Sixteenth Century*. Baton Rouge: Louisiana State University Press, 1990. On the Pánuco area the main work remains Donald E. Chipman, *Nuño de Guzmán and the Province of Pánuco in New Spain, 1518–1533*. Glendale, CA: Arthur H. Clark Company, 1967. See also Donald E. Chipman, "Alonso Alvarez de Pineda and the Río de las Palmas: Scholars and the Mislocation of a River" *Southwestern Historical Quarterly* 98:3 (January 1995), 369–385.

Florida was the first region visited by the expeditioners. For a general introduction to the precontact peoples inhabiting this peninsula see Jerald T. Milanich, *Archaeology of Precolumbian Florida*. Gainesville: University Press of Florida, 1994. A recent collection of essays explore the connections between Florida and other coastal areas. Nancy Marie White, ed., *Gulf Coast Archeology*. Gainesville: University Press of Florida, 2005. James Axtell provides a wide-ranging overview of the impact of early Europeans on the indigenous populations of what is now the U.S. South in *The Indian's New South: Cultural Change in the Colonial Southeast*. Baton Rouge: Louisiana State University Press, 1997; as does Jerald T. Milanich in *Florida Indians and the Invasion from Europe*. Gainesville: University Press of Florida, 1995. Essays describing the overall route and activities of the Narváez expedition in Florida include Paul E. Hoffman, "Narváez and Cabeza de Vaca in Florida" in *The Forgotten Centuries: Indians and Europeans in the American South, 1521–1704*. Edited by Charles Hudson and Carmen Chaves Tesser. Athens: University of Georgia Press, 1994, 50–73; and Rochelle A. Marrinan, John F. Scarry, and Rhonda L. Majors, "Prelude to de Soto: The Expedition of Pánfilo de Narváez" in *Columbian Consequences: Archaeological and Historical Perspectives on the Spanish Borderlands East*. Edited by David Hurst

Thomas, II, 71–82. For an interesting analysis of what the Indians of western Florida may have made of the arrival of Europeans during the first half of the sixteenth century see Sylvia L. Lilton, "Los indios de Tocobaga y Timucua (Florida occidental) ante sus primeros contactos con los hombres blancos" in *Congreso de Historia del descubrimiento, actas*. Madrid: Real Academia de la Historia, 1992, I, 343–403. There is tantalizing archaeological evidence of the earliest Spanish presence in Florida. This evidence is considered in Jeffrey M. Mitchem, "Initial Spanish-Indian Contact in West Peninsular Florida: The Archaeological Evidence" in *Columbian Consequences: Archaeological and Historical Perspectives on the Spanish Borderlands East*. Edited by David Hurst Thomas, II, 49–59; and Jeffrey M. Mitchem, "Artifacts of Exploration: Archaeological Evidence from Florida" in *First Encounters: Spanish Explorations in the Caribbean and the United States, 1492–1570*. Edited by Jerald T. Milanich and Susan Milbrath. Gainesville: University of Florida Press, 1991, 99–109. A great deal of information relevant to the Narváez expedition can be gleaned from the expedition led by Hernando de Soto a little over a decade later. Interested readers can turn to Jerald T. Milanich and Charles Hudson, *Hernando de Soto and the Indians of Florida*. Gainesville: University Press of Florida, 1993, 227–228; and Charles R. Ewen and John H. Hann, *Hernando de Soto among the Apalachee: The Archaeology of the First Winter Encampment*. Gainesville: University Press of Florida, 1998. The largest indigenous polity visited by Narváez and his men has received some scholarly attention in John F. Scarry, "The Apalachee Chiefdom" in *The Forgotten Centuries: Indians and Europeans in the American South, 1521–1704*. Edited by Charles Hudson and Carmen Chaves Tesser. Athens: University of Georgia Press, 1994, 156–178; and John H. Hann, "The Apalachee of the Historic Era" in *The Forgotten Centuries: Indians and Europeans in the American South, 1521–1704*. Edited by Charles Hudson and Carmen Chaves Tesser. Athens: University of Georgia Press, 1994, 327–354. First-hand accounts of the Hernando de Soto expedition are available in *The de Soto Chronicles: The Expedition of Hernando de Soto to North America in 1539–1543* 2 vols. Edited by Lawrence A. Clayton, Vernon James Knight, Jr., and Edward C. Moore. Tuscaloosa: University of Alabama Press, 1993. El Inca Garcilaso de la Vega interviewed some of the survivors of the de Soto expedition and wrote a history of Florida simply entitled *La Florida*. Madrid: Alianza Editorial, 1988.

The passage of the Narváez expedition through present-day Texas has received considerable scholarly attention. As noted earlier, many authors have debated the precise route followed by the survivors and the identities of the indigenous groups that the expeditioners met along the way. Unfortunately, in some instances it is impossible to establish a direct connection between the peoples mentioned by Cabeza de Vaca in the early sixteenth century and indigenous groups later documented in the seventeenth, eighteenth, and nineteenth centuries. In any event, the region where the rafts of the Narváez expedition landed was later inhabited by at least five separate bands collectively known as Karankawas. For brief but enlightening descriptions of the Karankawa Indians see William W. Newcomb, "Karankawa" in *Handbook of North American Indians*. Washington, DC: Smithsonian Institution, 1983, X, 360; and the relevant section in W. W. Newcomb, Jr., *The Indians of Texas: From Prehistoric to Modern Times*. Austin: University of Texas Press, 1961. Some scholars believe that Cabeza de Vaca and some of the others landed in what is now Galveston Island. Robert A. Ricklis has conducted a detailed archaeological study of a site on the island entitled *Aboriginal Life and Culture on the Upper Texas Coast: Archaeology at the Mitchell Ridge Site, 41GV66, Galveston Island*. Corpus Christi, TX: Coastal Archaeological Research, Inc., 1994. Ricklis has also published the most comprehensive study of the Karankawas: *The Karankawa Indians of Texas: An Ecological Study of Cultural Tradition and Change*. Austin: University of Texas Press, 1996. Ricklis specifically addresses the issue of how the archaeological findings on Galveston Island and surrounding areas relate to the Indian practices described by the expeditioners in an essay entitled "Cabeza de Vaca's Observations of Native American Lifeways: Correspondences in the Archaeological Record of the Texas Coast" in *Windows to the Unknown: Cabeza de Vaca's Journey to the Southwest*. Symposium hosted by the Center for the Study of the Southwest at Southwest Texas State University, San Marcos. (http://wp29.english.swt.edu/css/CSSINDEX.HTM). Thomas R. Hester has written on the same subject in "Artifacts, Archaeology and Cabeza de Vaca in Southern Texas and Northeastern Mexico" in *Windows to the Unknown: Cabeza de Vaca's Journey to the Southwest*. Symposium hosted by the Center for the Study of the Southwest at Southwest Texas State University, San Marcos. (http://wp29.english.swt.edu/css/CSSINDEX.HTM). For the more recent history of the Karankawa Indians see Kelly F. Himmel, *The*

Conquest of the Karankawas and the Tonkawas, 1821–1859. College Station: Texas A & M University Press, 1999. T. N. Campbell and T. J. Campbell go to great lengths to reconcile archaeological and historical information in a valuable and lengthy study somewhat obscurely entitled *Historic Indian Groups of the Choke Canyon Reservoir and Surrounding Area, Southern Texas.* San Antonio: Center for Archaeological Research, University of Texas at San Antonio, Choke Canyon Series, 1981. Later European expeditions offer additional insight into the native world of what is now the Lone Star State. See especially William C. Foster, *Spanish Expeditions into Texas, 1689–1768.* Austin: University of Texas Press, 1995; William C. Foster, ed., *The La Salle Expedition on the Mississippi River: A Lost Manuscript of Nicolas de La Salle, 1682.* Austin: Texas State Historical Association, 2003; and François Simars de Bellisle, "De Bellisle on the Texas Coast." Edited by Henri Folmer. *Southwestern Historical Quarterly* 44:2 (October 1940), 204–231.

The expeditioners passed through the confluence of the Rio Grande and the Conchos River, an area known as La Junta de los Rios that is located in the vicinity of the present-day towns of Presidio, Texas, and Ojinaga, Chihuahua. In the sixteenth century this area constituted an agricultural oasis in the middle of a nomadic sea. On the native inhabitants of La Junta area see J. Charles Kelley, *Jumano and Patarabueye: Relations at La Junta de los Rios.* Ann Arbor: Anthropological Paper Number 77, Museum of Anthropology, University of Michigan, 1986; and Nancy Parrott Hickerson, *The Jumanos: Hunters and Traders of the South Plains.* Austin: University of Texas Press, 1992. A later Spanish expedition specifically noted that the Indians of La Junta still remembered the passage of three Spaniards and a black person. See Antonio de Espejo, "Account of the Journey to the Provinces and Settlements of New Mexico, 1583," in Herbert Eugene Bolton, ed., *Spanish Exploration in the Southwest 1542–1706: Original Narratives of Early American History.* New York: Barnes & Noble, Inc., 1946; and Diego Pérez de Luxán, *Expedition into New Mexico Made by Antonio de Espejo 1582–1583: As Revealed in the Journal of Diego Pérez de Luxán, a Member of the Party.* Edited by George M. Hammond and Agapito Rey. Los Angeles: The Quivira Society, 1929. For a later expedition into La Junta see Joseph de Ydoiaga, *Expedition to La Junta de los Ríos, 1747–1748.* Austin: Texas Historical Commission, 1992.

The expeditioners ascended through the Rio Grande and ventured into the area once dominated by the imposing city of Paquimé or Casas Grandes on their way to northwest Mexico. The classic work on Paquimé is Charles C. di Peso, John B. Rinaldo, and Gloria J. Fenner, *Casas Grandes: A Fallen Trading Center of the Gran Chichimeca*. Flagstaff: The Amerind Foundation, Inc. and the Dragoon Northland Press, 1974. Recent archaeological investigations of other sites in the area have shed light on the regional connections and have led to a reconsideration of the periodization of Paquimé itself. See Ronna Jane Bradley, "Recent Advances in Chihuahuan Archaeology" in Michael S. Foster and Shirley Gorenstein, eds., *Greater Mesoamerica: The Archaeology of West and Northwest Mexico*. Salt Lake City: University of Utah Press, 2000, 221–239; and Paul E. Minnis and Michael E. Whalen, "Chihuahuan Archaeology: An Introductory History" in Gillian E. Newell and Emiliano Gallaga, eds., *Surveying the Archaeology of Northwest Mexico*. Salt Lake City: University of Utah Press, 2004, 113–126. For an introduction to the indigenous peoples of northwest Mexico see Susan M. Deeds, "Legacies of Resistance, Adaptation, and Tenacity: History of the Native Peoples of Northwest Mexico" in *The Cambridge History of the Native Peoples of the Americas*. Vol. II, Part 2. New York: Cambridge University Press, 2000, 44–88. Long-distance trading networks of such items as copper bells and shells are clearly noted by Cabeza de Vaca and his companions. Relevant studies of these trading networks include J. Charles Kelley, "The Aztatlán Mercantile System: Mobile Traders and the Northwestward Expansion of Mesoamerican Civilization" in Michael S. Foster and Shirley Gorenstein, eds., *Greater Mesoamerica: The Archaeology of West and Northwest Mexico*. Salt Lake City: University of Utah Press, 2000, 137–154; Jeremiah F. Epstein, "Cabeza de Vaca and the Sixteenth-Century Copper Trade in Northern Mexico" *American Antiquity* 56:3 (July 1991), 474–482; and Victoria D. Vargas, *Copper Bell Trade Patterns in the Prehispanic U.S. Southwest and Northwest Mexico*. Tucson: Arizona State Museum/University of Arizona Press, 1995.

There are only a handful of studies on Nuño de Guzmán and his involvement in Nueva Galicia. A rich source is José López Portillo y Weber's *La rebelión de la Nueva Galicia*. Mexico City: Colección Peña Colorada, 1980. On the arduous task of administering and ruling this territory see J. H. Parry, *The Audiencia of New Galicia in the Sixteenth Century*.

Cambridge: Cambridge University Press, 1948. On his way to the West Coast Nuño de Guzmán passed through the rich province of Michoacán, wrecking havoc there. See J. Benedict Warren, *The Conquest of Michoacán: The Spanish Domination of the Tarascan Kingdom in Western Mexico, 1521–1530.* Norman: University of Oklahoma Press, 1985. On the overall route followed by Guzmán on that fateful first *entrada* into Nueva Galicia see Carl Sauer and Donald Brand, *Aztatlán: Prehistoric Mexican Frontier on the Pacific Coast.* Berkeley: University of California Press, 1932. Important insights into the exploration of Mexico's northwest can be found in Arthur S. Aiton, *Antonio de Mendoza: First Viceroy of New Spain.* Durham: Duke University Press, 1927; and in the *Documents of the Coronado Expedition, 1539–1542.* Edited, translated, and annotated by Richard Flint and Shirley Cushing Flint. Dallas: Southern Methodist University Press, 2005, especially in Antonio de Mendoza, "Instructions to Fray Marcos de Niza," 59–88. Primary sources pertaining to the violent founding of Nueva Galicia are scattered in various published and unpublished collections including the *Documentos para la historia de México*, edited by Joaquín García Icazbalceta. Mexico City: Editorial Porrúa, 1980. 2 volumes. The most relevant documents include the relación de la entrada de Nuño de Guzmán que dio García del Pilar, su intérprete, II, 248–261; the relación de la conquista de los Teules Chichimecas que dio Juan de Sámano, II, 262–287; the primera relación anónima de la jornada que hizo Nuño de Guzmán a la Nueva Galicia, II, 288–295; the segunda relación anónima de la jornada que hizo Nuño de Guzmán a la Nueva Galicia, II, 296–306; the tercera relación anónima de la jornada que hizo Nuño de Guzmán a la Nueva Galicia, II, 439–460; and the cuarta relación anónima de la jornada que hizo Nuño de Guzmán a la Nueva Galicia, II, 461–483. Also valuable are some documents included in the *Espistolario de Nueva España.* Edited by Francisco del Paso y Troncoso. Mexico City: Porrúa, 1939. 3 volumes, such as the testimonio de tres provisiones expedidas por Nuño de Guzmán a favor de Francisco Verdugo . . . Chiametla, January 18, 1531, II, 9–14; and an indispensable letter from Nuño de Guzmán to Empress Isabel, Compostela, June 12, 1532, II, 142–173. In the *Colección de documentos inéditos relativos al descubrimiento, conquista y organización de las antiguas posesiones españolas de América y Oceanía.* Madrid, 1864–1884. 42 Volumes. One can find such key documents as the Carta de Nuño de Guzmán a Su Majestad, diciéndole que el

Marqués del Valle había entrado en su gobernación con pendón en mano, a manera de descubridor y conquistador. Valle de Banderas, June 8, 1535, IV, 150–152; and the probanza "Ad Perpetuam Rei Memoriam" sobre la tierra del Marqués del Valle e indios que de la Nueva Galicia a ella llevaron. Autos entre Nuño de Guzmán y Hernando Cortés, Compostela, Nueva Galicia, December 10, 1535, IV, 153–161. The Archivo General de Indias contains important sources such as the carta de la reina doña Isabel al presidente y oidores de la audiencia de la Nueva España, Ocaña, January 25, 1531. México 1088 L. 1 Bis, F. 45 v–49r; the real provisión al gobernador y oficiales de las tierras y provincias de Galicia de la Nueva España, para que no se haga esclavos a los indios . . . Ocaña, January 25, 1531. Indiferente General 422, L. 15, f.8v; the carta del cabildo secular de Compostela sobre la necesidad de hacer esclavos a los indios rebeldes y su aprovechamiento para el trabajo en las minas, Compostela, Nueva Galicia, February 28, 1533. Guadalajara 30, No. 1/ 1/1–4; and the provisión real ordenando a Nuño de Guzmán, gobernador de Nueva Galicia, haga cumplir la ordenanza expedida en Toledo el 4 de diciembre de 1528, en la que se prohíbe el empleo de indios para el trabajo en las minas, donde sólo se autoriza el de esclavos, n.p., September 28, 1534. Indiferente General 422, L. 16, f.126–137. For a primary source by a near contemporary containing a wealth of information see Antonio Tello, *Crónica Miscelánea de la Sancta Provincia de Xalisco* 2 vols. Guadalajara: Gobierno del Estado de Jalisco/Universidad de Guadalajara/ INAH, 1973.

The sources compiled in this essay are far from comprehensive. They are intended as mere suggestions for interested readers and as a resource for scholars wishing to pursue this endlessly fascinating episode. Additional references can be found in the relevant endnotes.

NOTES

INTRODUCTION

1. Cabeza de Vaca says that the slavers experienced a "great shock." Cabeza de Vaca, *Relación of 1542*, edited by Rolena Adorno and Patrick Charles Pautz, 3 vols. (Lincoln: University of Nebraska Press, 1999), I, 245 [hereafter cited as Cabeza de Vaca, *Relación of 1542*, 245]. Antonio Tello also recounts this encounter in his *Crónica Miscelánea de la Sancta Provincia de Xalisco*, 2 vols. (Guadalajara: Gobierno del Estado de Jalisco, Universidad de Guadalajara, INAH, 1973), I, 249–257. Friar Tello wrote his account in 1652, more than a century after the facts. However, when he wrote his *Crónica Miscelánea*, he was already eighty-six years old and had been a longtime resident of Nueva Galicia where the events took place and therefore must have had access to some of the lore surrounding the arrival of Cabeza de Vaca and his companions. Friar Tello based his account on preexisting documents but also offers details that are not found anywhere else.

2. Cabeza de Vaca, *Relación of 1542*, 245.

3. A flashpoint of this ongoing debate occurred in 1550–1551 when several jurists and theologians gathered in Valladolid, Spain, to argue over the rationality and humanity of Native Americans. It is easy to forget, however, that this so-called great debate would not be the first nor the last time when the related questions of the nature of the indigenous inhabitants of America and Spain's right to subdue them would be aired. It was a recurrent concern throughout the sixteenth century and even later. The *junta* at Valladolid itself could not reach a clear-cut conclusion because those who took part in the debate remained far apart in their positions and failed to persuade one another. For a synthetic treatment of this most interesting disputation, see Lewis Hanke, *All Mankind Is One* (De Kalb: Northern Illinois University Press, 1974), passim.

4. Oviedo's *Historia general* was published only in the nineteenth century, although handwritten copies of some portions circulated since the sixteenth century. Of the two sources, Cabeza de Vaca's *Narrative* was easily the most influential.

5. Quotes from Andrés Pérez de Ribas, *Historia de los triunfos de nuestra Santa Fe* (Mexico City: Siglo Veintiuno, 1992), 24. Pérez de Ribas's account was first published

in Madrid in 1645. As Ralph Bauer has noted, Cabeza de Vaca's *Narrative* has recently "become a favorite among New Historicist literary critics, who have been intrigued by its representation of new alterities and identities produced in the Euro-American colonial encounter. . . ." For a brief appraisal of this literature, see Ralph Bauer, "Mythos and Epos: Cabeza de Vaca's Empire of Peace," in *The Cultural Geography of Colonial American Literatures: Empire, Travel, Modernity*, edited by Ralph Bauer (New York: Cambridge University Press, 2003), 30–76. From a strictly literary perspective, there is much that the *Narrative* can offer. Although steeped in the medieval tradition of heroic romances and chivalric accounts, the *Narrative* breaks new ground by placing the action in the Americas. Thus it can be conceived as the first "captivity" account of the Americas and even a pioneer in the letters of the New World. As William T. Pilkington has put it, "Cabeza de Vaca was not only a physical trailblazer; he was also a literary pioneer, and he deserves the distinction of being called the Southwest's first writer. His narrative turned out to be a prototype of much American writing to come." William T. Pilkington, "Epilogue," in *Cabeza de Vaca's Adventures in the Unknown Interior of America*, translated and edited by Cyclone Covey (Albuquerque: University of New Mexico Press, 1961), 146. See also José Rabasa, *Writing Violence on the Northern Frontier: The Historiography of Sixteenth-Century New Mexico and Florida and the Legacy of Conquest* (Durham: Duke University Press, 2000), chapter 1.

6. For the daring attempt to locate the route of Cabeza de Vaca, see Cleve Hallenbeck, *Álvar Núñez Cabeza de Vaca: The Journey and Route of the First European to Cross the Continent of North America, 1534–1536* (Glendale, CA: The Arthur H. Clark Company, 1940), 159. Unfortunately for him, we now know that the climate of the sixteenth century was quite different from ours and therefore any inference derived from this painstaking exercise must be judged invalid. More generally, the protracted exchange over the route followed by the survivors has generated all the trappings of scholarly warfare: a group advocating a "northern route" across Texas and New Mexico, a subversive camp proposing a "southern route" through what is now northern Mexico, and various intermediate positions bordering on betrayal and heresy. Occasionally nonacademics joined the fray. In the 1930s the president of the Texas Geographic Society became incensed by the suggestion that the trekkers may have somehow slipped out of Texas and into present-day Mexico and spearheaded a journalistic crusade to "relocate the scene of Cabeza's route upon the Texas map where it justly belongs, and from where it was most unjustly and wrongfully removed." See Robert T. Hill, quoted in Donald E. Chipman, "In Search of Cabeza de Vaca's Route across Texas: An Historiographical Survey," *Southwestern Historical Quarterly* 91:2 (October 1987), 138.

7. With regard to possible sexual encounters, we know that Estebanico requested young women from the Indians in a later expedition. It is almost certain that he acquired this habit during his sojourn across the continent. During the 1540s, when the first edition of Cabeza de Vaca's account was published, the Inquisition formally reviewed manuscripts intended for publication.

8. I am fortunate to be able to count on an abundant literature devoted to reconciling textual, geographic, and archaeological information relating to the Florida expedition. Even though some disagreements linger with respect to the castaways' route, recent breakthroughs have narrowed the possibilities. This book would not be possi-

ble without the contributions of many scholars, including Donald E. Chipman, Alex D. Krieger, T. N. Campbell, T. J. Campbell, Paul E. Hoffman, William C. Foster, Jerald T. Milanich, and others. I wish to single out the landmark, three-volume set published in 1999 by Rolena Adorno and Patrick C. Pautz, *Álvar Núñez Cabeza de Vaca: His Account, His Life, and the Expedition of Pánfilo de Narváez*. This work constitutes yet another edition and translation of Cabeza de Vaca's *Narrative* plus—literally—two-and-a-half volumes of "notes." These volumes have taken our understanding of this survival experience to a new level. This work contains biographical information of the protagonists, a detailed study of Cabeza de Vaca's genealogy, relevant historical background, and a textual analysis of the different accounts of the expedition, among other things. It constitutes the single most important source for the present book project. I have also relied on their transcription of Cabeza de Vaca's *Narrative*, first published in 1542, and often cite their translations. With regard to the lost art of storytelling, some academic historians have tried to revive it. For a good example see John Demos, *The Unredeemed Captive: A Family Story from Early America* (New York: Vintage Books, 1994).

9. The demographic decline of the indigenous peoples living north of Mesoamerica is both evident and difficult to quantify with precision. Level-headed discussions can be found in Peter Gerhard, *La Frontera Norte de la Nueva España* (Mexico City: UNAM, 1996), 420–422, and more recently in David Frye, "The Native Peoples of Northeastern Mexico," and Susan M. Deeds, "Legacies of Resistance, Adaptation, and Tenacity: History of the Native Peoples of Northwest Mexico," both in *The Cambridge History of the Native Peoples of the Americas*, vol. II, part II (New York: Cambridge University Press, 2000), 89–135 and 44–88, respectively. See also Russell Thornton, "Health, Disease, and Demography," in Philip J. Deloria and Neal Salisbury, eds., *A Companion to American Indian History* (Malden, MA: Blackwell Publishing Ltd., 2002); and Ann F. Ramenofsky, Alicia K. Wilbur, and Anne C. Stone, "Native American Disease History: Past, Present, and Future Directions," *World Archaeology* 35:2 (October 2003), 241–257. For information about the demography of specific locations, see later citations and the brief bibliographical discussion at the end of this book. To gain an appreciation of the importance of Cabeza de Vaca's account, let's consider the case of Texas. After Cabeza de Vaca's early visit to the future Lone Star State, there are significant hiatuses. The De Soto–Moscoso expedition passed through what is now east Texas in 1542. But after that brief visit, it would take more than a century before the great French explorer René-Robert Cavelier, Sieur de La Salle set foot in Texas, leaving us another detailed account. On La Salle's voyage, see Isaac J. Cox., ed., *The Journeys of René-Robert Cavelier, Sieur de La Salle*, 2 vols. (New York: A. S. Barnes and Company, 1905), passim.

10. William M. Denevan, "The Pristine Myth: The Landscape of the Americas in 1492," *Annals of the Association of American Geographers* 82:3 (September 1992), 369–385.

11. Richard White first launched this notion in his appropriately titled *The Middle Ground: Indians, Empires, and Republics in the Great Lakes Region, 1650–1815* (New York: Cambridge University Press, 1991). Since then the term has acquired a life of its own. For more recent elaborations—and similarly titled books—see Kathleen DuVal, *The Native Ground: Indians and Colonists in the Heart of the Continent*

(Philadelphia: University of Pennsylvania Press, 2006); and Alan Taylor, *The Divided Ground: Indians, Settlers and the Northern Borderland of the American Revolution* (New York: Knopf, 2006). For a recent retrospective, see "Forum: The Middle Ground Revisited," *William and Mary Quarterly* 63:1 (January 2006), 3–96. For a comparative consideration of first encounters, see Bruce G. Trigger, "Early Native North American Responses to European Contact: Romantic versus Rationalistic Interpretations," *The Journal of American History* 77:4 (March 1991), 1195–1215; and Bruce G. Trigger and William R. Swagerty, "Entertaining Strangers: North America in the Sixteenth Century," in *The Cambridge History of the Native Peoples of the Americas*, vol. 1 part 1 (New York: Cambridge University Press, 1996), 325–398.

CHAPTER 1

1. The Dominican friar Bartolomé de Las Casas spent time with Diego Velázquez both in Española and Cuba and got to know him well over the years. Las Casas described Velázquez's character as follows: "Of all the Spaniards that he had under his orders, he [Velázquez] was greatly appreciated and beloved because of his cheerful disposition and his conversation of pleasure and mischief as if among lads who lacked discipline." Bartolomé de las Casas, *Historia de las Indias* (Mexico City: Fondo de Cultura Económica, 1986), 2, 506.

2. On Narváez's physical appearance, see Bartolomé de Las Casas, *Historia de las Indias*, II, 525; and Bernal Díaz del Castillo, *Historia Verdadera de la Conquista de La Nueva España*, 2 vols. (Mexico City: Editorial Porrúa, S.A., 1977), I, 171. For a discussion of Narváez's probable age, see Adorno and Pautz, *Álvar Núñez Cabeza de Vaca: His Account, His Life, and the Expedition of Pánfilo de Narváez*, III, 208. See also Frank Goodwyn, "Pánfilo de Narváez, a Character Study of the First Spanish Leader to Land an Expedition to Texas," *Hispanic American Historical Review* 29:1 (February 1949), 150–156. The fact that Velázquez and Narváez came from nearby towns (Valladolid and Cuéllar) mattered greatly in an environment in which loyalty and trust were paramount. For a discussion of Narváez's birthplace, see Adorno and Pautz, *Álvar Núñez Cabeza de Vaca: His Account, His Life, and the Expedition of Pánfilo de Narváez*, III, 205–208. Whether Velázquez and Narváez knew each other in Spain remains a conjecture. Hugh Thomas states that Narváez "was probably a childhood friend of that governor [Velázquez]" but provides no further evidence. Hugh Thomas, *Conquest: Montezuma, Cortés, and the Fall of Old Mexico* (New York: Simon and Schuster, 1993), 354.

3. The history of the conquest of Cuba has to be pieced together from just a handful of sources, including (1) two letters from Diego Velázquez dated April 1, 1514, and August 10, 1515, both at the *Colección de documentos inéditos relativos al descubrimiento, conquista y organización de las antiguas posesiones españolas de América y Oceanía...*, 42 vols. (Madrid, 1864–1884), XI, 412–29 [hereafter cited as CDI]; (2) the account provided by Bartolomé de Las Casas in his *Historia de Indias* as well as other writings; (3) royal edicts published in José María Chacón y Calvo, ed., *Cedulario Cubano* (Madrid, 1929); and (4) some letters of King Ferdinand that allude to Cuba, also at CDI. See also Hortensia Pichardo Viñals, *La fundación de las primeras villas de la isla de Cuba* (La Habana: Editorial de Ciencias Sociales, 1986),

passim; and Irene A. Wright, *The Early History of Cuba* (New York: Macmillan, 1916), passim. As early as 1513, Velázquez received instructions to make a first distribution of Indians among his fellow conquerors. The crown left enormous discretion in the hands of Velázquez. See Esteban Mira Caballos, *El indio antillano: repartimiento, encomienda y esclavitud (1492–1542)* (Seville: Muñoz-Moya Editor, 1997), 159–160.

4. Bernal Díaz del Castillo participated in all three expeditions to Yucatán and provides the most detailed narrative. Bernal Díaz del Castillo, *Historia verdadera de la conquista de la Nueva España*, I, 39–101. My information also comes from Wright, *The Early History of Cuba*, 74–75; and Henry R. Wagner, *The Rise of Fernando Cortés* (New York: Kraus Reprint Co., 1969), 26–27. On the excitement caused in Cuba by the explanations provided by one of the two Maya Indians, see Bernaldino de Santa Clara to Secretary Francisco de los Cobos, October 20, 1517, in CDI, XI, 557.

5. On the events leading to Cortés's appointment, see the testimonies of Francisco de Montejo and Alonso Hernández Portocarrero in *Información recibida en La Coruña sobre la armada que Diego Velázquez dispuso para el descubrimiento de Nueva España y nombramiento de capitán general de ella a Hernán Cortés*, La Coruña Spain, April 29–30, 1520, in Francisco del Paso y Troncoso, ed., *Epistolario de Nueva España, 1505–1818* (Mexico City: José Porrúa e Hijos, 1939), I, 44–50.

6. José Luis Martínez, *Hernán Cortés* (Mexico City: FCE-UNAM, 1990), 117–118.

7. Quote from Las Casas, *Historia de Las Indias*, II, 528.

8. Wagner, *The Rise of Fernando Cortés*, 27, 32; Martínez, *Hernán Cortés*, 130–131. Chronicler Bernal Díaz del Castillo provides a different version of this final farewell. There is no question, however, that Cortés left the port of Santiago in a hurry, without sufficient provisions, and against Velázquez's will. Andrés de Tapia, another participant in the expedition who would later write a brief chronicle, sheds additional light on the deepening rivalry between Velázquez and Cortés: "As Diego Velázquez saw that the marqués [Cortés] was liberally investing his own fortune and enlisting more men than seemed necessary, he grew wary and tried to prevent the marqués' departure. And so the marqués sailed from the port of the city of Santiago, Cuba, not as well provisioned as was necessary, and, as we have said, went the length of the island gathering supplies, ships, and men. Andrés de Tapia, "Chronicle," in *The Conquistadors: First-Person Accounts of the Conquest of Mexico*, edited and translated by Patricia de Fuentes (New York: Orion Press, 1963), 27.

9. We can surmise this from a letter that Miguel de Pasamonte, the royal treasurer based in Española, wrote to King Ferdinand, as explained in Adorno and Pautz, *Álvar Núñez Cabeza de Vaca*, III, 221–222. For the objectives of Narváez at court, see also Las Casas, *Historia de las Indias*, III, 103.

10. Ferdinand's grandson and future monarch Charles V best represents this trend. In his dual role as King of Spain and holy Roman emperor, he went to every nation in Western Europe and visited parts of Africa, made eleven sea voyages, and spent one of every four days of his reign on the road. On the day of his abdication he summed it all up: "My life has been one long journey." Henry Kamen, *Empire: How Spain Became a World Power 1492–1763* (New York: HarperCollins, 2003), 50. Grandees traveled with extended families, servants, and jesters. The entourage of the Duke of Béjar included Francesillo de Zúñiga, the famous jester who would later join the retinue of Emperor Charles V. Don Francesillo would go on to write a unique book about life at

the court describing the looks and magnificence of different delegations and passing on valuable gossip. Francesillo de Zúñiga, *Crónica burlesca del emperador Carlos V* (Barcelona: Editorial Crítica, 1981).

11. Antonio de Guevara, *Libro llamado aviso de privados y doctrina de cortesanos* (Antwerp: Martij, 1545), 37. It is a remarkable source on the court's functioning.

12. Guevara, *Libro llamado aviso de privados y doctrina de cortesanos*, chapter 12.

13. On the gold consignment from Cuba, see the relación de cartas que los oficiales reales de la isla de Cuba escribieron a Su Alteza sobre el gobierno de ella, 1515, in CDI, XI, 456. On Bishop Rodríguez de Fonseca's character, see Las Casas, *Historia de las Indias*, I, 333. Although the Council of the Indies was formally founded as late as 1523, ever since the days of Columbus the bishop had surrounded himself with some members of the Council of Castile who advised the King on matters of Spain's overseas possessions and in effect functioned as the Council of the Indies before it was formally founded as such. See Juan Manzano, "Un documento inédito relativo a cómo funcionaba el Consejo de Indias," *Hispanic American Historical Review* 15:3 (August 1935), 313–351; and Hayward Keniston, *Francisco de los Cobos, Secretario de Carlos V* (Madrid: Editorial Castalia, 1980), 44–45, 53–54. On Velázquez's short-lived marriage and amorous life, see Las Casas, *Historia de las Indias*, II, 497, and III, 256; and Díaz del Castillo, *Historia verdadera de la conquista de la Nueva España*, II, 78, 88, although the name given in his version of the gossip is Petronila de Fonseca.

14. We don't know the exact date that Narváez joined the court, but he had delivered the gold to King Ferdinand by November 1515.

15. This is the most traditional account, based on some primary sources like the "Deuxième voyage de Phillipe le Beau en Espagne en 1506," 463, as quoted in Bethany Aram, *Juana the Mad: Sovereignty and Dynasty in Renaissance Europe* (Baltimore: Johns Hopkins University Press, 2005), 89. Aram observes that although historians have long used Juana's procession as proof of her "excessive love" and "mad devotion" to her husband, there were other, more earthly motivations at work. By keeping Philip's mortal remains disinterred, Juana was able to fend off eager suitors as she wished to remain a widow. Moreover, by insisting on reburying Philip's corpse in Granada, alongside her mother's, Juana "probably hoped to secure her rights, and those of her eldest son, Charles, to the southern kingdom." Aram, *Juana the Mad*, 89. Especially fascinating is Aram's suggestion that Juana's erratic behavior may have drawn strength from one of the *Letters* of Saint Jerome, a hermetic text contained in her library. Saint Jerome recommended that the widow "quench the fire of the devil's shafts with the cold streams of fast and vigil" and observed that "if it should happen that you have sons by your second husband, domestic warfare and internecine feuds will be the result. You will not be allowed to love your own children, or to look kindly on those to whom you gave birth." Aram, *Juana the Mad*, 97.

16. Laurent Vital, *Premier Voyage de Charles-Quint en Espagne, de 1517 a 1518,* in Louise-Prosper Gachard et Charles Piot, eds., *Collection des Voyages des Souverains des Pays-Bas* (Brussels: F. Hayez, 1881), III, 94–105. The transfer of power was not seamless. In fact, Juana remained the proprietary queen of Castile until her death in 1555, and the Council of Castile at first opposed Charles's accession to the throne while Juana was alive. For an account of the meeting at Tordesillas, see Vital, *Premier Voyage de Charles-Quint en Espagne*, 134–137.

17. Narváez first tried to negotiate with the interim government that followed Ferdinand's death—a regency headed by Cardinal Francisco Jiménez de Cisneros—but instead was referred to a new tribunal of Jeronymite monks being established at Española. At that point Narváez must have decided to wait for the arrival of the new monarch.

18. *Ecclesiastes* 34:21–22, as quoted in Benno M. Biermann, *El padre las Casas y su apostolado* (Madrid: Fundación Universitaria Española, 1986), 19.

19. The most comprehensive treatment of these events can be found in Manuel Giménez Fernández, *Bartolomé de Las Casas: delegado de Cisneros para la reformación de las Indias, 1516–1517,* 2 vols. (Seville: Escuela de Estudios Hispanoamericanos de Sevilla, 1953), passim. For the position of Las Casas see the *Representación hecha al Rey por el clérigo Bartolomé de Las Casas, en que manifiesta los agravios que sufren los indios de la isla de Cuba de los españoles.* Narváez's quote comes from the *Informe de los procuradores de la isla de Cuba, Pánfilo de Narváez y Antonio Velázquez,* 1516, both in CDI, VII, 5–13. See also Las Casas, *Historia de las Indias,* III, 117.

20. Quotes from Las Casas, *Historia de las Indias,* III, 113. See also Giménez Fernández, *Bartolomé de Las Casas: delegado de Cisneros para la reformación de las Indias* Las Casas, II, 408–415.

21. Velázquez did not rely exclusively on Narváez but also sought the appointment of *adelantado* of the new lands through other agents. He sent Gonzalo de Guzmán to Spain to act in concert with Narváez.

22. Adorno and Pautz, *Álvar Núñez Cabeza de Vaca,* III, 224. See also King Charles to Diego Velázquez, Zaragoza, December 12, 1518, in Francisco del Paso y Troncoso, ed., *Epistolario de Nueva España, 1505–1818* (Mexico City: Porrúa, 1939), I, 38.

23. For an excellent discussion of Cortés's instructions and motivations, see Richard Konetzke, "Hernán Cortés como poblador de la Nueva España," in *Lateinamerika: Entdekung, Eroberrung, Kolonisation* (Böhlau Verlag: Viena, 1983), 157–171. For the instructions themselves, see Instrucciones de Diego Velázquez a Hernán Cortés, Santiago, October 23, 1518, in José Luis Martínez, ed., *Documentos Cortesianos* (Mexico City: UNAM and FCE, 1990), 45–59. On Velázquez's deteriorating relationship with Cortés, see Diego Veláquez to King Charles, Santiago of Cuba, October 12, 1519, in CDI, XII, 247. Adorno and Pautz observe that modern historians' reliance on pro-Cortés sources has resulted in a tendency to exaggerate the degree of Velázquez's suspicions about Cortés during much of 1519. Adorno and Pautz, *Álvar Núñez Cabeza de Vaca,* III, 249. The chronicle of Andrés de Tapia (admittedly, a pro-Cortés source) provides a very plausible scenario: "Diego Velázquez did not admit publicly that the marqués [Cortés] was embarking against his will, nor did the marqués make public that he was an enemy of Velázquez . . . for this reason Diego Velázquez made it appear that he had a claim to the marqués' enterprise, though he had actually not spent much on it. In fact, when I arrived at the Cuban port of the city of Santiago and told Diego Velázquez that I was there to serve him and wished to go on the expedition with the marqués del Valle, he said to me: 'I do not know what Cortés' intentions are toward me, but I think they are bad, because he has spent everything he had and is in debt, and has gathered in his service as many attendants as if he were one of the lords in Spain. Nevertheless I shall be pleased to have

you go in his company, and since it is no more than two weeks since he left this port you will soon overtake him.'" Andrés de Tapia, "Chronicle," in *The Conquistadors: First-Person Accounts of the Conquest of Mexico*, 27.

24. The story of the conquest of Mexico has been told many times before. For a recent and luminous telling, including a blow-by-blow account of the exchange between Cortés and Moctezuma, see Hugh Thomas, *Conquest*, 175–240.

25. For a detailed inventory, see Pietro Martire d'Anghiera (or Pedro Mártir de Angelería), *Décadas del Nuevo Mundo*, 2 vols. (Mexico City: Porrúa e Hijos, 1964), I, 425–431. Cortés's expedition had collected these varied objects from the Maya of Cozumel and Yucatán, along the Gulf of Mexico, from the Totonacs, and from the Aztecs. The sheer quantity was astonishing. But discerning eyes in Europe also noted the artistic sensibility and superb craftsmanship involved. The renowned painter and engraver Albrecht Dürer saw Cortés's gift in Brussels on August 27, 1520. The entire lot had been received in Seville, forwarded to Valladolid, and had traveled from there with King Charles and his court by way of England to the Low Countries, where Dürer saw it. In his diary, he wrote: "I have seen the things which they have brought to the King out of the new lands of gold: a sun all of gold, a whole fathom broad, and a moon, too, of silver, of the same size, also two rooms full of armour, and the people there with all manner of wondrous weapons, harness, darts, wonderful shields, extraordinary clothing, beds, and all kinds of wonderful things for human use, much finer to look at than prodigies. These things are all so precious that they are valued at 100,000 gulden, and all the days of my life I have seen nothing that reaches my heart so much as these, for among them I have seen wonderfully artistic things and have admired the subtle ingenuity of men in foreign lands." Roger Fry, ed., *Dürer's Records of Journeys to Venice and the Low Countries* (New York: Dover Publications, 1995), 47–48. Pietro Martire d'Anghiera, an Italian attached to the Spanish court and a member of the Council of the Indies, became similarly impressed by the fine Indian objects that he saw at Valladolid: "In truth, I do not so much admire the gold and the precious stones, what bedazzles me most is the craftsmanship and effort making these works of art transcend their materials." Mártir de Angelería, *Décadas del Nuevo Mundo*, I, 430. King Charles was delighted too. Perennially short of cash, he eventually had the gold pieces melted and turned into coinage—a course of action that makes art historians and archaeologists cringe to this day. On the fate of Cortés's gift see Martínez, *Hernán Cortés*, 187–188; and Thomas, *Conquest*, 353.

26. See the Instrucciones de Hernán Cortés a los procuradores Francisco de Montejo y Alonso Hernández Portocarrero, enviados a España, Veracruz, early July 1519, in *Documentos Cortesianos*, edited by José Luis Martínez (Mexico City: UNAM and FCE, 1990), 77–90. The subsequent narrative is based chiefly on Wagner, *The Rise of Fernando Cortés*, chapter 8; José Luis Martínez, *Hernán Cortés*, chapter 7; Adorno and Pautz, *Álvar Núñez Cabeza de Vaca*, III, 247–263; and Bernal Díaz del Castillo, *Historia verdadera de la conquista de la Nueva España*, I, chapters 109–123.

27. The witness in question was one Francisco Pérez. He estimated the objects to be worth anywhere between 270,000 and 300,000 *castellanos*. See Juan de Rojas, September 11, 1519, in CDI, XII, 155–160; and Diego Velázquez to King Charles I, October 12, 1519, in CDI, XII, 248.

28. On the events surrounding the preparations of this armada, see especially Diego Velázquez to Bishop Juan Rodríguez de Fonseca, Santiago of Cuba, October 12, 1519, in *Documentos Cortesianos*, 91–94.

29. It is fair to note that a smallpox epidemic was ravaging Cuba at the time. Velázquez may have chosen to stay on the island out of a sense of duty. See Thomas, *Conquest*, 340. Narváez's quote appears in Francisco Cervantes de Salazar, *Crónica de la Nueva España* (Mexico City: Editorial Porrúa, 1982), 388.

30. Wagner, *The Rise of Fernando Cortés*, 270–271.

31. The source actually says that six ships capsized, but from the context (and the fact that only forty men drowned) he must have meant that six vessels were damaged and only one capsized. See Thomas, *Conquest*, 360.

32. Robert S. Weddle, *Spanish Sea: The Gulf of Mexico in North American Discovery, 1500–1685* (College Station: Texas A&M University Press, 1985), 118.

33. On the Aztec lookouts, see Thomas, *Conquest*, 364.

34. Wagner, *The Rise of Fernando Cortés*, 270.

35. Thomas, *Conquest*, 361–362.

36. Díaz del Castillo, *Historia Verdadera*, I, 335. One of the four defectors was Diego Velázquez's former jester, a man referred to as Cervantes *el chocarrero* (the crude or vulgar). With more dramatic flare he egged on his newfound benefactor: "Oh, Narváez, Narváez, how blessed you are, and how timely your arrival!" Quoted in Díaz del Castillo, *Historia Verdadera*, I, 335.

37. The friendship between Narváez and Tlacochcalcatl was not devoid of ambiguity. Narváez actually confiscated the Spanish goods that Cortés had left in Cempoallan the year before. Tlacochcalcatl protested and became apprehensive of Cortés's reaction. But he still helped feed Narváez's army and consented to its presence in Cempoallan. One especially good and underutilized source on the Narváez expedition to Mexico is Cervantes de Salazar's *Crónica de la Nueva España*. He wrote it more than three decades after the events took place, but members of Narváez's party must have been among his informants. Cervantes de Salazar re-creates plausible dialogues between Narváez and the *licenciado* Vázquez de Ayllón or, in this case, between Narváez and the cacique of Cempoallan. Cervantes de Salazar, *Crónica de la Nueva España*, 391–392.

38. For these events, see Díaz del Castillo, *Historia Verdadera*, I, 352–355. See also Información promovida por Diego Velázquez contra Hernán Cortés, Santiago, Cuba, June 28–July 6, 1521, in *Documentos Cortesianos*, I, 198–199; and Thomas, *Conquest*, 374–375.

39. Thomas, *Conquest*, 368, 372.

40. Thomas, *Conquest*, 377; and Díaz del Castillo, *Historia Verdadera*, I, 364–365.

41. Cortés's men had received these long pikes from the chinantecos. Bernal Díaz del Castillo was an eyewitness to this battle and is easily our best source. My description is largely based on his account. Díaz del Castillo, *Historia Verdadera*, 355–373.

42. Narváez's quote comes from Díaz del Castillo, *Historia Verdadera*, 371.

43. Council member and historian Martire d'Anghiera would later interview some of the participants in the battle of Cempoallan. Somewhat cryptically, he noted that there were many rumors but that one day it would be known how a small band, however bold and resolute, had been able to vanquish a much larger force. He was clearly

hinting at the tangle of bribes and intrigues preceding the battle. What sketchy evidence we have suggests that more than anything else, Cortés's astonishing negotiating talent carried the day. Martire d'Anghiera suspected that the fighting had been rather limited. Martire d'Anghiera, *Décadas del Nuevo Mundo*, II, 490.

44. The eyewitness was Alonso Pérez de Zamora quoted in Adorno and Pautz, *Álvar Núñez Cabeza de Vaca*, III, 257. On the failed escape attempt see probanza sobre la fuga que intentaba Pánfilo de Narváez, preso en la Villa-Rica por orden de Hernando Cortés, February 10–16, 1521, in CDI, XXVI, 287–297.

45. Quote from Díaz del Castillo, *Historia Verdadera*, II, 79. Adorno and Pautz make the crucial point that Díaz del Castillo could not have been witness to this encounter and therefore his retelling had to be constructed from hearsay and therefore must be taken with a grain of salt. Adorno and Pautz, *Álvar Núñez Cabeza de Vaca*, II, 4.

46. Copy of Diego Velázquez's Testament, Santiago, Cuba, April 9, 1524, in *Epistolario de Nueva España*, I, 67.

47. Pánfilo de Narváez told the story of how his wife had tried to save him from Cortés to fellow conquistador and historian Gonzalo Fernández de Oviedo y Valdés in 1525. *Joint Report*, 87.

48. Oviedo met Narváez in Toledo sometime in 1525 or 1526 and exhorted him to go back home. *Joint Report*, 87.

CHAPTER 2

1. Quote from Pablo E. Pérez-Mallaína, *Spain's Men of the Sea: Daily Life on the Indies Fleets in the Sixteenth Century* (Baltimore: Johns Hopkins University Press, 1998), 1.

2. My description of Seville as a maritime hub is based on María del Carmen Mena García, *Sevilla y Las Flotas de Indias: La Gran Armada de Castilla del Oro (1513–1514)* (Seville: Universidad de Sevilla/Fundación El Monte, 1998); Pérez-Mallaína, *Spain's Men of the Sea*; Eduardo Trueba, *Sevilla marítima (siglo XVI)*, 2d ed., (Seville: Padilla Libros, 1990); and Clarence H. Haring, *Trade and Navigation Between Spain and the Indies in the Times of the Hapsburgs* (Mansfield Centre, CT: Martino Publishing, 2004). The estimate of the average lifespan of a vessel corresponds to the sixteenth century and is provided by Pero Veitia Linaje, a member of the House of Trade and presumably well acquainted with such nautical statistics. Mena García, *Sevilla y las Flotas de Indias*, 263. The subject of measurements is especially convoluted as terms proliferated: *toneles de Vizcaya, salmas de trigo, barricas, sacas de lana, cahices de sal*, etc. In the early sixteenth century, the terms *tonelada* and *tonel* were used interchangeably in Seville. One *tonel* corresponded to two *pipas* full of water or wine, amounting to 55 *arrobas* or 887 liters of water, which is close to our modern, decimal metric ton. See Mena García, *Sevilla y Las Flotas de Indias*, 243–244; and Trueba, *Sevilla marítima*, 68. There was a small crane on a stone platform at the base of the famous Torre de Oro (Golden Tower), which had been used to lift large blocks of stone in the previous century. But this was hardly appropriate considering Seville's considerable shipping volume. In contrast, Antwerp boasted seven piers and at least three cranes while London in the second

half of the sixteenth century possessed no less than seven or eight cranes. Pérez-Mallaína, *Spain's Men of the Sea*, 5–6.

3. Pérez-Mallaína, *Spain's Men of the Sea*, 5.

4. For a discussion of Seville's demographic data by parishes, see Ruth Pike, *Aristocrats and Traders: Sevillian Society in the Sixteenth Century* (Ithaca, NY: Cornell University Press, 1973), chapter 1. See also Pérez-Mallaína, *Spain's Men of the Sea*, 15–16. The quote comes from Miguel de Cervantes, "El coloquio de los perros" in *Novelas Ejemplares*, cited in Pike, *Aristocrats and Traders*, 17. The characters come from one of Cervantes's *Novelas ejemplares* entitled precisely *Cortadillo y Rinconete* (Madrid: Edimat Libros, S. A., 2004), 99–123 and is also mentioned in Pérez-Mallaína, *Spain's Men of the Sea*, 27.

5. On Cortés's campaigns of territorial expansion, see Martínez, *Hernán Cortés*, 348–358; and Adorno and Pautz, *Álvar Núñez Cabeza de Vaca*, III, 298–302.

6. The quote comes from the first petition of Pánfilo de Narváez to Emperor Charles V, Toledo, 1525, in CDI, X, 40. For a fuller explanation of the geographic meaning of the places named, see below in the chapter. The second quote comes from Narváez's third petition, no place, no date, CDI, X, 46. In a second petition, and against the backdrop of newly introduced legislation aimed at protecting the American natives, Narváez restated his right to make slaves out of those Indians who "insisted on rebelling even after repeated warnings." Second petition, no place, no date, CDI, X, 41. Narváez may have drafted this petition around the time when the crown introduced a set of new ordinances regulating Indian slavery issued in November of 1526.

7. Narváez's charter was actually signed by Francisco de los Cobos, a powerful secretary and erstwhile ally of Bishop Rodríguez de Fonseca (who had died in 1524 as stated) and therefore was probably well disposed toward Narváez. For a full legal discussion of these charters, see Milagros del Vas Mingo, *Las Capitulaciones de Indias en el siglo XVI* (Madrid: Instituto de Cooperación Iberoamericana, 1986), passim.

8. On the flour problems, see Archivo General de Indias [hereafter AGI] Justicia 1159 R. 2/1527–28; and AGI Indiferente 421, L. 12, f67r–67v.

9. Quote from the Real Cédula a los oficiales de la Casa de Contratación, Madrid, December 28, 1514, in Mena García, *Sevilla y las flotas de Indias*, 185. The scarcity of expert pilots was nothing new. See Mena García, *Sevilla y las flotas de Indias*, 45–46.

10. On Narváez's whereabouts and activities at this time, see Adorno and Pautz, *Álvar Núñez Cabeza de Vaca*, II, 5–27. Having a crier announce a colonization venture and conducting the recruiting at the cathedral steps were standard procedures. Pedraria Dávila's large armada for Castilla del Oro was organized in this way. Mena García, *Sevilla y las flotas de Indias*, 49–50.

11. These scraps of information come from a variety of sources. On Pedro Lunel, see Real cédula a Pedro Lunel para que pueda pasar cuatro esclavos negros, Valladolid, March 29, 1527, in Indiferente 421, L. 12, F50-v–51r at the AGI; on Mari Hernández and Francisco de Quevedo, see Mari Hernández to the viceroy of New Spain, Toledo, August 2, 1539, in Mexico 1088, L. 3/1/256 r and v in AGI; on Doroteo Teodoro, see Cabeza de Vaca, *Relación of 1542*, I, 73, 78; on don Pedro, see Cabeza de Vaca, *Relación of 1542*, 67; on Juan Velázquez de Salazar, see "Título de regidor del primero pueblo que descubriese y poblase Pánfilo de Narváez," n.p., 1527, in Patronato 19, R. 1/1/2–4 in the AGI; on Hernando de Esquivel, see "Relación de la Florida" (inquiry

undertaken by Vicente de Zaldívar on behalf of Juan de Oñate), Mexico City, n.d., Patronato 19, R 33 /1/1–8 in the AGI.

12. Narváez had been free to recruit anyone "within our kingdoms" as well as "from the outside"—a perplexing clause considering that the Crown's overall policy was to keep Spain's rivals out of the Indies. But foreign seamen represented a substantial percentage of early crews. For an enlightening precedent, see Mena García, *Sevilla y las flotas de Indias*, 147–155. For a discussion about the possible meanings of the phrase quoted in the paragraph, see Adorno and Pautz, *Álvar Núñez Cabeza de Vaca*, II, 16–18.

13. On the social composition of early expeditions, see Bernard Grunberg, *L'Univers des Conquistadores: Les hommes et leur conquête dans le Mexique du XVIe siècle* (Paris: L'Harmattan, 1993), 45–47; James Lockhart, *The Men of Cajamarca: A Social and Biographical Study of the First Conquerors of Peru* (Austin: University of Texas Press, 1973), 37–39; and James Lockhart and Stuart B. Schwartz, *Early Latin America: A History of Colonial Spanish America and Brazil* (New York: Cambridge University Press, 1983), 80.

14. For a detailed discussion of Cabeza de Vaca's age as can be deduced by triangulating various sources and ascertaining the precise meaning of terms like "guardianship" and "trusteeship," see Adorno and Pautz, *Álvar Núñez Cabeza de Vaca*, I, 343–346. We don't have any explicit description of his looks, but it can be deduced from occasional clues contained in his narrative. A seventeenth-century genealogist calls it "the ancient and noble house of Cabeza de Vaca." See José Pellicer de Ossau Salas y Tovar, cited in Adorno and Pautz, *Álvar Núñez Cabeza de Vaca*, I, 319. By the sixteenth century, the Cabeza de Vaca family had split into different branches, not all of equal standing. For instance, the Cabeza de Vaca lineage based in the city of Zamora belonged to that most exclusive circle of titled nobility. They had been honored as lords of Arenillas for generations and through marriage became related to the marquises of Flores-Dávila. In contrast, the Andalusian branch of the Cabeza de Vaca house, to which Álvar belonged, represented only middle- and lower-ranking nobility—and as such untitled. Adorno and Pautz have written the most comprehensive treatment of Álvar's genealogy. *Álvar Núñez Cabeza de Vaca*, I, 319, and more generally I, 295–340. For the role of Luis Cabeza de Vaca in the Spanish court, see Hayward Keniston, *Francisco de los Cobos: Secretario de Carlos V*, 25; and Adorno and Pautz, *Álvar Núñez Cabeza de Vaca*, I, 323. Luis Cabeza de Vaca was also a member of the Council of the Indies in the 1520s. For the importance of the Canary Islands as an antecedent to the exploration and conquest of the New World, see Felipe Fernández-Armesto, *The Canary Islands after the Conquest* (Oxford: Oxford University Press, 1982); and Fernández-Armesto, *Before Columbus: Exploration and Colonisation from the Mediterranean to the Atlantic, 1229–1492* (London: Macmillan, 1987), 207–212. For the relationship between Cabeza de Vaca and his illustrious grandfather, see Hipólito Sancho de Sopranis, "Datos para el estudio de Álvar Núñez Cabeza de Vaca," *Revista de Indias* 8 (1947), 81. See also Adorno and Pautz, *Álvar Núñez Cabeza de Vaca*, I, 329–333.

15. For an assortment of biographical details, see Sancho de Sopranis, "Datos para el studio de Álvar Núñez Cabeza de Vaca," 90. Adorno and Pautz make the point that Álvar began his service in the house of Medina Sidonia as early as 1503, before the

death of his parents, and also note that other members of the Cabeza de Vaca family were in the duke's service. Adorno and Pautz, *Álvar Núñez Cabeza de Vaca*, I, 351. For a general treatment of the Comunero movement, see Stephen Haliczer, *The Comuneros of Castile: The Forging of a Revolution, 1475–1521* (Madison: University of Wisconsin Press, 1981). For Cabeza de Vaca's activities in the Comunero revolt and his marriage to María Marmolejo, see Adorno and Pautz, *Álvar Núñez Cabeza de Vaca*, I, 359–360, 366–369.

16. In fact, there were three officials of the royal treasury. Cabeza de Vaca was the chief treasurer, Alonso Enríquez was the comptroller, and Alonso de Solís was the factor and inspector of mines.

17. We know that Cabeza de Vaca received his commission in Valladolid on February 15, 1527, during a period when Emperor Charles V held court there. Narváez could not have been present, as he was almost certainly in Seville at that time. For instance, on February 19, 1527, Narváez had a power of attorney drawn up. Adorno and Pautz, *Álvar Núñez Cabeza de Vaca*, II, 26.

18. See Adorno and Pautz, *Álvar Núñez Cabeza de Vaca*, II, 408; and Baltasar Dorantes de Carranza, *Sumaria relación de las cosas de la Nueva España* (Mexico City: Imprenta del Museo Nacional, 1902), 266. Adorno and Pautz also note that Dorantes was appointed councilman to the first town founded in Florida. Adorno and Pautz, *Álvar Núñez Cabeza de Vaca*, II, 409.

19. The phrase comes from one of the witnesses in Alonso del Castillo's *probanza* (investigation) conducted in 1547. Quoted in Adorno and Pautz, *Álvar Núñez Cabeza de Vaca*, II, 423. On Castillo's background, see also Adorno and Pautz, *Álvar Núñez Cabeza de Vaca*, II, 422–427.

20. See real cédula a Fray Juan Suárez, Burgos, February 15, 1528, L. 13/1/131 (60r) at the AGI. Fray Juan de Palos is mentioned in the *Relación of 1542*, I, 46.

21. Richard Konetzke, "La emigración de mujeres españolas a América durante la época colonial," in *Lateinamerika: Entdeckung, Eroberung, Kolonisation* (Böhlau Verlag: Viena, 1983), 1–28.

22. The quote is by Ambassador Andrés Navagero in Pérez-Mallaína, *Spain's Men of the Sea*, 18. On female workers in Seville, see also Konetzke, "La emigración de mujeres españolas a América durante la poca colonial," 13.

23. For the women on Narváez's expedition to Mexico, see Grunberg, *L'Univers des Conquistadores*, 37–39. For the expedition to Florida, see Cabeza de Vaca, *Relación of 1542*, I, 272. It is not clear whether all these ten women departed from Spain or some took passage in the Caribbean.

24. Leo Africanus, *The History and Description of Africa*, 3 vols. (London: Hakluyt Society, 1896), II, 293, 379–381. It was first published in Italian in 1526, the year before the expedition's departure.

25. On the Portuguese occupation of Azamor, see David Lopes, *A Expansão em Marrocos* (Lisbon: Editorial Teorema, n.d.), 31–40.

26. Adorno and Pautz provide a detailed analysis of Estebanico's ethnic and cultural background in *Álvar Núñez Cabeza de Vaca*, II, 414–422. The interpretation offered here adds a few elements based on the enlightening works of Aurelia Martín Casares, *La esclavitud en la Granada del siglo XVI: género, raza y religion* (Granada: Universidad de Granada y Diputación Provincial de Granada, 2000), especially 167–173; and

Alfonso Franco Silva, *La esclavitud en Andalucía, 1450–1550* (Granada: Universidad de Granada, 1992).

27. Matthew Restall, "Black Conquistadors: Armed Africans in Early Spanish America," *Americas* 57:2 (October 2000), 171–205; and Peter Gerhard, "A Black Conquistador in Mexico," in *Slavery and Beyond: The African Impact on Latin America and the Caribbean* (Wilmington: SR Books, 1995), 1–9.

28. I assume that the Narváez expedition followed the usual route, as there is no specific documentation on this phase of the voyage. On navigating the Guadalquivir, see Pérez-Mallaína, *Spain's Men of the Sea*, 8–9; and Trueba, *Sevilla marítima*; 35–38.

29. Pérez-Mallaína, *Spain's Men of the Sea*, 8.

30. The quote comes from Diego García de Palacio, *Instrucción náutica para navegar* (Madrid: Instituto de Cultura Hispánica, 1944), III, 112. This treatise was originally published in 1587. See also Antonio de Guevara, *Arte de marear y de los inventores della con muchos avisos para los que navegan en ellas* (Valladolid, 1539), especially chapters 5 and 6.

31. Oviedo, *Historia General y Natural de las Indias*, book 2, chapter 9.

32. These dimensions correspond to a *nao* (a particular type of ship) of 106 toneladas, according to House of Trade regulations. Naturally, there were different sizes. Moreover, tonnage tended to increase in the course of the century. For tonnage increase see Pérez-Mallaína, *Spain's Men of the Sea*, 130; for my description of the overcrowded conditions on board, see Pérez-Mallaína, *Spain's Men of the Sea*, 131–140. Regarding eating on board, see Pérez-Mallaína, *Spain's Men of the Sea*, 132–133; Guevara, *Arte de marear*, 263; and especially Mena García, *Sevilla y las flotas de Indias*, 409–425.

33. Quote from Mena García, *Sevilla y las flotas de Indias*, 425. On sleeping and eating arrangements, see Pérez-Mallaína, *Spain's Men of the Sea*, 140–143; and Guevara, *Arte de marear*, 259–260.

34. Eugenio Salazar, *La mar descrita por los mareados* (1573), 287–288, quoted in Pérez-Mallaína, *Spain's Men of the Sea*, 143.

35. Guevara, *Arte de marear*, 262–263.

36. Cabeza de Vaca, *Relación de 1542*, I, 22.

37. Cabeza de Vaca, *Relación de 1542*, I, 23.

38. First petition of Pánfilo de Narváez to Emperor Charles V, Toledo, 1525, in CDI, X, 41.

39. Quote from the Relación del Bachiller Alonso de Parada, Valladolid, July 2, 1527, in CDI, XL, 266. Adorno and Pautz estimate that this report was penned in early 1525. See also *Álvar Núñez Cabeza de Vaca*, II, 47. The depopulation of the Caribbean islands, including some regions of Española, was a real phenomenon. See *licenciados* Espinoza and Suazo to Emperor Charles V, Santo Domingo, March 30, 1528, in *Santo Domingo en los Manuscritos de Juan Bautista Muñoz* (Santo Domingo: Ediciones Fundación García Arévalo, Inc., 1981), 277–290. Adorno and Pautz further point out that Española was struggling with a declining Indian population and, at the time of Narváez's arrival, was reeling from the effects of a hurricane and an Indian revolt. Adorno and Pautz, *Álvar Núñez Cabeza de Vaca*, II, 48. Notwithstanding these problems, the sources do present a favorable economic picture of Española. The dominant historical narrative emphasizing the overall decline of the Caribbean islands in

NOTES

the wake of Spain's continental conquests has prevented scholars from fully appreciating the prosperity and vibrancy of Española's economy through much of the sixteenth century.

40. Members of the Florida expedition had tangible proof. Scarcely a few days after their arrival, Española's royal treasurer sent to Spain a large remittance of 21,706 pesos in gold as well as "504 marks [255 pounds] of common pearls and another lot of round ones." Pasamonte, Juan de Ampiés, and Fernando Caballero to Emperor Charles V, Santo Domingo, September 12, 1527, Patronato 174, R.33, AGI. For a modern investigation, see Aldemaro Romero et al., "Cubagua's Pearl-Oyster Beds: The First Depletion of a Natural Resource Caused by Europeans in the American Continent," *Journal of Political Ecology* 6 (1999), 57–78.

41. There had been prior attempts to establish sugar mills in Española in 1505 or 1506, but Vellosa's facility was the first that succeeded. See Las Casas, *Historia de las Indias*, III, 273–276; Oviedo, *Historia general y natural de las Indias*, I, 106–111; Relación del Bachiller Parada, CDI, XL, 262; and for the larger context, see Sydney W. Mintz, *Sweetness and Power: The Place of Sugar in Modern History* (New York: Penguin, 1985), 32–35.

42. Queen Isabel (not to be confused with Charles's mother, Isabella) to Vasco Porcallo, Madrid, December 22, 1529, in AGI Santo Domingo 1121, L. 1 f. 13v. Vasco Porcallo's prominence is easy to establish. When Diego Velázquez had sought out partners with whom to explore Mexico jointly in the late 1510s, Vasco Porcallo, along with Cortés and then Narváez, had been among his principal choices. For additional information on Vasco Porcallo's biography see Adorno and Pautz, *Álvar Núñez Cabeza de Vaca*, II, 48–51. See also Cabeza de Vaca, *Relación of 1542*, I, 24.

43. National Oceanic and Atmospheric Administration, *Hurricane Basics* (Washington, DC: U.S. Department of Commerce, 1999); and Jay Barnes, *Florida's Hurricane History* (Chapel Hill: University of North Carolina Press, 1998), 6–9, 17.

44. Cabeza de Vaca's account is decidedly apologetic at this point. He emphasizes his reluctance to leave the ships, pointing out that he did it only after his crew urged him to do so in order to expedite the transfer of provisions.

45. Barnes, *Florida's Hurricane History*, 6, 40. See also Louis A. Pérez, Jr., *Winds of Change: Hurricanes and the Transformation of Nineteenth-Century Cuba* (Chapel Hill: University of North Carolina Press, 2001).

46. Cabeza de Vaca, *Relación of 1542*, I, 29.

47. The first quote comes from Fray Ramón Pané, *An Account of the Antiquities of the Indians* (Durham: Duke University Press, 1999), 29. The second quote comes from Oviedo, *Historia general y natural de las Indias*, I, 147.

48. Cabeza de Vaca dutifully reported the loss to the emperor on November 28, 1527. See Real cédula a Álvar Núñez Cabeza de Vaca, Madrid, March 27, 1528, in AGI Indiferente 421, L. 13, 1, 520.

CHAPTER 3

1. Quote from Cabeza de Vaca, *Relación of 1542*, 31. The second quote is from Alonso de Chaves, *Espejo de Navegantes*, reproduced in Mena García, *Sevilla y las flotas de Indias*, 182.

2. I want to express my gratitude to Kevin Boothby, my only friend who has actually circumnavigated the world powered only by the wind and without a GPS for the most part. He graciously read this chapter and gave thoughtful suggestions about navigational matters. On pilots' salaries, see Pérez-Mallaína, *Spain's Men of the Sea*, 122.

3. Narváez could only dream about recruiting Antón de Alaminos, the pilot who had almost single-handedly unlocked the secrets of sailing the Gulf of Mexico coast. Alaminos had guided Ponce de León's expedition of the discovery of Florida of 1513. He had also served as chief pilot in *all three* expeditions sponsored by Diego Velázquez that ended up discovering Yucatán and the coast of Mexico in the late 1510s. No other navigator could match Alaminos's comprehensive knowledge of that entire coast from Yucatán to Florida. But, alas, he was not available. To be sure, there were other pilots familiar with portions of the Gulf shore. On Alaminos's career, see Weddle, *Spanish Sea*, 40–41, 56, 96–97; and Adorno and Pautz, *Álvar Núñez Cabeza de Vaca*, III, 214–221, 237–239, 245–246. Donald E. Chipman notes that Spain lacked a centralized (or at least a systematic) way of storing and disseminating geographic information of the New World. For instance, the Pineda map of 1519 established the peninsularity of Florida. Yet, the House of Trade did not seem to know that information through the 1520s. A similar situation existed with regard to the peninsularity of Baja California. Donald E. Chipman, personal communication.

4. Quote from Cabeza de Vaca, *Relación of 1542*, 30–32. It is possible that Miruelo had piloted a ship that Ponce de León encountered while returning from Florida in 1513. A certain "Diego Fernández de Mirnedo" is also listed as the chief pilot of the 1523 expedition that actually discovered the Rio de las Palmas and may have been this same individual. Early writers, including El Inca Garcilaso and Andrés González de Barcia, clouded the identity of Diego Miruelo by making unwarranted assumptions and outright mistakes and inventions. See discussion in Adorno and Pautz, *Álvar Núñez Cabeza de Vaca*, II, 62–69.

5. For the slaving activities in the Bahamas, Florida, and farther north, see Paul A. Hoffman, "A New Voyage of North American Discovery: Pedro de Salazar's Visit to the 'Island of Giants,'" *Florida Historical Quarterly* 58:4 (April 1980), 415–426; and *A New Andalusia and a Way to the Orient: The American Southwest during the Sixteenth Century* (Baton Rouge: Louisiana State University Press, 1990), especially part one.

6. A series of calamities prevented Ponce de León from launching another expedition to Florida until eight years later. And as fate would have it, he died in the second attempt. Oviedo writes about Ponce de León and the "fountain of youth" as follows: "Juan Ponce went with two caravels to discover the islands of Bimini on the northern quadrant, and then the fable spread about the fountain that turned old men into young ones." Oviedo, *Historia general y natural de las Indias*, II, 103. However, there is no direct evidence indicating that Ponce de León *himself* thought that he was looking for the "fountain of youth." See Douglas T. Peck, "Anatomy of an Historical Fantasy: The Ponce de León-Fountain of Youth Legend," *Revista de Historia de América* 123 (1998). For a detailed account of Ponce de León's exploits and the myths surrounding the exploration of the New World, see Juan Gil, *Mitos y utopías del descubrimiento* (Madrid: Editorial Alianza, 1989), I, 24–56, 251–269. For Ponce de León's voyage, see also Weddle, *Spanish Sea*, 38–42; and Douglas T. Peck, "Reconstruction and Analysis

of the 1513 Discovery Voyage of Juan Ponce de León," *Florida Historical Quarterly* 71:2 (1992), 133–154.

7. On the identity of the Rio de las Palmas, see Donald E. Chipman, "Alonso Alvarez de Pineda and the Rio de las Palmas: Scholars and the Mislocation of a River," *Southwestern Historical Quarterly* 98:3 (January 1995), 368–385; and Donald E. Chipman, *Nuño de Guzmán and the Province of Pánuco in New Spain, 1518–1533* (Glendale, CA: Arthur H. Clark Company, 1967), passim. For explicit testimonies about slaving in Santiesteban del Puerto, see "Información que hizo la villa de Santiesteban del Puerto sobre la conveniencia de enviar esclavos a las islas para cambiarlos por caballos, yeguas y otros ganados, Santiesteban del Puerto," October 9, 1529, in *Espistolario de Nueva España*, I, 153–166. See also Weddle, *Spanish Sea*, chapter 6; and Adorno and Pautz, *Álvar Núñez Cabeza de Vaca*, III, 278–281.

8. Quote from Cortés comes from his letter to Charles V, Coyoacán, May 15, 1522, in Martínez, *Documentos Cortesianos*, I, 231. The geographic report is included in the Carta de Don Luis de Cárdenas sobre la división geográfica de la Nueva España, Seville, August 30, 1527, in CDI, 40, 273–287. The Rio de las Palmas marked the southern boundary of Narváez's *adelantamiento*. Its northern limit is not so easily established. Hoffman observes that Florida was known to extend north to only about 28°30' on the basis of testimony provided by Pedro de Quejo. Hoffman, "A New Voyage of North American Discovery: Pedro de Salazar's Visit to the 'Island' of Giants,'" 421. However, one must note that Quejo's interest lay in pushing Florida's northern limit as far south as possible; he was hardly an impartial observer. It seems more reasonable to assume that Florida extended at the very least as far north as Ponce de León's first landing site, which is given at 30°08' in the voyage account (Weddle, *Spanish Sea*, 42) and more properly to a latitude that would include the entire peninsula, that is, 31°, which is what I use in my calculations.

9. Cortés to Emperor Charles V, Coyoacán, May 15, 1522, in Martínez, *Documentos Cortesianos*, I, 231.

10. On Vázquez de Ayllón's background, including the quote, see Hoffman, *A New Andalusia and a Way to the Orient*, chapter 2; and "A New Voyage of North American Discovery," 417. For Vázquez de Ayllón's sugar plantations and mill in Puerto Plata, see Oviedo, *Historia general y natural de las Indias*, I, 110.

11. Hoffman, *A New Andalucia and a Way to the Orient*, 8, 44; and "A New Voyage of North American Discovery," 415–426, and especially chapter 3.

12. José Epigmenio Santana, a twentieth-century historian, listed among Guzmán's chief characteristics "cruelty of the highest order, ambition without limit, a refined hypocrisy, great immorality, ingratitude without equal, and a fierce hatred for Cortés." The quote appears in Chipman, *Nuño de Guzmán and Pánuco*, 142.

13. On Guzmán's genealogy and early career, see Chipman, *Nuño de Guzmán and Pánuco*, chapter 4. On Guzmán's royal appointment, departure from Spain, and exploration of the Rio de las Palmas, see Chipman, *Nuño de Guzmán and Pánuco*, 131, 137, 157–164.

14. Quote from Cabeza de Vaca, *Relación of 1542*, 33.

15. Cabeza de Vaca, *Relación of 1542*, 33.

16. In his first voyage, Columbus did try to take three latitude sights on Polaris, which were all hopelessly off. In his second and third voyages, he used the quadrant on

five different occasions with mixed results. Celestial navigation was clearly not the basis of Columbus's remarkably accurate sailing. For a colorful discussion by someone who is both a sailor and a historian, see Douglas T. Peck, *Cristoforo Colombo: God's Navigator* (Columbus, WI: Columbian Publishers, 1993), 27–30.

17. Italian and Catalan chartmakers were the first to introduce portolan charts in the 1200s, perfecting them in the course of the following three centuries and turning them into one of the most significant navigational developments of that era. For an overview of the evolution of portolan charts, see Edward Luther Stevenson, *Portolan Charts: Their Origin and Characteristics with a Descriptive List of Those Belonging to the Hispanic Society of America* (New York: Knickerbocker Press, 1911), passim.

18. On the literacy of pilots, see Pérez-Mallaína, *Spain's Men of the Sea*, 231.

19. The latitude, that is the distance traveled north or south from the Equator, was the only measurement that pilots could obtain at sea in the sixteenth century. Measuring longitude, that is, the distance traveled east or west from a fixed meridian, was beyond the abilities of any sailor until the eighteenth century. As it turns out, in the case of Miruelo's specific problem of finding the Rio de las Palmas, determining his longitude would have been more crucial. In the early 1500s, virtually no pilots were able to find latitude at sea; by the 1540s many could. The 1520s constitute a transitional decade. But even well after the 1520s, navigating by the sun and the stars was not especially central to pilots' practice. On the abilities of pilots in the sixteenth century, see Alison Sandman, "Cosmographers vs. Pilots: Navigation, Cosmography, and the State in Early Modern Spain," Ph. D. diss., University of Wisconsin, Madison, 2001, especially chapter 2. See also Pérez-Mallaína, *Spain's Men of the Sea*, 84–87.

20. There were portolan charts of the Gulf of Mexico at least since 1519. See Richard Uhden, "An Unpublished Portolan Chart of the New World, A.D. 1519," *Geographical Journal* 91:1 (January 1938), 44–50. Miruelo probably did not aim *exactly* at the Rio de las Palmas. The uncertainties of sixteenth-century navigation were such that he would not have been able to tell whether he had missed the mark to the south or to the north. Instead of steering directly to his objective, Miruelo had to point his compass toward one side or the other; that way he would know how to correct. This traditional navigational technique, called "aiming off," is employed even today to find rivers, paths, and other linear features. Miruelo could have chosen to overshoot to the right and correct to the left. That is, he could have aimed for the northwest at 10:00 or 11:00 o'clock—well to the right of the Rio de las Palmas—and then turned the ships to the left at the sight of the coast. That may well have been Miruelo's plan. In his narrative Cabeza de Vaca clearly tells us that from Havana, the expedition crossed "by the way of the Florida coast," meaning that it approached the Rio de las Palmas by the Florida side.

21. My calculation assumes that the flow rate of the Mississippi River is 593,286 cubic feet per second. For the general characteristics of the Gulf Stream, see Joanna Gyory, Arthur J. Mariano, and Edward H. Ryan, "The Gulf Stream," Ocean Surface Currents. http://oceancurrents.rsmas.miami.edu/atlantic/gulf-stream.html. I am indebted to Susan E. Welsh at Louisiana State University who graciously pointed me to some useful sources of information on the Gulf Stream, and to Kevin Boothby for providing additional data from a sailor's perspective.

22. Quote from Weddle, *Spanish Sea*, 42, 292.

23. With regard to the expedition's passage from Havana to the Gulf of Mexico coast, Cabeza de Vaca's text is somewhat opaque, giving rise to different interpretations. Adorno and Pautz state that upon making landfall, the pilots "evidently believed that the expedition had reached the coast on the Rio Pánuco [i.e., south] side of the mouth of the Rio de las Palmas." These authors go on to explain that after "a few days" of travel, "they evidently changed their opinion about where they had landed, deciding that they had come to shore on the *Florida* (i.e., northern) side of the mouth of the Rio de las Palmas rather than on the Rio Pánuco." Adorno and Pautz, *Álvar Núñez Cabeza de Vaca*, II, 75–76. Unfortunately, there is nothing *evident* about these assertions. Adorno and Pautz reach this conclusion by interpreting the ambiguous phrase "la vía de la Florida" as "the way of Florida," meaning *in the direction* of Florida. To be sure, they are to some extent correct. There are instances in which "la vía" does refer to direction, as in "y que los navíos con la otra gente se irían la misma vía hasta llegar al mismo puerto." Indeed, one of the cornerstones of this interpretation is Oviedo's *seemingly* straightforward phrase: "otro día adelante envió el gobernador un bergantín que llevaban, para que fuesse costeando la vía de la Florida é buscasse un puerto quel piloto Miruelo decía que sabía . . . É mandóle que assi buscando atravesase á la isla de Cuba. . . ." This sentence *appears* to indicate that the brigantine was to sail to the south, looking for the port, and ultimately all the way to Cuba. However, I propose an alternative interpretation, based on a careful reappraisal of the meaning of these key sentences, as well as on the facts of the expedition. As far as semantics are concerned, I want to start out by noting that Cabeza de Vaca provides the most important clue of the expedition's understanding of place one line earlier, when he tells us quite candidly and unambiguously that from Havana, the expedition crossed "by way of the Florida coast" ("atravessamos por la costa de la Florida"), obviously implying that the expedition members were well aware from the very beginning that they were on the *Florida side* of the Rio de las Palmas. If we take this statement at face value—and there's no reason not to—then Cabeza de Vaca's next line, "y fuimos costeando la vía de la Florida," cannot mean direction but rather that they continued to sail on the Florida "side" or "coast" but in the direction of the Rio de las Palmas. A close examination of the usage of "la vía" throughout Cabeza de Vaca's narrative will reveal that at times it refers to "side" or "coast" and *not* direction. For instance, the passage "pues los pilotos dezían que no estaría sino diez o quinze leguas de allí la vía de Pánuco" can only mean that the Pánuco "coast" was near. Bearing in mind that "la vía" can also mean "side" or "coast" in certain contexts, we can reexamine Oviedo's cornerstone phrase and acknowledge its ambiguity, as it is open to two different interpretations: one in which the brigantine was to go to the south, seeking the port, and then continue on to Cuba, or, alternatively, that the brigantine was to sail to the north and then head for Cuba. This ambiguity is even more obvious when we consider the equivalent of Oviedo's phrase in Cabeza de Vaca: "el gobernador mandó que el vergantín fuesse costeando la vía de la Florida y buscasse el puerto . . . y fuéle mandado al vergantín que si no lo hallasse, travessasse a la Havana." In this phrase there is no implicit continuity of direction at all. One could understand perfectly that the brigantine was to sail to the north and *then* would head to Cuba. I'm afraid that semantics alone cannot settle this question. We must therefore turn to the facts of the expedition for additional meaning. We know that the expedition

first saw land on a Tuesday, that it coasted until Thursday, and that on Friday it took possession of the land. First of all, the ceremony of land possession indicates to us—beyond any doubt—that by Friday the expedition members were convinced that they were on the Florida side of the Rio de las Palmas, that is, somewhere within Narváez's *adelantamiento* (otherwise, they would have been taking possession of Pánuco!). Narváez's royal charter of conquest was quite explicit. He was to found two settlements *within* his *adelantamiento*. There is simply no possibility that Narváez would have raised the banners and gone through the sacred ceremony of land possession and founded a town, had he not been completely persuaded that the expedition was within his *adelantamiento*, that is, on the Florida side. If the expedition members already knew that they were on the Florida side by Friday, then it follows that the brigantine that was dispatched a couple of days later had to sail to the *north* (in the direction of the Rio de las Palmas, which was their objective) rather than to the south (back to Cuba), as Adorno and Pautz and others would have us believe. Having settled this point, the question remains as to whether between Tuesday and Thursday the fleet zigzagged, looking for the Rio de las Palmas. I believe that this is highly unlikely; it makes no sense from a navigational point of view. Since the coastline was completely unfamiliar to the pilots, they would have had no grounds whatsoever to turn the ships 180 degrees after only one or two days of coastal sailing just because they hadn't found the Rio de las Palmas. *The only way* they could have known on which side of the Rio de las Palmas they were is if they had "aimed off" from the very beginning. There is no reason to doubt Cabeza de Vaca when he tells us that the expedition crossed "by way of the Florida coast." In fact, the expedition members were so certain that they were on the Florida side that they would subsequently travel for more than 1,200 miles in the right direction, always convinced that Pánuco lay ahead—as it did.

24. Cabeza de Vaca, *Relación of 1542*, 40. This conversion results by assuming that 1 Spanish league equals a little over 3 miles or 4.8 kilometers. For a discussion of the approximate length of a league in Cabeza de Vaca's account, see Alex D. Krieger, *We Came Naked and Barefoot: The Journey of Cabeza de Vaca Across North America* (Austin: University of Texas Press, 2002), 42–44.

25. Cabeza de Vaca, *Relación of 1542*, 35.

26. Quote from Cabeza de Vaca, *Relación of 1542*, 35. Additionally, see pp. 32–34; and *Joint Report*, 91–92. Once again, there is considerable debate about the landing site of Narváez's party. For a lengthy discussion of the different alternatives, see Adorno and Pautz, *Álvar Núñez Cabeza de Vaca*, 77–83. In the absence of evidence, all we can do is speculate. I join the camp of those who propose Sarasota Bay as the point of debarkation and Tampa Bay proper (not Old Tampa Bay) as "the bay that seemed to go far inland." Certain passages in Cabeza de Vaca's *Narrative* support this interpretation. Cabeza de Vaca specifically writes: "We followed to the north until, at the hour of vespers, we arrived at a very large bay that seemed to us to go far inland." This description fits admirably well the impression one would gain by walking from Sarasota Bay to Tampa Bay, as one would be forced inland by the contours of this enormous bay. Had the expedition landed on Pinellas Peninsula, they would have been able to march directly to the north unimpeded and may even have missed Tampa Bay and Old Tampa Bay altogether. To be sure, Oviedo does mention that the party traveled to the "northeast" rather than to the "north"; but he may have been referring to

the actual direction that the party followed—as they were forced inland by the contours of Tampa Bay—rather than their intended course, which must have been along the coast. Toward the end of his narrative, Cabeza de Vaca provides the most convincing clue that what he is describing is Tampa Bay, and not the smaller Old Tampa Bay, when he writes that the ships in the end "found the port that entered seven or eight leagues inland, and it was the same one that we had discovered." Such a length could only refer to Tampa Bay proper. Old Tampa Bay measures only half as much. There is one additional consideration. If the ships veered to the left upon reaching the coast and never changed direction—as explained before—then they would have first sailed across the mouth of the enormous Tampa Bay during the coastal passage before landing at Pinellas Peninsula. Yet both first-hand accounts make it clear that the "large bay" was discovered by overland parties rather than during the coastal passage, thus suggesting that the fleet stopped before reaching the mouth of Tampa Bay. In short, there is no scholarly agreement about the location of the point of debarkation at present. For another work in support of Tampa Bay as "the bay that seemed to go far inland," see Weddle, *The Spanish Sea*, 188–189. For works supporting Pinellas Peninsula as the first landing site, see Adorno and Pautz, *Álvar Núñez Cabeza de Vaca*, 77–83; Jerald T. Milanich, *Florida Indians and the Invasion from Europe* (Gainesville: University Press of Florida, 1995), 115–125; and Jerald T. Milanich and Charles Hudson, *Hernando de Soto and the Indians of Florida* (Gainesville: University Press of Florida, 1993), 23. I thank Jerald T. Milanich for taking the time to elaborate on his views about Narváez's first landing site. We both agree that although the exact landing site cannot be determined with certainty, it is important to speculate on the basis of what we currently know. Perhaps archaeological evidence will one day solve this riddle. For an overview of the archeological evidence with respect of Spain's early presence on the west coast of Florida, see Jeffrey M. Mitchem, "Initial Spanish-Indian Contact in West Peninsular Florida: The Archaeological Evidence," in *Columbian Consequences: Archaeological and Historical Perspectives on the Spanish Borderlands East*, edited by David Hurst Thomas (Washington DC: Smithsonian Institution Press, 1990), II, 49–59. See also the fine essay by Sylvia L. Hilton, "Los indios de Tocobaga y Timucua (Florida occidental) ante sus primeros contactos con los hombres blancos," in *Congreso de historia del descubrimiento, actas* (Madrid: Real Academia de la Historia), I, 343–403.

27. The map elaborated by Alonzo Álvarez de Pineda after surveying the entire Gulf Coast in 1519 does show Tampa Bay, but obviously quite far from the Rio de las Palmas.

28. Quote from Cabeza de Vaca, *Relación of 1542*, 39. James Axtell was among the first to note the deferential treatment that these Indians had accorded to the dead Europeans. Axtell, *The Indian's New South: Cultural Change in the Colonial Southeast* (Baton Rouge: Louisiana State University Press, 1997), 12.

29. Quote from Cabeza de Vaca, *Relación of 1542*, 39. See also pp. 36–38.

30. On Narváez's strategy during the occupation of Cuba, see Hortensia Pichardo Viñals, *La fundación de las primeras villas de la isla de Cuba* (Havana: Editorial de Ciencias Sociales, 1986), 14.

31. For Fray Suárez's quote and a description of the acquiescence of the others, see Cabeza de Vaca, *Relación of 1542*, 40–43.

32. Cabeza de Vaca, *Relación of 1542*, 41.

33. The notary's minutes were lost, and the other men involved in the meeting all perished and left no records. See Adorno and Pautz, *Álvar Núñez Cabeza de Vaca*, II, 92–95.

34. Quotes from Cabeza de Vaca, *Relación of 1542*, 43 and 45, respectively.

35. Quote from Cabeza de Vaca, *Relación of 1542*, 273.

36. Cabeza de Vaca, *Relación of 1542*, 273, 275.

CHAPTER 4

1. Quote from Cabeza de Vaca, *Relación of 1542*, 47.

2. Sources vary with respect to the amount of food received by each expedition member. The *Joint Report* indicates that each man received 1 pound of hardtack and half a pound of pork. The *Joint Report*, 95. Quote from Cabeza de Vaca, *Relación of 1542*, 56. Even today, the Florida peninsula ranks second within the continental United States, only after California, in richness of native plants. Florida constitutes a bridge between the tropical Caribbean and the U.S. mainland. The state's floral diversity arises from its tropical vegetation in the south gradually giving way to a more temperate one toward the north. I want to acknowledge the gracious help that I received from my biologist friend Diego Pérez Salicrup.

3. The sabal, or cabbage palm is so named because at the top of its trunk, it has a large leaf bud that becomes edible when cooked. For the reference to the palms of Andalusia, see Cabeza de Vaca, *Relación of 1542*, 47.

4. As usual, scholars have argued over the identity of this river. Although the overland party surely crossed several rivers while walking the length of Florida from Tampa Bay to Apalachee, Cabeza de Vaca mentions only two. These two rivers were singled out precisely because of their size, depth, and difficulty in crossing. These facts are especially important if we consider that the trekkers were looking for the Rio de las Palmas, which was known to be a large, navigable river. Simply by matching the explorers' expectations with the geography of Florida, we find that the two largest rivers between Tampa Bay and Apalachee were the Withlacoochee and the Suwannee. A consideration of the chronology of the expedition's progress will also reveal that these two rivers are the most likely candidates in terms of the distance conceivably traveled. Once again, although it is not possible to rule out completely other alternatives, these are the most reasonable, given what we know today. For a levelheaded discussion, see Adorno and Pautz, *Álvar Núñez Cabeza de Vaca*, II, 111–113. Quote from Cabeza de Vaca, *Relación of 1542*, 47.

5. Quote from Cabeza de Vaca, *Relación of 1542*, 47.

6. See Oviedo, *Joint Report*, 95; and Cabeza de Vaca, *Relación of 1542*, 47.

7. Quote from Cabeza de Vaca, *Relación of 1542*, 46.

8. Cabeza de Vaca, *Relación of 1542*, 48.

9. Cabeza de Vaca, *Relación of 1542*, 51.

10. Cabeza de Vaca writes that Velázquez's death "gave us much grief because up to that point none of us had perished." Cabeza de Vaca, *Relación of 1542*, 50–51. As Adorno and Pautz note, it was a curious statement, given that a number of other men, including sixty during the hurricane in Cuba, had already perished.

11. Quote from Cabeza de Vaca, *Relación of 1542*, 55.

12. Archaeologists have defined a type of material and cultural expression that they call the Safety Harbor culture. It emerged after around A.D. 900 and extends into the colonial period. Geographically, the Safety Harbor archaeological culture is distributed along the Gulf Coast and adjacent inland areas from Charlotte Harbor in the south to as far north as the Withlacoochee River in Citrus County. See Jerald T. Milanich, *Archaeology of Precolumbian Florida* (Gainesville: University Press of Florida, 1994), especially 389–412.

13. The Apalachee Chiefdom began around A.D. 1100 and flourished during the Fort Walton period. It developed out of an earlier regional culture known as the Weeden Island Wakulla. Archaeologists have identified two phases within the Fort Walton period, chiefly on the basis of changing pottery styles: the Lake Jackson phases (A.D. 1100–1500) and the Velda phase (A.D. 1500–1633). Milanich, *Archaeology of Precolumbian Florida*, 355–387.

14. In addition to Milanich, see John F. Scarry, "The Apalachee Chiefdom" and John H. Hann, "The Apalachee of the Historic Era," both in *The Forgotten Centuries: Indians and Europeans in the American South, 1521–1704*, edited by Charles Hudson and Carmen Chaves Tesser (Athens: University of Georgia Press, 1994), 156–178 and 327–354, respectively. Once the center of Apalachee and the place where the Hernando de Soto expedition spent the winter of 1539–1540, Anhaica faded into oblivion in more recent times. Only in the 1980s did serendipity permit its rediscovery. For this remarkable tale, see Charles R. Ewen and John H. Hann, *Hernando de Soto among the Apalachee: The Archaeology of the First Winter Encampment* (Gainesville: University Press of Florida, 1998).

15. See Timothy R. Pauketat and Thomas E. Emerson, *Cahokia: Domination and Ideology in the Mississippian World* (Lincoln: University of Nebraska Press, 1997), 269–278. A scholarly debate revolves around whether European contact—in the form of direct violence or epidemics—resulted in the disappearance of many indigenous societies or if it was simply one factor among many. See especially Henry F. Dobyns, *Their Number Became Thinned: Native American Population Dynamics in Eastern North America* (Knoxville: University of Tennessee Press, 1983); and Ann F. Ramenofsky, *Vectors of Death: The Archaeology of European Contact* (Albuquerque: University of New Mexico Press, 1987). More recent studies have shown that even though the arrival of Europeans always brought about depopulation of native peoples, the scope and timing of such demographic declines varied from one region to the next. Apalachee, for instance, appears to have fared rather well despite the Spanish *entradas* of the first half of the sixteenth century. See John H. Hann, "The Apalachee of the Historic Era," 330. It is only fitting that the first publication ever issued by the Smithsonian Institution was a study of the "mound builders." It was originally published in 1847 during the U.S. war with Mexico. Its very title captures the excitement and romanticism associated with the early study of these cultures. Ephraim G. Squier and Edwin H. Davis, *Ancient Monuments of the Mississippi Valley*, edited and with an introduction by David J. Meltzer (Washington: Smithsonian Institution Press, 1998), passim. For recent studies of the *Mississippian tradition*, see Timothy R. Pauketat and Thomas E. Emerson, eds., *Cahokia: Domination and Ideology in the Mississippian World* (Lincoln: University of Nebraska Press, 1997); and Frank F. Schambach, *Pre-Caddoan*

Cultures in the Trans-Mississippi South (Fayetteville: Arkansas Archeological Survey, 1998). Pauketat rightly warns about the racism implicit in the "Moundbuilder Myth" and the perils of making invidious distinctions between "chiefdoms" and "kingdoms" and "empires." Pauketat, *Ancient Cahokia and the Mississippians* (New York: Cambridge University Press, 2004), 3.

16. Like other Mississippian centers, Apalachee was already undergoing considerable turmoil even before the arrival of the Narváez expedition. Around 1500, Apalachee's longtime political center, a major site graced by mounds called Lake Jackson, was abandoned and replaced by Anhaica. The latter site never attained the magnificence of the former, as mound building was generally discontinued.

17. See Jerald T. Milanich and Charles Hudson, *Hernando de Soto and the Indians of Florida* (Gainesville: University Press of Florida, 1993), 227–228; and Hoffman, "Narváez and Cabeza de Vaca in Florida," 37. For a more skeptical interpretation see Adorno and Pautz, *Álvar Núñez Cabeza de Vaca*, II, 119–127. Two main reasons support the notion that the settlement reached by Narváez was not Anhaica. First, there is the question of size. Both Cabeza de Vaca's *Relación* and the *Joint Report* categorically state that the town of "Apalachee" was modest and contained 40 houses. Anhaica was almost certainly much larger and imposing. El Inca Garcilaso de la Vega, an author of the second half of the sixteenth century who wrote an account of a subsequent expedition to Apalachee conducted by Hernando de Soto eleven years after Narváez's expedition, directly states that Anhaica consisted of 250 houses and comments in passing that Narváez's "Apalachee" must have been a different, much smaller community. That seems reasonable, although we must take Garcilaso's assertions with a grain of salt, as he based his account on the documentation available to him, as well as on interviews of some of the survivors of de Soto's expedition, but not on direct observation. Some scholars have deemed Garcilaso's account unreliable and have pointed to instances in which his account is clearly in error. Yet, as far as the population of Anhaica is concerned, Garcilaso's statement jibes well with other historical sources. The Gentleman of Elvas wrote that the province was "heavily settled." Early seventeenth-century sources estimate Apalachee's total population at between 30,000 and 34,000. Anhaica had to possess more than forty houses. For population estimates of Apalachee, see Hann, "The Apalachee of the Historic Era," 329–330. The second reason has to do with location. Narváez's "Apalachee" was the first settlement reached by the expedition. We know, however, that Anhaica was located on the western side of the province, and since Narváez's men were approaching from the eastern side, they would have needed to pass through other settlements in this "densely populated" province before running into Anhaica. Hernando de Soto's expedition, for instance, stumbled on various settlements as it traversed the province including the town of Vitachuco [or Ivitachuco], which served as a main center of the eastern half of Apalachee. See Lawrence A. Clayton, Vernon James Knight, Jr., and Edward C. Moore, eds., *The de Soto Chronicles: The Expedition of Hernando de Soto to North America in 1539–1543*, I, 70–71. The identification of Narváez's "Apalachee" with Ivitachuco harkens back to John R. Swanton in the late 1930s; an identification that contemporary archaeologists have not contradicted. See Rochelle A. Marrinan, John F. Scarry, and Rhonda L. Majors, "Prelude to de Soto: The Expedition of Pánfilo de Narváez," in *Columbian Consequences*, edited by David Hurst Thomas (Washington DC: Smith-

NOTES

sonian Institution Press, 1990), II, 74. See also arguments advanced by Hoffman, "Narváez and Cabeza de Vaca in Florida," 60–61. Such arguments do not constitute absolute proof, but they do point to the more likely scenario.

18. Cabeza de Vaca, *Relación of 1542*, 55.
19. Cabeza de Vaca, *Relación of 1542*, 58–60.
20. Cabeza de Vaca, *Relación of 1542*, 58; *Joint Report*, 97. I am grateful to Nancy White for pointing out to me that the cloth mantles found by the Florida expedition were not made out of cotton, as I originally had it. Cotton existed in Mexico and the Southwest—and of course became crucial to the Southeast's economy in colonial times—but for some reason there are no precontact samples of cotton in the Southeast.
21. Cabeza de Vaca, *Relación of 1542*, 59.
22. See Gentleman of Elvas, *True Relations of the Hardships Suffered by Governor Don Hernando de Soto . . .* in *The De Soto Chronicles*, 69–74. See also Hoffman, "Narváez and Cabeza de Vaca in Florida," 60–61. To be sure, it seems that Apalachee weathered the epidemics much better than other indigenous groups. See Hann, "The Apalachee of the Historic Era," 330.
23. Scarry, "The Apalachee Chiefdom," 158.
24. Quote from Cabeza de Vaca, *Relación of 1542*, 61. See Mitchem, "Artifacts of Exploration: Archaeological Evidence from Florida," 103. James Axtell asserts that Narváez's expedition "was constantly misled by native guides away from the populous, well-fed Apalachee towns of the Panhandle until they despaired and retreated to the sea." James Axtell, *The Indians' New South: Cultural Change in the Colonial Southeast* (Baton Rouge: Louisiana State University Press, 1997), 9. Milanich and Hudson are of the same opinion, adding that eleven years later the de Soto expedition was subjected to the same treatment: "a guide tricked them and continually got them lost, leading them on a wild goose chase through the estuarine and coastal marches." *Hernando de Soto and the Indians of Florida*, 220.
25. Both quotes from Cabeza de Vaca, *Relación of 1542*, 63.
26. Adorno and Pautz, *Álvar Núñez Cabeza de Vaca*, II, 135. Henry F. Dobyns first ventured the identification of the illness as typhoid or typhus. *Their Number Became Thinned*, 261; and Marrinan, Scarry, and Majors, "Prelude to de Soto: The Expedition of Pánfilo de Narváez," II, 75.
27. Cabeza de Vaca, *Relación of 1542*, 66. My translation.
28. Although some clues point to the general location of this camp, its precise whereabouts continues to elude scholars. Any attempt to narrow the search needs to take into account four important statements made in the historical sources: (1) from "Apalachee" it would take the Narváez expedition ten days to reach the coast (nine days to Aute plus one more day); (2) Aute was a large indigenous settlement one day away from the coast; (3) the open sea could not be seen from the place where Narváez and his men set up camp; and (4) it would later take the Spaniards seven days of travel on makeshift rafts on waist-deep water before they were able to reach an island located very close to the mainland, beyond which was the open sea. This last-mentioned detail is strongly reminiscent of present-day Indian Pass, formed between the continent and St. Vincent Island at the western end of Apalachicola Bay. No other part of the Florida panhandle fits this description so well (to be sure, these barrier islands are very

dynamic, and it is conceivable that their contours may have been different 500 years ago). In any event, today anyone looking out from a beach anywhere between the present-day town of Carrabelle and the western edge of the Apalachicola Bay will gain a distinctive impression of a shallow bay separated from the sea by barrier islands. It is still possible that Narváez and his men may have emerged farther east. See Hoffman, "Narváez and Cabeza de Vaca in Florida," 62–63; and especially Adorno and Pautz, *Álvar Núñez Cabeza de Vaca*, II, 144–145. Jeffrey M. Mitchem argues that the village of Aute was probably located in what is now the Work Place site within the present-day St. Marks National Wildlife Refuge and makes the case that the expeditioners emerged at the mouth of the St. Marks River. Mitchem makes these identifications on the basis of archaeological evidence, particularly the discovery of Clarksdale bells found in the St. Marks Wildlife Refuge Cemetery site, which are characteristic of early sixteenth-century European artifacts and thus could only have come from either the Narváez or the de Soto expeditions. Jeffrey M. Mitchem, "Artifacts of Exploration: Archaeological Evidence from Florida," in *First Encounters*, 99–109. See also Marrinan, Scarry, and Majors, "Prelude to de Soto: The Expedition of Pánfilo de Narváez," II, 76–77. Still, it is difficult to tell whether these artifacts belonged to the Narváez or the de Soto expeditions. Moreover, contrary to Cabeza de Vaca's description, the open sea would have been visible to the expeditioners from the mouth of the St. Marks River. Jerald T. Milanich and Nancy Marie White went over this and other chapters and graciously took the time to discuss the possible identity of Aute. Both these archaeologists were skeptical of the idea that Aute may have been a major ceremonial center from the Fort Walton period, located in the lower delta of the Apalachicola River and known today as the Pierce Mounds. On this topic see also Nancy Marie White, "Protohistoric and Historic Native Cultures of the Apalachicola Valley, Northwest Florida," paper presented at the annual meeting of the Southeastern Archaeological Conference, October 2004, St. Louis.

29. Cabeza de Vaca, *Relación of 1542*, 69.

30. I have generally followed the version of these events provided by the Gentleman of Elvas in Clayton, Knight, and Moore, eds., *The de Soto Chronicles*, I, 59–60. Yet, I could not resist adding some additional elements from the more detailed rendition given in El Inca Garcilaso de la Vega, *La Florida* (Madrid: Alianza Editorial, 1988), 146–154. However, this account must be taken with a grain of salt, as it has been found to be unreliable in some instances. Yet, given that Garcilaso interviewed some members of the de Soto expedition, it is quite possible that many of the details in his account are true.

31. Garcilaso, *La Florida*, 149. In many ways Ortiz's ordeal prefigures what other members of the Narváez expedition would later experience. On the powerful feelings generated by captivity and return to "civilization," see John Demos, *The Unredeemed Captive: A Family Story from Early America* (New York: Vintage Books, 1994).

32. Deposition of Manuel Hojas, San Salvador, April 29, 1530, in *Información hecha en la Isla de Cuba a pedimento de María de Valenzuela, la muger de Pánfilo de Narváez, contra Hernando de Ceballos sobre dos bergantines, e bastimentos y municiones*, Cuba, 1530, in reel 1, the Stetson Collection, Bancroft Library.

33. Ceballos held a power of attorney that Narváez had left with him before departing for the New World. See *Poder que otorgó Pánfilo de Narváez, gobernador de*

la Florida, Rio de Las Palmas y Espíritu Santo, en Sevilla, A su criado Hernando Caballos, para pedir, demandar y cobrar lo que le corresponda, y sustitución del mismo, Seville, March 8, 1528, in CDI, XII 86–91.

34. María de Valenzuela's rescue efforts and her litigation against Hernando de Ceballos can be found in the *Información hecha en la Isla de Cuba a pedimento de María de Valenzuela, la muger de Pánfilo de Narváez, contra Hernando de Ceballos sobre dos bergantines, e bastimentos y municiones,* Cuba, 1530, in reel 1, the Stetson Collection, Bancroft Library. This is a microfilmed edition of Justicia 972, 51–2/12 at the AGI. See also Hernando de Ceballos to the King of Spain, Cuba, March 16, 1531, Indiferente General 1203, No. 28, folios 1–11 at the AGI. Although they did not consult these sources, Adorno and Pautz scrupulously cite them, greatly facilitating the elucidation of this episode. Adorno and Pautz, *Álvar Núñez Cabeza de Vaca,* II, 100–104.

CHAPTER 5

1. These descriptions were provided by Antonio Fernandez de Biedma and Juan de Añasco, respectively, both in Clayton, Knight, and Moore, eds., *The de Soto Chronicles,* I, 72 and note 90.

2. Quotes from Cabeza de Vaca, *Relación of 1542,* 68.

3. For a brief but enlightening discussion of Spain's military edge, see Lockhart and Schwartz, *Early Latin America,* 80–83.

4. Adorno and Pautz, *Álvar Núñez Cabeza de Vaca,* II, 135.

5. For millennia the Indians of Ecuador and Peru have used an extremely light type of wood known as *balsa* to fashion their rafts. Balsa is the Spanish word for raft. This material is so light, sturdy, and seaworthy that in 1947 the colorful Norwegian anthropologist/adventurer, Thor Heyerdahl, crossed the Pacific Ocean on a raft made out of balsa logs to prove that South American Indians had colonized Polynesia (a theory that has been proven wrong more recently).

6. By Archimedes's principle, we know that an object will float at such a depth that its submerged part displaces a volume of water equal to the object's weight. I performed the calculations in the decimal system. The volume of the wood employed (X), times the density of the wood (380 kilograms per cubic meter), plus 5 metric tons (5,000 kilograms) must have been equal to the volume of water displaced (Y) times the density of the ocean water (let's assume that it was 1,027 kilograms per cubic meter). At the same time we know that 18 centimeters of wood remained above the waterline. From that, it must follow that the total volume of wood (X), minus the volume of water displaced (Y), divided by the surface of the raft (in this case 10 meters by 10 meters) must have equaled 0.18 meters. By solving these two simultaneous equations, it turns out that the total volume of wood employed must have been 36.29 cubic meters and that the volume of water displaced must have been 18.29 cubic meters. By multiplying the volume of wood with its density, we arrive at a figure of 13.79 metric tons. Converting from metric to U.S. tons, we arrive at a total weight of 15.15 US tons.

7. Indeed, in the Florida panhandle there is a type of pine called slash or pitch pine (Pinus elliottii) from which resin can be extracted by scoring the trunk. Narváez's men

must have poured this pitch on the oakum and between the logs. Cabeza de Vaca, *Relación of 1542*, 72.

8. As Cabeza de Vaca points out, "from the savins growing there [possibly bold cypress] we made the oars that it seemed to us were necessary." Cabeza de Vaca, *Relación of 1542*, 73.

9. Cabeza de Vaca states that the men at the Bay of Horses were able to gather 400 *fanegas* of maize. They must have eaten much of this during their stay, but were able to keep enough for the passage. See Cabeza de Vaca, *Relación of 1542*, 71. For a general idea, it can be assumed that a *fanega* equals 1.6 bushels and that a bushel of corn equals 56 pounds. four hundred *fanegas* would amount to almost 18 tons of corn.

10. Cabeza de Vaca, *Relación of 1542*, 73.

11. Cabeza de Vaca, *Relación of 1542*, 75.

12. Quote from Cabeza de Vaca, *Relación of 1542*, 77. As stated before, none of these places can be located with certainty. In a personal communication, Florida archaeologist Nancy Marie White endorses the identification of this island with St. Vincent. She notes that St. Vincent Island not only conforms to the description provided in the sources but also was the most heavily occupied of the barrier islands possessing shell midden sites from all time periods during the last 4,000 years.

13. Cabeza de Vaca, *Relación of 1542*, 77.

14. Cabeza de Vaca, *Relación of 1542*, 77.

15. Cabeza de Vaca, *Relación of 1542*, 79. Here there are some inconsistencies between the two main sources. The *Joint Report* claims that the men spent only three days on the small island and that five or six men died from drinking seawater.

16. Quotes from Cabeza de Vaca, *Relación of 1542*, 79.

17. Cabeza de Vaca, *Relación of 1542*, 79.

18. Cabeza de Vaca, *Relación of 1542*, 79.

19. *Joint Report*, 104.

20. Cabeza de Vaca, *Relación of 1542*, 81, 83.

21. Minor inconsistencies continue. Cabeza de Vaca claims that they stayed one more day while the *Joint Report* indicates that it was two days.

22. Cabeza de Vaca, *Relación of 1542*, 85, 87.

23. Clayton, Knight, and Moore, eds., *The de Soto Chronicles*, I, 292. See discussion in Adorno and Pautz, *Álvar Núñez Cabeza de Vaca*, II, 148–151.

24. *Joint Report*, 105–106; and Cabeza de Vaca, *Relación of 1542*, 89. My translation.

25. Cabeza de Vaca, *Relación of 1542*, 88, 89, 90. The translation is mine.

26. Cabeza de Vaca, *Relación of 1542*, 91. In this paragraph I have used some details from the *Joint Report*, 22.

27. Quote from Cabeza de Vaca, *Relación of 1542*, 93.

28. Quote from Cabeza de Vaca, *Relación of 1542*, 150. The translation is mine. Cabeza de Vaca does not recount the fate of the other rafts in chronological order. Instead, he inserts flashbacks as he learns about these events from other survivors days, months, or even years later. The allusions are brief, and therefore it is quite difficult to locate where the other rafts landed. Vague allusions to inlets and islands and bays lend themselves to educated guesses at best. I have relied on the reconstructions provided by Adorno and Pautz in *Álvar Núñez Cabeza de Vaca*, II, 183–190.

29. Cabeza de Vaca says that the men of the comptroller's raft traveled 60 leagues (more than 180 miles), which is probably an overestimation. Cabeza de Vaca, *Relación of 1542*, 130.

30. Cabeza de Vaca, *Relación of 1542*, 133.

31. Cabeza de Vaca, *Relación of 1542*, 133. My translation.

32. Quote from *Joint Report*, 31.

CHAPTER 6

1. Quote from Cabeza de Vaca, *Relación of 1542*, 93,95.

2. Scholars have debated the identity of this island. Galveston Island is one obvious candidate. But as Davenport and Wells have pointed out, there are at least four inconsistencies between Galveston Island and Cabeza de Vaca's description: (1) Galveston Island "is doubly too wide," (2) "three times too long," (3) "too far from the first of the four rivers" that the castaways would later cross, and (4) "there are no woods opposite on the mainland," as Cabeza de Vaca asserts. Harbert Davenport and Joseph K. Wells, "The First Europeans in Texas, 1528–1536," *Southern Historical Quarterly* 22:2 (October 1918), 121. None of these objections apply to the smaller island just to the south called San Luis. Today it is no longer an island but a peninsula that, as Krieger points out, "lies between Oyster Bay and the Gulf of Mexico and is unnamed on most ordinary maps. It has been called Oyster Bay Peninsula, San Luis Peninsula, and Velasco Peninsula. The fact that it is now joined to the mainland does not mean that it was so in 1528, for every authority on Texas coast geology knows what changes have been wrought by tides, currents, hurricanes, and shifts in river channels, even within recent years." Alex D. Krieger, *We Came Naked and Barefoot: The Journey of Cabeza de Vaca across North America*, edited by Margery H. Krieger (Austin: University of Texas Press, 2002), 29. For a succinct but very insightful historiographical discussion of what scholars have had to say for more than a century about Cabeza de Vaca's whereabouts, see Donald E. Chipman, "In Search of Cabeza de Vaca's Route across Texas: An Historiographical Survey," *Southwestern Historical Quarterly* 91:2 (October 1987), 127–148. In one way or another all these authors have contributed to the identification of the island where Cabeza de Vaca and his companions first landed with what is now Follets Island. The same view is held by Adorno and Pautz, *Álvar Núñez Cabeza de Vaca*, II, 190, 198.

3. Cabeza de Vaca, *Relación of 1542*, 95.

4. Cabeza de Vaca, *Relación of 1542*, 95.

5. Cabeza de Vaca, *Relación of 1542*, 97.

6. Quote from Cabeza de Vaca, *Relación of 1542*, 97.

7. Cabeza de Vaca, *Relación of 1542*, 96. My translation.

8. By studying tree rings and measuring receding glaciers, scholars have learned a great deal about past weather patterns. In North America 1529 marked the beginning of a cold spell that would last until the early 1550s. See discussion of moraine advances and stabilization in Jean Grove, *Little Ice Ages: Ancient and Modern*, 2 vols. (London: Routledge, 2nd ed., 2004), I, 260. Similarly, Europe went through a cold spell between 1527 and 1529. Wine harvests in France were disastrous in 1527 and quite bad in 1528 and 1529. Emmanuel Le Roy Ladurie, *Times*

of Feast, Times of Famine: A History of Climate Since the Year 1000 (New York: Doubleday, 1971), 66.

9. Quote from Cabeza de Vaca, *Relación of 1542*, 99.

10. Cabeza de Vaca, *Relación of 1542*, 101.

11. Cabeza de Vaca, *Relación of 1542*, 101.

12. Quote from Cabeza de Vaca, *Relación of 1542*, 103.

13. Quote from Cabeza de Vaca, *Relación of 1542*, 103.

14. Cabeza de Vaca, *Relación of 1542*, 103.

15. Cabeza de Vaca, *Relación of 1542*, 103.

16. Cabeza de Vaca, *Relación of 1542*, 105.

17. DNA scholars argue that the source population of the Americas most probably lived in the Lake Baikal and Altai regions of south-central Siberia, simply because that is where the five mitochondrial DNA lineages common in America can all be found. Naturally, the Asian populations have also moved in the intervening thousands of years, so this geographic location is just a rough approximation. I want to express my gratitude to Brian M. Kemp for introducing me to some of the mysteries of genetic research.

18. Estimates of the indigenous population of America at the time of contact come from Lockhart and Schwartz, *Early Latin America*, 36. DNA has recently shed considerable light on the origins and initial peopling of the Americas. For a pioneering work see D. C. Wallace et al., "Dramatic Founder Effects in Amerindian Mitochondrial DNA Species," *American Journal of Physical Anthropology* 68 (1985), 149–156. For an insightful and recent survey, see Herbert S. Klein and Daniel C. Schiffner, "The Current Debate about the Origins of the Paleoindians of America," *Journal of Social History* 37:2 (2003), 483–492. See also R. S. Malhi et al., "The Structure of Diversity within the New World Mitochondrial DNA Haplogroups: Implications for the Prehistory of North America," *American Journal of Human Genetics* 70 (2002), 905–919.

19. A key discussion revolves around the ethnic and linguistic identity of these two groups. Galveston and Follets Island lie at the northernmost range of the Karankawa Indians, who were known to La Salle in the 1680s and to the Spanish inhabitants of the Texas coast during the eighteenth and nineteenth centuries. Furthermore, the entire central coast of Texas is associated with a distinctive archaeological complex known as the Rockport Focus, spanning from the precontact era into the colonial period. W. W. Newcomb, Jr., was among the first to propose a correspondence between the groups mentioned in Cabeza de Vaca's account—Capoques and Hans, as well as other groups farther south that he would later visit—and the five bands that in the eighteenth and nineteenth centuries would comprise the Karankawa. From north to south, these five bands were: Cocos, Cujanes, Karankawa proper, Coapites, and Copanos. Largely on the basis of their approximate locations, Newcomb identifies the Capoques with the later Cocos, the Deguenes mentioned by Cabeza de Vaca with the later Cujanes, the Quevenes with the later Karankawa proper, the Guaycones of Cabeza de Vaca with the Coapites, and the Quitoles with the Copanos. Newcomb has also suggested, echoing previous scholars, that the *Han*—which spoke a language that was different from that spoken by the Capoques—were Akokisas (an Atakapa group) on the grounds that Han resembles an Atakapa word for "house." Newcomb, "Karankawa," in *Handbook of North American Indians*, vol. 10 (Washington, DC:

Smithsonian Institution, 1983), 360. More recently, Robert A. Ricklis has found Newcomb's correspondences reasonable, although somewhat speculative. Still, he finds especially significant that in both the sixteenth and the eighteenth centuries "there were five groups between Matagorda Bay and Corpus Christi Bay." Robert A. Ricklis, *The Karankawa Indians of Texas: An Ecological Study of Cultural Tradition and Change* (Austin: University of Texas Press, 1996), 8. Similarly, Kelly F. Himmel, in her study of the Karankawas and Tonkawas in the nineteenth century, asserts that Cabeza de Vaca and his companions "likely encountered the ancestors of the Karankawas." Himmel, *The Conquest of the Karankawas and the Tonkawas, 1821–1859* (College Station: Texas A & M University Press, 1999), 14. These authors are quite correct in refraining from establishing firm correspondences. After reading Cabeza de Vaca's account and the *Joint Report* and their enumeration of indigenous groups along the Texas coast, it is hard to place much confidence in any ethnic continuities between the sixteenth century and later times. For one thing, the arrival of Europeans led to precipitous population declines of these populations—already reported by Cabeza de Vaca—leaving the door open for other groups to move into the area. That is especially evident in the multiplicity of ethnonyms associated with the Texas coast in colonial times, as indigenous groups from Coahuila, east Texas, and elsewhere traveled through the region and stayed for lengthy periods of time. Sifting through the diaries and records left by various Spanish expeditions into Texas in the seventeenth and eighteenth centuries, William C. Foster has compiled an impressive—and unsettling—list of indigenous groups sighted in this region at one point or another. Foster, *Spanish Expeditions into Texas, 1689–1768* (Austin: University of Texas Press, 1995), especially his appendix on "Indian Tribes Reported on Spanish Expeditions into Texas, 1689–1768," 265–289. One gets a similar sense of bewilderment after reading the list of nations encountered by La Salle along the central coast of Texas. Cox, *The Journeys of La Salle*, II, 114–115. Other scholars have already noted the difficulties of establishing direct correspondences between Cabeza de Vaca's named groups and later bands. See especially Albert. S. Gatschet, *The Karankawa Indians: The Coast People of Texas* (Cambridge, MA: Peabody Museum of American Archaeology and Ethnology, 1891), 23; and Adorno and Pautz, *Álvar Núñez Cabeza de Vaca*, II, 237–241. Having said all this, it is also important not to toss out the baby with the bathwater by being too focused on the cultural identification of the different bands. As Cabeza de Vaca also makes clear, groups like the Capoques and Hans, although linguistically and culturally unrelated, led practically identical lifestyles. The archaeological record underscores the homogeneity in the economic strategies and exploitation of the environment, regardless of the specific linguistic and cultural affiliation of these groups. For instance, the findings of a recent excavation at Mitchell Ridge Site on Galveston Island jibe exceedingly well with the lifestyle described by Cabeza de Vaca and other survivors of the Pánfilo de Narváez expedition. Among other things, remains at Mitchell Ridge Site provide evidence of seasonal occupation in the fall-winter, reveal the presence of aboriginal structures with a round-to-oval floor plan in which one side may have been left open, and show debris deposits with abundant fish bones (no remains of aquatic roots would be expected after nearly 500 years). Information about indigenous occupation patterns, economic activities, commonly used household implements, burial practices, and other aspects of life relevant to Cabeza de Vaca's story can be gleaned from this site. Robert A. Ricklis, *Aboriginal Life and Culture on the Upper Texas Coast: Archaeology at the Mitchell Ridge Site, 41GV66, Galveston Island* (Corpus Christi, TX: Coastal Archaeological Research, Inc., 1994), passim. At the very least, this work indicates that the Capoque-Han-type of cultural expression described by Cabeza de Vaca was quite representative of the lifestyle prevalent throughout the area that would later become the homeland of the Karankawa. My retelling of the Capoques and Hans, while based largely on Cabeza de Vaca's own account, will occasionally and cautiously draw on other sources pertaining to the Karankawa in the understanding that this particular cultural identity represented a broader set of material and environmental adaptations of diverse groups living on the coast of Texas. The Spaniards' impression that the coastal peoples of Texas were very tall is corroborated by skeletal evidence. See Ricklis, *The Karankawa Indians of Texas*, 9–10. In contrast, the average heights of northern Europeans (I could not find data for residents of the Iberian Peninsula) apparently decreased from the early Middle Ages through the seventeenth century, from 68.27 inches to 65.75.

20. These numbers are very rough estimates. They stem from Cabeza de Vaca's observation that the Spaniards were greeted by about one hundred Indian warriors and considering that the ratio of adult males to the total population must have been about 1 to 4; 400 or 500 are relatively high numbers for mobile hunter-gatherers. See discussion in Ricklis, *Aboriginal Life and Culture on the Upper Texas Coast*, 26.

21. Cabeza de Vaca, *Relación of 1542*, 108. My translation. Ricklis notes that cattails are quite common along the shallow bays of the area. Their roots are starchy and thus constitute a good source of carbohydrates. They are edible until midwinter. Ricklis, *The Karankawa Indians of Texas*, 107.

22. Quote from Cabeza de Vaca, *Relación of 1542*, 105, 107.

23. Quotes from the *Joint Report*, 110; and Cabeza de Vaca, *Relación of 1542*, 113, respectively. The sources do not specifically tell us where the groups spent the summer months, but the archaeological evidence is quite clear in this regard. See especially Ricklis, *The Karankawa Indians of Texas*, 72–100. Cabeza de Vaca's statement that the Indians inhabited the island "from October to the end of February" suggests another trip to the mainland between the summer months and September.

24. In the eighteenth century, a French officer named Simars de Bellisle was shipwrecked in or near Galveston Bay. For fifteen months between 1719 and 1721, the Frenchman lived with an Indian group not unlike the Capoques and Hans and left a description that could well have been penned by Cabeza de Vaca and his companions. This lonesome European noted that the Indians had no cabins or fields but instead moved incessantly from one place to another in search of food: "They travel in this manner the entire summer. The men kill a few deer and a few buffaloes and the women search for wild potatoes [possibly the cattail roots]." For an English translation of de Bellisle's account, see Henri Folmer, "De Bellisle on the Texas Coast," *Southwestern Historical Quarterly* 44:2 (October 1940), 216. As one scholar has noted, "The indigenous peoples of the Texas Gulf Coast are gone, yet they will forever stir our imaginations. Perhaps this is because, unlike ourselves, they faced daily and directly the stark realities of remaining alive. To those who have seldom been too cold, hot, or wet, never really hungry, and confidently expect to see many tomorrows, a people who had

none of these advantages come as something of a shock." W. W. Newcomb, Jr., *The Indians of Texas: From Prehistoric to Modern Times* (Austin: University of Texas Press, 1961), 81.

25. See Mariah Wade, "Go-between: The Roles of Native American Women and Álvar Núñez Cabeza de Vaca in Southern Texas in the 16th Century," *Journal of American Folklore* 112 (Summer 1999), 445, 332–342.

26. Cabeza de Vaca, *Relación of 1542*, 105, 107. My translation.

27. Quote from Cabeza de Vaca, *Relación of 1542*, 106. My translation.

28. Cabeza de Vaca, *Relación of 1542*, 106.

29. Cabeza de Vaca, *Relación of 1542*, 106.

30. Cabeza de Vaca, *Relación of 1542*, 119.

31. Quotes from the *Joint Report*, 40; Cabeza de Vaca, *Relación of 1542*, 137; and the *Joint Report*, 42, respectively. According to the *Joint Report*, only one Christian died for moving from one house to another, the other two were killed in different circumstances but just as arbitrarily. See also Adorno and Pautz, *Álvar Núñez Cabeza de Vaca*, II, 210–213.

32. Indians did not readily enslave the castaways. Captains Andrés Dorantes and Alonso del Castillo and the African Estebanico, for instance, were at one point "thrown out and told to go to other Indians which were said to be on another inlet six leagues farther on . . . [and] these two *hidalgos* and the black man went to that *rancho*, and they believed that the Indians would want them for their purposes, that is, to carry wood and water and serve as slaves. But these Indians also threw them out within three or four days, and they wandered for some days being lost and without hope of finding help." See *Joint Report*, 123. My translation. Two centuries later, Bellisle's enslavement experience was remarkably similar to that of Cabeza de Vaca and his companions. It is worth quoting him at length: "It was at that place that they began to treat me much worse than before. If they needed water or wood they ordered me to go and get it. In the beginning I told them to go and get it themselves because I knew a little of their language. When I told them this the second time, there was one who gave me a blow with all his force. I understood then that I should obey without replying. I went therefore to get wood for them. As soon I returned, a woman told me to fetch some water. I did this. Since they began to treat me badly, I could not say a word without receiving a slap or a blow with a stick or being beaten with any object upon which they could lay their hands. The big ones as well as the little ones beat me, and the ones to whom I was kind beat me most." Folmer, "De Bellisle on the Texas Coast," 216–217.

33. Cabeza de Vaca, *Relación of 1542*, 119.

34. Cabeza de Vaca, *Relación of 1542*, 118.

35. On Cabeza de Vaca's trading activities, see J. X. Corgan, "Cabeza de Vaca, Dealer in Shells," *American Malacological Union, Annual Reports for 1968* (1969), 13–14. Thomas R. Hester notes that Cabeza de Vaca got involved in an ancient trading system in southern Texas. Hester, "Artifacts, Archaeology and Cabeza de Vaca in Southern Texas and Northeastern Mexico," in *Windows to the Unknown: Cabeza de Vaca's Journey to the Southwest*. Symposium hosted by the Center for the Study of the Southwest at Southwest Texas State University, San Marcos. (http://wp29.english.swt.edu/css/CSSINDEX.HTM)

36. Cabeza de Vaca, *Relación of 1542*, 120.
37. Cabeza de Vaca, *Relación of 1542*, 122.
38. Cabeza de Vaca, *Relación of 1542*, 125.
39. Quote from Cabeza de Vaca, *Relación of 1542*, 127. For a careful consideration of the season when this gathering occurred, see note 2 of next chapter.
40. Cabeza de Vaca, *Relación of 1542*, 81.
41. For a more detailed discussion of the identities of these survivors, see Adorno and Pautz, *Álvar Núñez Cabeza de Vaca*, II, 196–198. Naturally, these numbers varied over time. There were fourteen castaways on Malhado in the spring of 1529, but only twelve of them crossed to the mainland. Out of this group of twelve, two men drowned, but subsequently the group met another Christian who joined them, and so on.
42. Quote from Cabeza de Vaca, *Relación of 1542*, 127.

CHAPTER 7

1. The *Joint Report* provides the best description of these pecan groves: "On those river shores there are many nuts, which they eat during the season, because the nut tree there bears fruit one year and another year, not. Sometimes there will be a year or two without a crop. But when there is, there are plentiful nuts, and they are a delicacy for these Indians come from a distance of twenty and thirty leagues, from all that region to eat them . . . and eat nothing but nuts during that month. These nuts are small, much smaller than those from Spain, and very difficult to get the meat out of the shell." *Joint Report*, 43–44. There is some controversy about the dating of this encounter as the sources are somewhat vague on this point. Adorno and Pautz assert that the reunion occurred "in the spring of 1533." Adorno and Pautz, *Álvar Núñez Cabeza de Vaca*, II, 218. However, the biology of pecan trees rules out this possibility. Pecan nuts have to be harvested in a well-defined, two-month period that runs from early October to early December. Try to harvest the pecans before and you'll find stubby twigs crowned with underdeveloped green husks filled with a jelly-like, tannic substance that could not have satisfied anyone's hunger. Try to harvest the pecan nuts after the two-month period and squirrels would have made short work of them. Since the identification of the "nuts" with pecans is beyond dispute, the gathering must have occurred in October, November, or early December at the latest. This is consistent with other passages in the *Relación*. Cabeza de Vaca remarks no less than three times that it was necessary for him to remain with the Mariames for six months before the escape plan could be put into effect. Adorno and Pautz speculate that this period must have been from "about April until September 1533." Cabeza de Vaca, *Relación of 1542*, 129 and note 1. But we know that this cannot be true as there would have been no pecans in April. The alternative interpretation of Cabeza de Vaca's six-month waiting period is between around November—at the height of the pecan season—to about May or June, when the Mariames, Yguases, and others would be traveling south to visit a prickly-pear ground located farther south as we shall see below. Krieger is closer to the mark in affirming that the gathering of the four castaways took place "in or about January 1533" on the grounds that "the next tuna season was to start in six months." Krieger, *We Came Naked and Barefoot*, 35. It is now necessary to turn to the matter of the

year. Did the reunion at the "river of nuts" occur in 1533 or 1532? To settle this question, one has to work back from April 1536, when we are positively certain that the castaways regained Spanish-controlled territory in what is now northwestern Mexico. We know that the castaways lived with the Mariames and Yguases (or with some other neighboring groups) for one and a half years. Both Cabeza de Vaca and the *Joint Report* allude to a first failed escape attempt six months after Cabeza de Vaca's arrival at the "river of nuts" and to a successful escape one year later. See below for specific citations. Cabeza de Vaca also writes categorically that the castaways spent eight lunar months with the Avavares: "We were with those Avavares Indians eight months. And this reckoning we made by the moon." Cabeza de Vaca, *Relación of 1542*, 163. These two periods alone add up to two years and two months. If the reunion at the "river of nuts" had occurred in the fall of 1533—say October at the earliest—and we add the two years and two months, we get to January of 1536, leaving only three months for the foursome to cross the entire continent by foot, clearly an impossibility. Therefore, the gathering at the "river of nuts" must have occurred in the fall of 1532. As usual, route students have debated the identity of "the river of nuts." Early scholars like Ponton and McFarland proposed the Colorado River. Miss Brownie Ponton and Bates H. McFarland, "Álvar Núñez Cabeza de Vaca: A Preliminary Report on His Wanderings in Texas," *Southwestern Historical Quarterly* 1:3 (1898), 166–186. More recently, Baskett, Krieger, and T. N. Campbell and T. J. Campbell have all argued compellingly in favor of the lower courses of the San Antonio and Guadalupe rivers, most especially the latter. James Newton Baskett, "A Study of the Route of Cabeza de Vaca," *Texas State Historical Association Quarterly* 10 (1907), 246–279; Krieger, *We Came Naked and Barefoot*, 39, 152; and T. N. Campbell and T. J. Campbell, *Historic Indian Groups of the Choke Canyon Reservoir and Surrounding Area, Southern Texas* (San Antonio: Center for Archaeological Research, University of Texas at San Antonio, Choke Canyon Series, 1981), 5–6. See also discussion in Adorno and Pautz, *Álvar Núñez Cabeza de Vaca*, II, 217–218. Presently, most scholars agree that the "river of nuts" must have been the lower Guadalupe River. Pecans are indigenous to North America and found in great profusion in Texas. Indeed, the pecan became the official tree of Texas in 1919.

2. Unfortunately, this large *tunal* in the lower Nueces River has largely disappeared. A severe freeze in 1899 reduced the stands greatly. For an insightful discussion of the location of this food paradise and excellent quotes describing the massiveness of the prickly-pear plants as late as the nineteenth century see Campbell and Campbell, *Historic Indian Groups of the Choke Canyon Reservoir*, 6–8. Cabeza de Vaca described the prickly pears as being "the size of an egg, vermilion or black, and of very good flavor." Cabeza de Vaca, *Relación of 1542*, 129.

3. Cabeza de Vaca, *Relación of 1542*, 151.

4. *Joint Report*, 44.

5. Cabeza de Vaca's description of the large "cows" with "small horns" appears in *Relación of 1542*, 147.

6. Cabeza de Vaca, *Relación of 1542*, 141. T. N. Campbell and T. J. Campbell have gathered all the available ethnographic material pertaining to the Mariames, Yguases, and other Indian groups in the area. The Campbells estimate the population size of the Mariames as "not exceeding 200 individuals." They deduce this population size

through one fleeting statement in the *Joint Report* describing a deer hunt that involved sixty men. The Campbells assume that these sixty individuals were all the adult males of the group. They also assume the average size of a Mariame family to be 5 and somewhat reduce the resulting number to allow for the practice of female infanticide, as will be discussed below. These are reasonable speculations. Campbell and Campbell, *Historic Indian Groups of the Choke Canyon Reservoir*, 27–28.

7. Cabeza de Vaca, *Relación of 1542*, 141, 143.

8. Quote from Cabeza de Vaca, *Relación of 1542*, 141. See also Cabeza de Vaca, *Relación of 1542*, 129, 139.

9. Quote from Cabeza de Vaca, *Relación of 1542*, 137, 138. My translation. Although rare, female infanticide was practiced by other societies in the Americas and around the world.

10. The state of Texas has more species of mosquitoes—eighty-one in all—than any other state in the United States or any place in Canada and Alaska. See Richard F. Darsie, Jr., and Ronald A. Ward, *Identification and Geographical Distribution of the Mosquitoes of North America, North of Mexico* (Fresno, CA: American Mosquito Control Association, 1981), especially the synopsis of the occurrence of mosquito species in the western United States on pp. 227–230. In addition to weakening the body, mosquitoes contribute to the spread of viral and bacterial diseases. Mosquitoes continued to be a pest through the centuries of colonization of the Americas. In the eighteenth century, a Frenchman shipwrecked on Galveston Bay recalled how in the summer, "there were so many mosquitoes that I thought I would die. I was obliged to hide under water to my neck and I passed the night in this manner." Henri Folmer, "De Bellisle on the Texas Coast," *Southwestern Historical Quarterly* 44:2 (October 1940), 216.

11. Cabeza de Vaca, *Relación of 1542*, 143, 145.

12. Cabeza de Vaca, *Relación of 1542*, 146. My translation.

13. Quote from Cabeza de Vaca, *Relación of 1542*, 147, 149.

14. Quote from Cabeza de Vaca, *Relación of 1542*, 147, 149.

15. The spelling of this group's name varies: Anagados, Eanagados, Ganegados, etc. A useful compilation of what little information there is about this group can be found in T. N. Campbell and T. J. Campbell, *Historic Indian Groups of the Choke Canyon Reservoir*, 27–28. Adorno and Pautz observe that although the *Joint Report* and Cabeza's *Relación* diverge at times, in this particular case they complement each other perfectly well. Adorno and Pautz, *Álvar Núñez Cabeza de Vaca*, II, 245–247.

16. *Joint Report*, 130. My translation.

17. Krieger considers the castaways' escape from the Mariames and Yguases as the beginning of their overland journey across North America. Adorno and Pautz dispute this notion by stating that the four men "made no forward progress on their trip," spending eight lunar months with another group in the area known as the Avavares. "We reject Krieger's scheme of the journey's beginning at this first area of prickly pears"—Adorno and Pautz write—"since the narratives give virtually no information about the men's whereabouts and travels during the winter of 1534–35." Adorno and Pautz, *Álvar Núñez Cabeza de Vaca*, II, 247. Although it may be true from a purely geographical vantage point, it is impossible to overlook the men's motivations. Both the *Joint Report* and Cabeza de Vaca's *Relación* quite explicitly describe the survivors' removal from the Mariames and Yguases as an "escape" or "flight" and

clearly state the goal of reaching Pánuco. There is little doubt that, at least retrospec-
tively, the four castaways no longer regarded their movements as a rotation from one
group to another within a restricted region of Texas, but as an attempt to reach Christian lands. On the beginnings of the castaways as healers, see Cabeza de Vaca,
Relación of 1542, 113. It is difficult to establish the precise chronology of these curing ceremonies. Adorno and Pautz have perceptively noted some discrepancies between Cabeza de Vaca's *Relación* and the *Joint Report*. Cabeza de Vaca claims that he
had first cured at the island of Malhado and that he had performed at least one more
cure at the "river of nuts." However, the *Joint Report* mentions no curing ceremonies
until the castaways left the Avavares, sometime in the summer of 1535. Both accounts
are also at odds about the reasons why the Avavares treated the castaways so well.
Cabeza de Vaca claims that he and his companions already enjoyed a reputation as
healers, but the *Joint Report* merely states that the Avavares knew very little about
how badly the outsiders had been treated previously. From such discrepancies,
Adorno and Pautz go on to posit that, although Cabeza de Vaca's account of the curing was probably accurate, the former Royal Treasurer shifted this entire sequence of
events backward all the way to the castaways' arrival at the coast of Texas. Adorno
and Pautz, *Álvar Núñez Cabeza de Vaca*, II, 283–285. This is a possibility, although
it is just as likely that the discrepancies between the *Relación* and the *Joint Report*
stem simply from the castaways' diverging experiences. Cabeza de Vaca is very clear
about the fact that he and Castillo were the first castaways to heal while Estebanico
and Dorantes were the last. It would not be surprising then that the *Relación* reflects
the perspective of someone involved in curing early on while the *Joint Report*—which
often presents Dorantes's viewpoint—tells the same tale from the standpoint of the
last castaway to cure. There is simply not enough information in the two accounts to
support one interpretation over the other. Moreover, it is unclear why Cabeza de Vaca
would have wanted to shift the timing of the cures. As Adorno and Pautz admit,
Cabeza de Vaca never exalts the cures as overtly as other chroniclers of these events.
If his intention had been to draw attention to his medical abilities and miracles, he
could have done so in far less oblique ways than misrepresenting the chronology of
his healing ceremonies. Adorno and Pautz also seem to question Cabeza de Vaca's account of his early cures on the grounds that he had been a mere slave at the time.
These authors emphasize the consistency between the *Narrative* and the *Joint Report*
regarding the poor treatment received by the castaways prior to 1535 and observe
that such a scenario is somehow less consistent with Cabeza de Vaca's claims "about
beginning the curing on Malhado and continuing it without hiatus afterward."
Adorno and Pautz, *Álvar Núñez Cabeza de Vaca*, II, 283. And yet, this is not necessarily the case. It is entirely possible that the Indians treated the castaways as slaves
and *at the same time* believed that they possessed special powers. Cabeza de Vaca's
specific mention that the Indians compelled them to cure by withdrawing food from
them points to just such a situation. Although superficially contradictory, it is
nonetheless entirely possible. As it will become clear in the rest of this chapter, I take
the view that the curing ceremonies performed by Cabeza de Vaca and the others occurred when he says they did, since there isn't sufficient evidence to persuade me of
any other chronology.
    18. *Joint Report*, 46.

19. The exact date of the apparition of the Virgin Mary in the outskirts of León is lacking, and only a few details are known. The shepherd's name was Álvar Simón. The pope would later allude to this occurrence, thereby adding the church's imprimatur, when he wrote about that "certain shepherd to whom, whether in dreams or divinely, it was revealed that on a certain public road out of the city of León, a shrine or hermitage or oratory should be built in honor of the Blessed Virgin Mary." Papal bull of 1517, as quoted in William A. Christian, Jr., *Apparitions in Late Medieval and Renaissance Spain* (Princeton: Princeton University Press, 1981), 150. Similar apparitions through the fifteenth and sixteenth centuries had led to the construction of scores of Marian shrines in Spain, Italy, and elsewhere on the continent. A translation of the testimonies of the investigation surrounding Juan de Rabe's allegations can be found in Christian, *Apparitions*, 152–159. For the Virgin's apparition in 1523 see also Christian, *Apparitions*, 159–179. In addition to the venerated Virgin—who was far and away the most common protagonist of such apparitions—from time to time Saint Anthony of Padua and Michael the Archangel made their own appearances in Spain. Christian, *Apparitions*, 94. Taken as a whole, these apparitions follow certain patterns. Except for a few extraordinary cases—Jeanne d'Arc, Bridget of Sweden, and Savonarola—the apparitions have been mostly local affairs that do not threaten the ecclesiastical and imperial establishments. Their timing is well defined. They have been most frequent from the late medieval period through the Renaissance, and again from the middle of the nineteenth century to the present. Christian, *Apparitions*, 3–9, 204–205. On the scope of the religious experience for the people at large, see William A. Christian, Jr., *Local Religion in Sixteenth-Century Spain* (Princeton: Princeton University Press, 1981), passim. Two excellent in-depth cases provide additional context: Richard L. Kagan, *Lucrecia's Dreams: Politics and Prophecy in Sixteenth-Century Spain* (Berkeley: University of California Press, 1990); and Sara Tilghman Nalle, *Mad for God: Bartolomé Sánchez, the Secret Messiah of Cardenete* (Charlottesville: University Press of Virginia, 2001).

20. It was an age of religious upheaval and experimentation. In the 1520s Christendom was rocked to the core by the Lutheran and Anabaptist revolutions. Theologians, princes, and devout Christians throughout Europe came to embrace these new religious ideas. The Christian world was torn asunder. But Spain tried to stay the course by becoming the champion of the Church of Rome and the epicenter of the Counter-Reformation.

21. First quote from Cabeza de Vaca, *Relación of 1542*, 99. Rolena Adorno has made this point before. Adorno, "The Negotiation of Fear in Cabeza de Vaca's *Naufragios*," *Representations* 33 (Winter 1991), 167–168. Second quote from *Joint Report*, 125. My translation.

22. Quote from Cabeza de Vaca, *Relación of 1542*, 173.

23. In addition to the four survivors, there surely were others like Lope de Oviedo. Even so, the number of survivors was appallingly small.

24. Cabeza de Vaca, *Relación of 1542*, 157.

25. First quote from Cabeza de Vaca, *Relación of 1542*, 157. Second quote from Cabeza de Vaca, *Relación of 1542*, 159.

26. First quote from Cabeza de Vaca, *Relación of 1542*, 113. Spain was one of the first European nations to create a board of physicians, *the Royal Protomedicato*,

charged with the training, licensing, and overseeing of all formal medical practitioners. See John Tate Lanning, *The Royal Protomedicato: The Regulation of the Medical Professions in the Spanish Empire*, edited by John Jay TePaske (Durham: Duke University Press, 1985). Second quote from Cabeza de Vaca, *Relación of 1542*, 113. Third quote from Cabeza de Vaca, *Relación of 1542*, 112. My translation.

27. John G. Bourke, *On the Border with Crook* (Lincoln: University of Nebraska Press, 1971), 133. Captain Bourke was a member of the staff of General George Crook. He became fascinated by Indians and wrote extensively about their customs and lifestyles. Learning about the specific beliefs, mindset, and techniques employed by medicine men at the time of the Florida expedition is exceedingly difficult. Both the *Relación* and the *Joint Report* provide some details. For the most detailed treatment of the subject, see Rafael Valdez Aguilar, *Cabeza de Vaca, chamán* (Mexico City: Editorial México Desconocido, 2002), passim. One can gain additional insight by investigating medicine men and women who lived in more recent times, even if certain Judeo-Christian elements were necessarily introduced into their healing practices after contact. See especially David E. Jones, *Sanapia: Comanche Medicine Woman* (Prospect Heights, IL: Waveland Press, 1972). My description of the general traits of shamanic practices is largely based on Sanapia, a medicine woman among the Comanches of Oklahoma who provided much insight about her trade. The existence of shamans can be easily detected in the archaeological record. Much of the material remains of ancient cultures of the Americas focuses precisely on these extraordinary individuals and their ability to establish connections between the natural and supernatural realms. For instance, the Olmec culture farther south in the Gulf of Mexico is notably rich in artistic manifestations depicting shamanic practices. See David A. Freidel, "Preparing the Way," in *The Olmec World: Ritual and Rulership* (Princeton: Art Museum, Princeton University Press, 1996), 3–9. Similar examples can be found in the Maya, Toltec, Nahua-Mexica, and other native cultures farther north.

28. Quote from Cabeza de Vaca, *Relación of 1542*, 153.

29. Quote from Cabeza de Vaca, *Relación of 1542*, 154. My translation.

30. Cabeza de Vaca, *Relación of 1542*, 115. See also Cabeza de Vaca, *Relación of 1542*, 165.

31. Quotes from Cabeza de Vaca, *Relación of 1542*, 167, 169. See discussion of Mala Cosa in Adorno, "The Negotiation of Fear in Cabeza de Vaca's *Naufragios*," 173–176.

32. Quote from Cabeza de Vaca, *Relación of 1542*, 161, 163.

33. First quote from Cabeza de Vaca, *Relación of 1542*, 161, 163. Second quote from Cabeza de Vaca, *Relación of 1542*, 161, 162. My translation.

34. First and second quotes from Cabeza de Vaca, *Relación of 1542*, 165. For a general discussion of fear among both Spaniards and Indians, see Adorno, "The Negotiation of Fear in Cabeza de Vaca's *Naufragios*," 163–199.

35. Early contacts between Europeans and Native Americans were likely to generate creative mutual misunderstandings. In fact, this process has been crucial in the creation of early colonial settings. For the most insightful elaboration of this phenomenon, see Richard White, *The Middle Ground: Indians, Empires, and Republics in the Great Lakes Region, 1650–1815* (New York: Cambridge University Press, 1991), passim. Adorno and Pautz arrive at a similar formulation of "mutual

cross-fertilization of gesture and comportment," in Adorno and Pautz, *Álvar Núñez Cabeza de Vaca*, II, 299.

36. Quote from Cabeza de Vaca, *Relación of 1542*, 165. The Council of Letrán in 1515 established that all book manuscripts had to be reviewed by a competent ecclesiastical authority before publication. But it was not until 1536 that the Inquisition assumed the primary task of reviewing the manuscripts and issuing the licenses. After 1550 the Inquisition reconsidered its position, scaled down its formal review process, and simply condemned those texts deemed in error. Interestingly, the second edition of Cabeza de Vaca's *Relación* was published in 1552, only two years after the Inquisition reduced its role.

37. First quote from Francisco López de Gómara, cited in Jacques Lafaye, "Los 'milagros' de Álvar Núñez Cabeza de Vaca (1527–1536)," in *Mesías, cruzadas, utopías: el judeo-cristianismo en las sociedades ibéricas* (Mexico City: Fondo de Cultura Económica, 1984), 76. In the *Joint Report*, Oviedo did use the word "miracle," for instance, when he wrote that "the Christians . . . up to that point were more used to hard work than making miracles." The *Joint Report*, 133. My translation. The beatification of Cabeza de Vaca and the others had already begun. Second quote from Garcilaso de la Vega, *Historia de la Florida*, cited in Lafaye, "Los 'milagros' de Álvar Núñez Cabeza de Vaca," 77. Third quote from Andrés Pérez de Ribas, *Historia de los triunfos de nuestra Santa Fe*, cited in Lafaye, "Los 'milagros' de Álvar Núñez Cabeza de Vaca," 79. Fourth quote from Gabriel de Cárdenas Cano, *Ensayo cronológico para la historia general de la Florida*, cited in Lafaye, "Los 'milagros' de Álvar Núñez Cabeza de Vaca," 81.

38. Krieger, *We Came Naked and Barefoot*, 47–49; and Campbell and Campbell, *Historic Indian Groups*, 6–9. As the Campbells insightfully observe, "the references [in Cabeza de Vaca's narrative] to terrain, vegetation, and surface water do not suggest that any part of the Sand Plain was traversed." Campbell and Campbell, *Historic Indian Groups*, 8.

39. Quote from Cabeza de Vaca, *Relación of 1542*, 173. The *monte* is still there. But due to warmer temperatures, higher levels of carbon dioxide, overgrazing by livestock, and lack of recurring fires, today it is even thicker and more difficult to traverse. At the time of the Pánfilo de Narváez expedition, the brush areas of south Texas must have had a more open aspect.

40. Krieger, *We Came Naked and Barefoot*, 51.

41. Quote from Cabeza de Vaca, *Relación of 1542*, 171. My translation.

42. Cabeza de Vaca, *Relación of 1542*, 191.

43. First quote from Cabeza de Vaca, *Relación of 1542*, 183. Second quote from Cabeza de Vaca, *Relación of 1542*, 181. The Royal Treasurer said this advisedly. He had performed military service in Italy. He took part in the battle of Ravenna of 1512, where he had occasion to observe the fighting prowess of Italians. Adorno and Pautz have gathered what few records remain of Cabeza de Vaca's involvement in Italy. Adorno and Pautz, *Álvar Núñez Cabeza de Vaca*, I, 360–366.

44. The *Joint Report*, 134. Scholars have written profusely about the locations of the river "wider than the Guadalquivir in Seville" and the mountains. See especially Davenport and Wells, "The First Europeans in Texas," 111–142; Krieger, *We Came Naked and Barefoot*, 45–61; T. N. Campbell and T. J. Campbell, *Historic Indian*

Groups of the Choke Canyon Reservoir, 8–9; Chipman, "In Search of Cabeza de Vaca's Route across Texas," 127–148; and Adorno and Pautz, *Álvar Núñez Cabeza de Vaca*, II, 260–264, 290–293. To this day it is still an article of faith with Texas nationalists that the castaways pursued a completely trans-Texas route all the way to the El Paso area. All the authors cited above have helped to demolish this notion and have shown that much of this journey took place in what is now northeastern Mexico. Although none of the recent authors doubt the identification of the river "wider than the Guadalquivir in Seville" with the Rio Grande, a minor point of contention revolves around the precise place where the crossing occurred. The Campbells and Krieger have advocated the Falcón Reservoir basin, whereas Adorno and Pautz believe that it happened closer to the delta. Thomas R. Hester, in the afterword of *We Came Naked and Barefoot*, 152–152, has also come out in support of the Falcón Reservoir basin as the crossing point. Cabeza de Vaca mentions the presence of a substantial indigenous village of about one hundred houses just south of the crossing place. Archaeology may well settle this controversy one day. As for the identity of the mountains, there are two likely possibilities: the Sierra de Pamoranes in northern Tamaulipas, which is closer to the coast and somewhat smaller and the Sierra Cerralvo of northeastern Nuevo León, which is farther inland, more northerly, and more massive. Adorno and Pautz have argued in favor of the first alternative while Krieger—following Davenport and Wells—favor the second one. There is no firm evidence to settle this question at present, but Adorno and Pautz make a good case for why the castaways would have been inclined to remain relatively close to the coast, thus favoring the Sierra de Pamoranes. Krieger, *We Came Naked and Barefoot*, 59–61; and Adorno and Pautz, *Álvar Núñez Cabeza de Vaca*, II, 169–178, 293–295.

45. First quote from Cabeza de Vaca, *Relación of 1542*, 195. Second quote from Cabeza de Vaca, *Relación of 1542*, 199. The question of how Indians conceived of the strangers is both crucial and difficult to answer. Were Cabeza de Vaca and his companions regarded as gods? This same question has been posed for other instances of contact, including Columbus's first interactions with Caribbean natives and Cortés's conquest of Mexico and his identification with Quetzalcoatl. Although the Cortés/Quetzalcoatl case is by no means open and shut, recent scholarship has emphasized postconquest elaboration and has found precious little evidence supporting such an identification *during* and immediately after the events. See especially Camilla Townsend, "Burying the White Gods: New Perspectives on the Conquest of Mexico," *American Historical Review* 108:3 (June 2003), 1–56. Adorno and Pautz discuss this same question for the survivors of the Narváez expedition. The authors rightly note that Cabeza de Vaca is careful to distance himself from native beliefs in regard to their being gods. Cabeza de Vaca was understandably reluctant to come across as blasphemous in a published account. But at the same time, such protestations made repeatedly through the *Relación* clearly indicate that the natives themselves attributed supernatural powers to the outsiders, even if they did not consider them outright gods. See the discussion in Adorno and Pautz, *Álvar Núñez Cabeza de Vaca*, II, 297–300. Moreover, such beliefs in the castaways' supernatural powers would have been entirely consistent with Native Americans' long-held reliance on shamans and medicine men.

46. See Cabeza de Vaca, *Relación of 1542*, 193. The only inkling of sexual encounters with native women comes from Estebanico, who later in life took part in another

expedition into Sonora and possibly Arizona. Sixteenth-century Spanish accounts state that Estebanico requested pretty women from the villages that he visited, a habit that he could only have acquired during his incredible sojourn with Cabeza de Vaca and the other castaways. Pedro de Castañeda de Nájera, "Relación de la Jornada de Cíbola," in *Narrative of the Coronado Expedition*, edited by John Miller Morris, (Chicago: Lakeside Press, 2002), 34, 36.

47. The Sierra de Pamoranes begins about 110 miles due south from the Falcón Reservoir basin. Adorno and Pautz rightfully observe that the mountains must have been enormously encouraging to the castaways. Even before the Florida expedition departed from Spain, it was known that there were mountains along the coast of Pánuco, as revealed by a 1527 map commissioned by Charles V. It is likely, although not certain, that Cabeza de Vaca and his fellow travelers understood that the mountains had seen signified the proximity of the Rio de las Palmas. See Adorno and Pautz, *Álvar Núñez Cabeza de Vaca*, II, 290–295.

48. I agree with Adorno and Pautz in that Cabeza de Vaca's cryptic statement, "teníamos por mejor de atravessar la tierra," has often been misunderstood. This statement refers only to the castaways' decision to proceed to Pánuco by an inland route instead of through the coast and not to the entire crossing of the continent. Adorno and Pautz, *Álvar Núñez Cabeza de Vaca*, II, 291–292. Since the sources contain no explicit statement as to why the castaways chose to bypass Pánuco and go across the continent, any explanation has to be speculative in nature and based as much as possible on the few clues that do exist in the text.

CHAPTER 8

1. This large parrot with iridescent feathers lives in the humid lowland forests along the Gulf Coast. Archaeologists have found hundreds of scarlet macaw remains in present-day Chihuahua, Arizona, New Mexico, and parts of Colorado, even though its range does not extend that far north. Long-distance merchants procured the chicks in the Huasteca, placed them in burden baskets, and made their way across the Sierra Madre Oriental through well-worn paths, all the while feeding the animals and protecting them from excessive heat or cold. Eager customers in the middle of the continent must have made their efforts worth their while. They were in the habit of sacrificing newly fledged scarlet macaws, burying the remains beneath house floors, and using the brilliant feathers in important ceremonies. William C. Foster recently reviewed the extant research on the scarlet macaw trading system and used it effectively to argue that Cabeza de Vaca and his companions "were moving along a frequently followed east-west trade route that connected the American Southwest to eastern sources of scarlet macaws in the tropical rainforest of Tamaulipas and possibly Huasteca." William C. Foster, ed., *The La Salle Expedition on the Mississippi River: A Lost Manuscript of Nicolas de La Salle, 1682* (Austin: Texas State Historical Association, 2003), 69. As we shall see, other clues in Cabeza de Vaca's account point to the same conclusion. Archaeological research on remains of the scarlet macaws has provided a wealth of information. In a monumental study of the ruins of Paquimé (Casas Grandes), Charles C. Di Peso and his co-investigators recovered no less than 322 scarlet macaw skeletons. Their study provides clues of how these birds

may have been transported from Tamaulipas, kept at Paquimé, and sacrificed in the spring. Charles C. Di Peso, John B. Rinaldo, and Gloria J. Fenner, *Casas Grandes: A Fallen Trading Center of the Gran Chichimeca* (Flagstaff: Amerind Foundation and the Dragoon Northland Press, 1974), VIII, 272–278. Lyndon L. Hargrave has conducted the most comprehensive survey of scarlet macaw remains in sites north of the present-day international border. He was able to identify 145 macaws distributed throughout the Southwest with notable concentrations in Pueblo Bonito, Wupatki, and Point of Pines Ruin. Thus, Casas Grandes boasts roughly two-thirds of all the macaws found in the Southwest/northern Mexico. Indeed, the macaw-breeding facilities found in Paquimé are so substantial that for some time scholars believed that this site functioned as a regional supplier of scarlet macaw feathers and possibly live animals. Yet, two recent excavations in west-central and northwestern Chihuahua have shown that other centers also produced macaws and therefore must have received live animals from the Gulf of Mexico coast as well. Paul E. Minnis, Michael E. Whalen, Jane H. Kelley, and Joe D. Stewart, "Prehistoric Macaw Breeding in the North American Southwest," *American Antiquity* 58:2 (1993), 270–276. Scarlet macaws were also imported into the Mimbres area of New Mexico. Darrell Creel and Charmion McKusick, "Prehistoric Macaws and Parrots in the Mimbres Area, New Mexico," *American Antiquity* 59:3 (1994), 510–524. The exchange of scarlet macaw feathers and live animals is ancient. Charmion McKusick notes that the earliest known introduction of macaws into the Southwest was among the Hohokam at Snaketown dating from the A.D. 500s or 600s. Charmion R. McKusick, *Southwest Birds of Sacrifice* (Globe, AZ: Arizona Archaeological Society, 2001), 74. The trade intensified in the period around A.D. 1000–1150 in the Mimbres area and flourished in Paquimé during the Medio period in the centuries leading up to contact. Creel and McKusick, "Prehistoric Macaws and Parrots in the Mimbres Area, New Mexico," 516; and Di Peso et al., *Casas Grandes*, VIII, 272–273. The exchange continued through the colonial era. Cabeza de Vaca writes of "parrot's feathers" being traded, although he could have been referring to a different species. With more precision Father Luis Velarde observed in the early eighteenth century that the Pimas at San Xavier del Bac and its surrounding areas raised scarlet macaws "because of the beautiful feathers of red and of other colors . . . which they strip from these birds in the spring for their adornment." Father Luis Velarde, "*Relación* of Pimeria Alta of 1716," quoted in Hargrave, *Mexican Macaws*, 1.

2. Quote from Cabeza de Vaca, *Relación of 1542*, 203. Adorno and Pautz point out that this incident is absent in the *Joint Report* and emphasize that no corn had been sighted by the castaways since leaving Florida and that they would not find more until La Junta de los Rios. Based on these facts, the authors go on to propose that Cabeza de Vaca probably invented this incident to justify the new journey that they had embarked upon, "because it potentially provides the incontestable logic of the search for food and the quest for survival." Adorno and Pautz, *Álvar Núñez Cabeza de Vaca*, II, 296. It seems to me that Cabeza de Vaca's inclusion of a fictitious encounter to justify a route change left otherwise unexplained is unlikely. It is more plausible that the two women were real and were actually transporting corn flour from farther west and north. Foster speculates that the corn flour may have been brought from the Huasteca region to the east and south or that they may have obtained it from a long-distance

trading party that the castaways themselves encountered later on. Foster, *The La Salle Expedition on the Mississippi River*, 68.

3. The three quotes come from the *Joint Report*, 138; and Cabeza de Vaca, *Relación of 1542*, 206. My translation in all cases. Cabeza de Vaca's *Relación* does not clearly state that it was a traveling party, but the *Joint Report* does. See also Foster, *The La Salle Expedition on the Mississippi River*, 68–69. The actual phrase in the third quote is the following: "de lo qual se colige que de donde aquello se traia, puesto que no fuesse oro, avia assiento é fundian." It is somewhat ambiguous with respect to whether the author is referring to settlements or mines, but the general gist is clear. The long-distance merchants were telling the truth. Modern archaeology has established that the copper bell described in the *Relación* and the *Joint Report* must have been manufactured "across the land toward the South Sea." Di Peso and his co-researchers proposed in 1974 that copper bells were produced at Paquimé. Their argument rested on the identification of possible smelting workshop material, chemical analyses of local copper ores, and the existence of copper artifacts apparently unique to Paquimé. More recently Jeremiah F. Epstein has examined carefully the only three Spanish expeditions in the sixteenth century that reported copper artifacts—those of Cabeza de Vaca, Ibarra, and Rodríguez-Chamuscado—and proposes that these objects were probably looted from Paquimé or some site in the area. Jeremiah F. Epstein, "Cabeza de Vaca and the Sixteenth-Century Copper Trade in Northern Mexico," *American Antiquity* 56:3 (July 1991), 474–482. Even more recently, Victoria D. Vargas has raised doubts that Paquimé could have produced copper bells like the one given to the Cabeza de Vaca party. Vargas believes that the copper bells found throughout the American Southwest were actually manufactured in an area that is now located on the west coast of Mexico, where a long copper-producing tradition existed. Victoria D. Vargas, *Copper Bell Trade Patterns in the Prehispanic U.S. Southwest and Northwest Mexico* (Tucson: Arizona State Museum/University of Arizona, 1995), passim. In either case the Indians who gave the copper bell to Dorantes were absolutely right.

4. Quote from Cabeza de Vaca, *Relación of 1542*, 206. My translation. For a full discussion of the location of this "iron slag," see Krieger, *We Came Naked and Barefoot*, 67. In fact, Mexico's preeminent smelting company (Altos Hornos de México), located in the nearby city of Monclova, continues to exploit those same iron deposits. Krieger, following in the footsteps of Davenport and Wells, identifies the "very beautiful river" as one of the northern branches of the Nadadores. The references to pine nuts in both the *Relación* and the *Joint Report* have given rise to much confusion. All studies prior to 1997 considered only two pine-nut species: the New Mexico piñón (Pinus edulis) and the Mexican piñón (Pinus cembroides). On one side, scholars supporting a trans-Texas and trans-New Mexico route have made much of the fact that the New México piñón—with its "moderately thin seed coat" that seemed to resemble the type described in the sources—can be found in Texas, New Mexico, Colorado, Utah, and northern Arizona, but rarely south of the present-day international border. Cleve Hallenbeck stated such a belief quite bluntly: "The pine nuts mentioned by Núñez [Cabeza de Vaca] are, of course, the fruit of the piñon pine, Pinus edulis." Cleve Hallenbeck, *Álvar Núñez Cabeza de Vaca: The Journey and Route of the First European to Cross the Continent of North America, 1534–1536* (Glendale, CA: Arthur H. Clark Company, 1940), 188. Previous and later scholars have made similar assertions.

In contrast, route-interpreters arguing for a mostly trans-Mexico course have chosen the Mexican piñón (Pinus cembroides), which has a more southerly range along both the Sierra Madre Oriental and the Sierra Madre Occidental. Adorno and Pautz, for instance, somewhat cautiously state that "their overlapping ranges [of Pinus edulis and Pinus cembroides] make these two species plausible choices, although the widespread occurrence in Mexico of Pinus cembroides suggests that it was the more likely candidate for the men's first acquaintance with the piñon nuts of Coahuila." Adorno and Pautz, *Álvar Núñez Cabeza de Vaca*, II, 309. The main problem with Pinus cembroides, of course, is that its "thick hard seed coat" hardly agrees with the descriptions provided in the sources, which are very specific in this regard. The riddle was finally solved with the identification of the Pinus remota. For a full discussion, see Donald W. Olson, Marilynn S. Olson, et al., "Piñon Pines and the Route of Cabeza de Vaca," *Southwestern Historical Quarterly* 101 (October 1997), 174–186.

5. Cabeza de Vaca, *Relación of 1542*, 208, 210.

6. Quote from Cabeza de Vaca, *Relación of 1542*, 208. My translation. On the medical significance of Cabeza de Vaca's intervention, see Jesse E. Thompson, "Sagittectomy: Operation Performed in America in 1535 by Cabeza de Vaca," *New England Journal of Medicine* 289:26 (December 27, 1973), 1404–1407.

7. Adorno and Pautz, *Álvar Núñez Cabeza de Vaca*, II, 292, 296.

8. Quotes from Cabeza de Vaca, *Relación of 1542*, 197, 199, and 211, respectively.

9. Quote from Cabeza de Vaca, *Relación of 1542*, 205. On the tensions between reverence and intimidation see Rolena Adorno, "The Negotiation of Fear in Cabeza de Vaca's Naufragios," *Representations* 33 (Winter 1991), 178–183.

10. Quote from Cabeza de Vaca, *Relación of 1542*, 211. See also Cabeza de Vaca, *Relación of 1542*, 203, 212.

11. Quotes in Cabeza de Vaca, *Relación of 1542*, 212, 202, and 204, respectively. See also Adorno, "The Negotiation of Fear in Cabeza de Vaca's Naufragios," 180–181.

12. Quotes in Cabeza de Vaca, *Relación of 1542*, 215. The precise route from the Sierra de la Gloria to La Junta de los Rios in what is now Presidio, Texas, and Ojinaga, Chihuahua, cannot be ascertained. For a fine discussion of the two most plausible trajectories, proposed by Davenport and Wells on the one hand and Krieger on the other, see Adorno and Pautz, *Álvar Núñez Cabeza de Vaca*, II, 310–313. It is possible that they may have crossed the Rio Conchos before it meets the Rio Grande. See Krieger, *We Came Naked and Barefoot*, 78–80.

13. Cabeza de Vaca, *Relación of 1542*, 202, 217, 219.

14. Cabeza de Vaca, *Relación of 1542*, 219; and *Joint Report*, 140–141.

15. Cabeza de Vaca, *Relación of 1542*, 221. See also the *Joint Report*, 141–142. Although the two main sources are largely in agreement about this episode, they provide complementary information, so the two must be read side by side.

16. Quote from Antonio Espejo, "Account of the Journey to the Provinces and Settlements of New Mexico, 1583," in Herbert Eugene Bolton, ed., *Spanish Exploration in the Southwest 1542–1706: Original Narratives of Early American History* (New York: Barnes and Noble, 1946), 173. Another member of the Espejo expedition wrote in his journal, "In this pueblo [the largest pueblo in the area, whose cacique was named Q. Bisise] and in all the others, they told us how Cabeza de Vaca and his two

companions and a negro had been there." George Meter Hammond and Agapito Rey, eds., *Expedition into New Mexico Made by Antonio de Espejo, 1582–1583: As Revealed in the Journal of Diego Pérez de Luxán, a Member of the Party* (Los Angeles: Quivira Society, 1929), 62. For a full discussion of the likelihood that the castaways passed through La Junta de los Rios, see Krieger, *We Came Naked and Barefoot*, 80–97.

17. Cabeza de Vaca, *Relación of 1542*, 221. On the damp islands and bays, see Hammond and Rey, eds., *Expedition into New Mexico Made by Antonio de Espejo*, 62.

18. Embarking on a full discussion of the "Jumano problem" is well beyond the scope of this footnote. But it is important to spell out how scholars have conceived the peoples encountered by Cabeza de Vaca, who lived in dwellings "with the semblance and appearance of houses." J. Charles Kelley has studied both the archaeology and the historical sources of La Junta de los Rios and has argued that two distinct peoples inhabited the area: a semi-sedentary, agricultural people that the Spaniards called Patarabueyes and a more nomadic folk known as Jumanos. Kelley is very much aware that the peoples encountered by Cabeza de Vaca "sound very much like the Patarabueyes culturally" and also acknowledges that the area described by Cabeza de Vaca and his companions, alongside a river with permanent settlements, resembles the world of La Junta de los Rios. Moreover, Kelley notes that the observations of the Espejo party with regard to Cabeza de Vaca and his companions help to establish their passage through La Junta de los Rios and further contribute to the identification of the people that they visited there with the Patarabueyes. However, Kelley himself objects to such an identification on the grounds that the Patarabueyes had pottery since the thirteenth century and the people visited by Cabeza de Vaca "had no pots in which to cook in the ordinary manner" and instead "boiled their food in gourd vessels by placing hot rocks in the stew therein." Above all, Kelley's skepticism stemmed from his reading of Hallenbeck's book, which argued that Cabeza de Vaca and his companions never went through La Junta de los Rios. Advocating a trans-Texas and trans-New Mexico route, Hallenbeck vigorously proposed that the villages visited by Cabeza de Vaca were located at the Pecos River and/or perhaps at the Rio Grande, but farther west and north by the El Paso area. Attempting to reconcile all this contradictory information, Kelley ventured the idea that the people visited by Cabeza de Vaca may have been Jumanos rather than Patarabueyes. J. Charles Kelley, *Jumano and Patarabueye: Relations at La Junta de los Rios* (Ann Arbor: Anthropological Paper Number 77, Museum of Anthropology, University of Michigan, 1986), 16–17. Nancy Parrott Hickerson has also revisited the "Jumano problem." After reviewing the literature and conceding that anthropologists have disagreed over the nature of the agricultural society found at La Junta de los Rios, she goes on to make some distinctions. She argues that the people encountered by Cabeza de Vaca were a less agricultural folk living upriver from La Junta proper, "near the half-way point between La Junta and El Paso," and that Luxán called Caguates. She reached this conclusion in part, once again, because of her reliance on Hallenbeck's route, which has come under attack more recently. Ultimately, her position is somewhat ambiguous. On the one hand, she states that the village visited by Cabeza de Vaca was "clearly not La Junta. There, the Rio Grande would not have appeared hemmed in by mountains, as

Cabeza de Vaca's description suggests. Further, the Rio Conchos, at that confluence, is broader than the Rio del Norte itself. Since the primary sources make no mention of the Conchos or of the joining of the rivers, it seems unlikely that the Spaniards visited there." But on the other hand, she admits that later reminiscences of Indian witnesses support the notion that Cabeza de Vaca did pass through La Junta de los Rios. Nancy Parrott Hickerson, *The Jumanos: Hunters and Traders of the South Plains* (Austin: University of Texas Press, 1992), 16, 66. Beyond the specific discussion of Cabeza de Vaca's precise route, Hickerson's work is important because it shows that a clear-cut distinction between Patarabueyes and Jumanos is all but impossible and that such terms were applied to different peoples at different times. The most recent route-interpreters are largely in agreement with regard to Cabeza de Vaca's party passing through La Junta de los Rios. If the travelers did pass through that area—and it is likely but not certain—then the people described in the *Relación* and the *Joint Report* (and later corroborated in the accounts of the Espejo expedition) could only refer to the more sedentary peoples of the Patarabuey-Jumano complex residing in the region. Indeed, all cultural traits mentioned in the sources except one—lack of pots—support such a notion (the villagers might have simply run out of pots when Cabeza de Vaca and his companions were visiting!). The other piece of information that calls into question Cabeza de Vaca's presence at La Junta de los Rios is that neither the Rio Grande nor the Rio Conchos flow between mountains where they meet. But Cabeza de Vaca says that such mountains existed *en route to* rather than *at* the village, so it is not an insurmountable objection. See the detailed geographic discussion in Krieger, *We Came Naked and Barefoot*, 84–108.

19. Quotes from the *Joint Report*, 60; and Cabeza de Vaca, *Relación of 1542*, 223, respectively. The exact same procedure to boil water is reported in Cabeza de Vaca, *Relación of 1542*, 227. See also Kelley, *Jumano and Patarabueye: Relations at La Junta de los Rios*, 121. As the author explains, both houses and tents occur at La Junta de los Rios. Kelley uses this evidence to argue that two distinct peoples lived there. Others believe that the two types of dwellings were used by the same people.

20. *Joint Report*, 144. My translation. See also Cabeza de Vaca, *Relación of 1542*, 224–225.

21. Quote from Cabeza de Vaca, *Relación of 1542*, 227, 229.

22. The journey from La Junta de los Rios to the town of Corazones remains extremely vague. First, it is difficult to pinpoint the precise location where the castaways left the Rio Grande valley and turned west. Some scholars believe that it may have happened as far north as the present-day El Paso area whereas others argue that such a place must have been located farther to the southeast. Krieger is among the latter, proposing that the turning point may have been located some 150 miles above La Junta, but still 75 miles downriver from El Paso. Krieger arrives at the conclusion by considering the distance that could reasonably be traveled by the castaways in seventeen days or so. He further notes that just at this place, there is a convenient ford and a gap (in the mountain ranges just south of the modern Sierra Blanca in Texas), which would have given the castaways access to northern Chihuahua. Krieger, *We Came Naked and Barefoot*, 107. After turning west the castaways could have taken a number of routes—all of them difficult—leading either to northwestern Chihuahua or northeastern Sonora. See also Adorno and Pautz, *Álvar Núñez Cabeza de Vaca*, II, 326–330.

23. Quotes from Baltasar de Obregón, *Historia de los descubrimientos antiguos y modernos de la Nueva España*, as it appears in Charles Di Peso, *Casas Grandes: A Fallen Trading Center of the Gran Chichimica*, III, 822; and the *Joint Report*, 61, respectively. Obregón's description was penned barely thirty years after Cabeza de Vaca went through the area. For a general description of the Francisco de Ibarra expedition to Paquimé, conducted during 1565–1567, see J. Lloyd Mecham, *Francisco de Ibarra and Nueva Vizcaya* (Durham: Duke University Press, 1927), 159–173. Paquimé is the best-studied site in all of northern Mexico thanks to the Joint Casas Grandes Project, spearheaded by Charles Di Peso and his co-investigators. The wealth of information available for Paquimé remains unmatched. However, more recent research has revised the basic chronology of Paquimé, establishing the end of the Medio period around 1450 to 1500 rather than a century earlier as Di Peso and his team would have it. The new scholarship has also investigated the nature of the relationships between this important city and its neighbors. It is clear that Paquimé established different ties with surrounding cities and villages, depending on their size and proximity. On the great trading routes passing through Paquimé, see Beatriz C. Braniff, ed., *La Gran Chichimeca: el lugar de las rocas secas* (Mexico City: CONACULTA, 2001), 237–248; and the ambitious formulation advanced by J. Charles Kelley in "The Aztatlán Mercantile System: Mobile Traders and the Northwestward Expansion of Mesoamerican Civilization," in Michael S. Foster and Shirley Gorenstein, *Greater Mesoamerica: The Archaeology of West and Northwest Mexico* (Salt Lake City: University of Utah Press, 2000), 137–154. For a survey of recent archaeological work conducted in Chihuahua see Paul E. Minnis and Michael E. Whalen, "Chihuahuan Archaeology: An Introductory History," in Gillian E. Newell and Emiliano Gallaga, eds., *Surveying the Archaeology of Northwest Mexico* (Salt Lake City: University of Utah Press, 2004), 113–126; and Ronna Jane Bradley, "Recent Advances in Chihuahuan Archaeology," in *Greater Mesoamerica*, 221–239.

24. Quote from Cabeza de Vaca, *Relación of 1542*, 229.

25. Quotes come from Cabeza de Vaca, *Relación of 1542*, 231; and the *Joint Report*, 146–147. These Indians have often been identified as the proto-historic Opata or have been more generally associated with the Rio Sonora archaeological tradition, which has been defined largely on the basis of the San José Baviácora site. See discussion in Adorno and Pautz, *Álvar Núñez Cabeza de Vaca*, II, 330–331. For an introduction to the Rio Sonora tradition, see Emiliano Gallaga and Gillian E. Newell, "Introduction," in *Surveying the Archaeology of Northwest Mexico*, 10–11. Krieger perceptively notes that Cabeza de Vaca's statement that Corazones "is the gateway to many provinces that are [near] the South Sea," together with evidence from later expeditions, has prompted historians to posit the existence of a "colonial highway" presumably inaugurated by Cabeza de Vaca. In the 1930s Carl Sauer pioneered this idea after having traveled extensively through Sonora. As he puts it, "The land passage through northwestern New Spain was mostly by one great arterial highway." Carl Sauer, *The Road to Cíbola* (Berkeley: University of California Press, 1932), 1. Sauer argued that early European explorers simply followed the footpaths beaten by many generations of Indian travel. If that is the case, then Corazones would have occupied a most strategic position. Scholars have attempted to pinpoint the location of Corazones by correlating historical with archaeological in-

formation. For instance, see Daniel T. Reff, "The Location of Corazones and Señora: Archaeological Evidence from the Rio Sonora Valley, Mexico," in David R. Wilcox and Bruce Masse, eds., *The Protohistoric Period in the North American Southwest, AD 1450–1700* (Tempe: Arizona State University, 1981), 94–112. Sauer and others have proposed that Corazones was located along the Sonora River in the immediacy of Ures, adding that anyone who had traveled through the region would have known instantly that it was "the most significant gateway of the state. Through this canyon passed almost all transport between the north and south of Sonora in the colonial period and for many years thereafter." Sauer, *The Road to Cíbola*, 17. As an alternative, Adorno and Pautz consider that the castaways traveled along the Bavispe and the Oposura (later renamed Moctezuma) Rivers and therefore locate Corazones farther south in the area of Onavas on the Yaqui River. See discussions in Adorno and Pautz, *Álvar Núñez Cabeza de Vaca*, II, 339–344; and especially Krieger, *We Came Naked and Barefoot*, 108–122. As all the authors concede, the location of Corazones cannot be established with precision on the basis of the scant information provided by the castaways.

26. Quote from Cabeza de Vaca, *Relación of 1542*, 233; and *Joint Report*, 145.

27. Cabeza de Vaca, *Relación of 1542*, 235.

28. Quote from Cabeza de Vaca, *Relación of 1542*, 237.

29. Cabeza de Vaca, *Relación of 1542*, 239. *Joint Report*, 65. My Translation.

CHAPTER 9

1. Nuño de Guzmán was appointed governor of Pánuco in 1525, reached the area in 1527, remained formally in charge of this jurisdiction until 1533, and retained considerable power even afterward. To be sure, the residents of Pánuco were already conducting a brisk trade of slaves before Guzmán's tenure. But Guzmán increased its scope and centralized the system issuing slaving licenses. In his *juicio de residencia* (the review after his tenure as governor) it was stated that as many as one-third of all slaves leaving the province belonged to him. Donald E. Chipman, *Nuño de Guzmán and the Province of Pánuco in New Spain 1518–1533* (Glendale, CA: The Arthur H. Clark Company, 1967), 197–204, 266.

2. Chipman, *Nuño de Guzmán and the Province of Pánuco in New Spain*, 221–222; and A. S. Aiton, *Antonio de Mendoza: First Viceroy of New Spain* (Durham: Duke University Press, 1927), 20. For a detailed account of Guzmán's abuses of the principal lords of Michoacán, see J. Benedict Warren, *The Conquest of Michoacán: The Spanish Domination of the Tarascan Kingdom in Western Mexico, 1521–1530* (Norman: University of Oklahoma Press, 1985), 138–156.

3. Estimates of the size of this expedition vary. See Warren, *The Conquest of Michoacán*, 213–214. See also Adorno and Pautz, *Álvar Núñez Cabeza de Vaca*, III, 346. A. S. Aiton has insightfully observed that "the general tenor of the royal orders addressed to Cortés and to the president and *oidores* of the second *audiencia* certainly indicate that Guzmán was in good standing at court despite the failure of his government, and that a successful conquest in New Galicia would have brought complete exoneration." Aiton, *Antonio de Mendoza*, 19. The same tenor can be appreciated in some of the documents cited below.

4. The quote comparing Cazonci with Moctezuma appears in the "Primera relación anónima de la jornada que hizo Nuño de Guzmán a la Nueva Galicia," in Joaquín García Icazbalceta, ed., *Documentos para la historia de México* (Mexico City: Editorial Porrúa, 1980), 295. The trial and death of Cazonci is an incredibly dramatic and important episode, told in great detail in Warren, *The Conquest of Michoacán*, 211–236. On the request for an additional 8,000 Indians see García del Pilar, "Relación de la entrada de Nuño de Guzmán," in *Documentos para la historia de México*, 248. Using additional documents, Warren observes that the actual number of men added to the expedition in Michoacán may have been 4,000 or 5,000 and that not all were put in chains, as it is doubtful that so many chains would have been available on such short notice, but that perhaps only the lords of the towns were chained. Warren, *The Conquest of Michoacán*, 228.

5. See "Primera relación anónima de la jornada que hizo Nuño de Guzmán a la Nueva Galicia," in *Documentos para la historia de México*, 288; and García del Pilar, "Relación de la entrada de Nuño de Guzmán," in *Documentos para la historia de México*, 255–256. Since there were no overarching indigenous polities in this area, it could be more properly—but cumbersomely—called the Aztatlán, Chametla, and Culiacán region. See Carl Sauer and Donald Brand, *Aztatlán: Prehistoric Mexican Frontier on the Pacific Coast* (Berkeley: University of California Press, 1932), 5. On the itinerary and scope of Guzmán's conquests see "Testimonio de tres provisiones expedidas por Nuño de Guzmán a favor de Francisco Verdugo," Chiametla, January 18, 1531, and Nuño de Guzmán to the Empress, Compostela, June 12, 1532, both in *Epistolario de Nueva España*, II, 9–14 and 142–173, respectively.

6. On Nuño de Guzmán's religious fervor, see José López Portillo y Weber, *La rebelión de la Nueva Galicia* (Mexico City: Colección Peña Colorada, 1980), 7. His devotion to the Holy Spirit can be appreciated in the many towns founded by him that bore the name "Holy Spirit," including the principal city of Nueva Galicia, which was originally named Espíritu Santo. On his megalomania and puritanical bent see Chipman, *Nuño de Guzmán and Pánuco*, 143, 176. Guzmán counted on the Crown's strong backing as revealed by the letter written by Empress Isabel (Charles's wife) to the *audiencia* of Mexico of January 1531. Among other things, the empress names Guzmán as governor of the newly conquered lands, giving him broad powers, and warns Cortés not to get involved in the lands being conquered by Guzmán. The letter also reveals a very cordial and frequent correspondence between Empress Isabel and Guzmán. Reina Doña Isabel to the president and *oidores* of the *audiencia* of Mexico, Ocaña, January 25, 1531, México 1088 L. 1 Bis, F. 45 v–49r. AGI.

7. For a detailed discussion of Guzmán's conquest of Nueva Galicia see Adorno and Pautz, *Álvar Núñez Cabeza de Vaca*, III, 325–381.

8. Quote in Cabeza de Vaca, *Relación of 1542*, 243.

9. Cabeza de Vaca, *Relación of 1542*, 245; and Tello, *Crónica Miscelánea de la Sancta Provincia de Xalisco*, I, 249–257.

10. Quote in Cabeza de Vaca, *Relación of 1542*, 246. My translation and emphasis. For the number of Spaniards and location of their encampment, see *Joint Report*, 150. In spite of Cabeza de Vaca's obvious interest in recording the precise date of his return to Christian-controlled territory, it has since been lost. Instead, scholars have been forced to estimate the date of arrival from the statement that "it was Christmas time"

when the four survivors were forced to pause due to the heavy rains after *Corazones*, by the passing mention "that it was hot even in January," and by the castaways' subsequent visit to Culiacán, which lasted until May 1536. The castaways' first meeting with the Spanish horsemen could have occurred any time between late February and April of 1536. For a consideration of the various chronologies, see Krieger, *We Came Naked and Barefoot*, 132–134.

11. Adorno and Pautz make this point in *Álvar Núñez Cabeza de Vaca*, II, 419–420.

12. Quote from Cabeza de Vaca, *Relación of 1542*, 249.

13. Both quotes from Cabeza de Vaca, *Relación of 1542*, 251.

14. Cabeza de Vaca, *Relación of 1542*, 248. My translation.

15. Quotes from Cabeza de Vaca, *Relación of 1542*, 249 and 251, respectively.

16. All three quotes from Cabeza de Vaca, *Relación of 1542*, 253. Cabeza de Vaca says that he and his companions were "under guard" on the way to Culiacán. But elsewhere in the *Narrative*, he characterizes their departure from the camp of the Spaniards as a "flight" or "escape." It is very likely that neither the castaways nor the slavers were completely in control of the situation.

17. Quote from Cabeza de Vaca, *Relación of 1542*, 255.

18. Cabeza de Vaca, *Relación of 1542*, 264. My translation.

19. Cabeza de Vaca, *Relación of 1542*, 265.

20. Nuño de Guzmán's rule of terror would soon come to an end and would be tried for several crimes ranging from embezzlement and extortion to illegal slaving. On the confrontation between the survivors and Guzmán, see Friar Tello, *Crónica Miscelánea*, I, 309. On the scope of the slaving activities in Compostela, see the revealing "Carta del cabildo secular de Compostela sobre la necesidad de hacer esclavos a los indios rebeldes y su aprovechamiento para el trabajo en las minas," Compostela, Nueva Galicia, February 28, 1533, AGI Guadalajara 30, No. 1/ 1/1–4. In the proceedings of 1537 Guzmán defended himself by stating that he had done many positive things citing, among others, the kindness he had shown toward the survivors of the Narváez expedition.

21. Cabeza de Vaca, *Relación of 1542*, 265. On the intense competition between don Antonio de Mendoza and Hernán Cortés, see A. S. Aiton, *Antonio De Mendoza*, chapter 5. There are only a few sources about the northern Indians who reached Mexico City with the castaways. Barcia writes the following: "In Mexico, Viceroy Antonio de Mendoza saw to it that the Indians who came out of Florida with Álvar Núñez and his companions were instructed in Christian doctrine so they could receive holy baptism. The charge was undertaken by Diego Muñoz Camargo who, though young in years, accomplished the assignment in short order." Andrés González de Barcia Carballido y Zúñiga, *Chronological History of the Continent of Florida* (Westport, CT: Greenwood Press, 1970), 21. Camargo must have indeed achieved his task in record time. By 1539 some of these Indians were being taken back to the north as auxiliaries. In the instructions that Viceroy Mendoza gave to Marcos de Niza in 1538–139, it is stated that "Governor Francisco Vázquez is taking the Indians who came with Dorantes, as well as others whom he has been able to gather from those places [in Nueva Galicia], so that if it happens to seem [appropriate] to him and to you that you take some in your company, you may do so and make use of them, if

you see that it is conducive to the service of God, Our Lord." *Instructions to and Account by Marcos de Niza, 1538–1539*, in Richard Flint and Shirley Cushing Flint, eds., *Documents of the Coronado Expedition, 1539–1542* (Dallas: Southern Methodist University Press, 2005), 65.

EPILOGUE

1. Alonso de la Barrera, a witness in Alonso del Castillo's *información de servicios*, recalled having seen the castaways dressed in skins. Quoted in Adorno and Pautz, *Álvar Núñez Cabeza de Vaca*, II, 392.

2. To fully grasp Cabeza de Vaca's vision of a peaceful occupation, it is necessary to study his actions in his subsequent voyage to the Rio de la Plata. The best treatment of this is David A. Howard, *Conquistador in Chains: Cabeza de Vaca and the Indians of the Americas* (Tuscaloosa: University of Alabama Press, 1997), passim.

3. Quote from Cabeza de Vaca, *Relación of 1542*, 269. See also Cabeza de Vaca, *Relación of 1542*, 265, 267; and Adorno and Pautz, *Álvar Núñez Cabeza de Vaca*, II, 395–397. Diego de Silveira, the Portuguese commander, gave a peppery but fair assessment: "You certainly come with great riches"—he told the Spaniards—"but you bring a very bad ship and very bad artillery! Son of a bitch, there's that renegade French ship and what a good mouthful she's lost!" Cabeza de Vaca, *Relación of 1542*, 271. For possible corroborating sources about the gold and silver carried by the ship, see Adorno and Pautz, *Álvar Núñez Cabeza de Vaca*, II, 398–400.

4. Quote from Gentleman of Elvas, "True Relation of the Hardships Suffered by Governor don Hernando de Soto and Certain Portuguese Gentlemen in the Discovery of the Province of Florida," in Clayton, Knight, and Moore, eds., *The de Soto Chronicles*, I, 48. De Soto turned out to be a conquistador in the mold of Narváez and Guzmán. In the 1520s he had taken part in exploration of Central America and had been involved in the trafficking of Indian slaves. Already a wealthy man, de Soto's star would rise even higher in the early 1530s when he joined Pizarro in the conquest of Peru. He played a prominent role in the taking of Cuzco, the capital of the Inca Empire. De Soto could have lived comfortably for the rest of his life. Yet a desire for adventure pulsed through his veins. In 1536 he returned to Spain to petition for lands in either Ecuador or Colombia. His efforts came to fruition on April 20, 1537, when he received a patent to colonize Florida. Cabeza de Vaca found de Soto outfitting a large fleet bound for North America. De Soto made Cabeza de Vaca "an advantageous proposal" to join his expedition. He was the first to acknowledge the obvious benefits of taking someone familiar with the land and able to communicate with the natives. It was less clear, however, what Cabeza de Vaca stood to gain from such a partnership. The Royal Treasurer had already traveled to Florida as a second-in-command, only to find himself trampled over by Narváez. Now Cabeza de Vaca needed an enlightened captain concerned not only with gold but with the well-being of the Indians. Yet nothing in de Soto's background suggested that he would be such a leader. De Soto's peripatetic expedition (1539–1543) turned out to be murderous for the natives and only slightly less disastrous than Narváez's foray for the Europeans. De Soto himself was stricken by a fever and died in May 1542. His body was cast into the turbid waters of the Mississippi River. As Las Casas sententiously wrote, "Thus the most unhappy cap-

tain died as if ill-fated, without confession, and we do not doubt but that he was buried in hell, unless maybe God did not sentence him secretly—according to His divine mercy and not his demerits—for such wickedness." Las Casas, quoted in Howard, *Conquistador in Chains*, 34.

5. Pero Hernández, "Comentarios de Álvar Núñez Cabeza de Vaca, adelantado y gobernador del Rio de la Plata," in *Naufragios y Comentarios* (Mexico City: Editorial Porrúa, S. A., 1988), 81.

6. On how the Indians of the Rio de la Plata feared the horses, see Hernández, *Naufragios y Comentarios*, 94–95. For a more detailed treatment of Cabeza de Vaca's method of conquest in South America, see Howard, *Conquistador in Chains*, 57, 161–199; and Adorno and Pautz, *Álvar Núñez Cabeza de Vaca*, I, 387–402.

7. Cabeza de Vaca's handling of the indigenous practice of giving women is very revealing. At contact, the Guaraní Indians did not subscribe to the notion of a monogamous marriage, nor did they abstain from establishing sexual relationships with women related to each other within the degree of affinity prohibited by cannon law. Instead, Guaraní Indians used women liberally to cement alliances and make peace with one another. As one witness put it, "Among these Indians the father sells his daughter, the husband his wife if she does not please him, and the brother sells or exchanges his sister." Ulrich Schmidel (Schmidt) quoted in Howard, *Conquistador in Chains*, 67. When Spaniards first explored the area, they were taken aback by the Indians' readiness to part with their female companions. But they adjusted quickly. By the time Cabeza de Vaca got to his *adelantamiento*, he found colonists living with as many as a dozen or more Indian women. Prominent conquistadors possessed harems often consisting of related women such as mothers and daughters, sisters, and cousins, all of whom were being exchanged like slaves. The sacrosanct institution of marriage was completely undermined. The new Governor could not tolerate it. He had a cleric examine this "serious sin and offense against God" and took many women away from the Spaniards. Howard, *Conquistador in Chains*, 68. This footnote is entirely based on Howard's *Conquistador in Chains*, chapter 10.

8. The Governor of the Rio de la Plata faced thirty-four criminal charges in four different lawsuits. In March 1551 he was found guilty on several counts. The examination of these charges against the Governor of the Rio de la Plata is beyond the scope of this epilogue. For a rundown of the accusations, see Morris Bishop, *The Odyssey of Cabeza de Vaca* (Westport, CT: Greenwood Press, 1971), 276–278. See also Adorno and Pautz, *Álvar Núñez Cabeza de Vaca*, I, 395–398.

9. Howard, *Conquistador in Chains*, 51–73 and conclusion.

10. On the last years of Cabeza de Vaca's life, see Adorno and Pautz, *Álvar Núñez Cabeza de Vaca*, I, 407–410. These authors correctly note that Cabeza de Vaca's ransom of Hernán Ruiz Cabeza de Vaca contradicts the depictions of Cabeza de Vaca's last years in poverty and obscurity.

11. Baltasar Dorantes de Carranza, *Sumaria relación de las cosas de la Nueva España* (Mexico City: Imprenta del Museo Nacional, 1902), 265; and *Traslado de la mitad del pueblo de Tehuacán a Alonso del Castillo Maldonado como marido de la viuda de Juan Ruiz de Alanís*, Madrid, February 11, 1540, AGI Patronato 275, R. 39/1/1–4. Castillo also bought land from neighboring indigenous communities, another unmistakable sign of his newfound prosperity. *Real provisión a Alonso del*

Castillo Maldonado dándole facultad para comprar heredades a los indios de Nueva España, Madrid, February 25, 1540, AGI Patronato 278, No. 2, R. 230.

12. Relación del distrito y pueblos del obispado de Tlaxcala, cited in Adorno and Pautz, *Álvar Núñez Cabeza de Vaca*, II, 411–412.

13. Adorno and Pautz, *Álvar Núñez Cabeza de Vaca*, II, 426–427.

14. Dorantes de Carranza, *Sumaria relación de las cosas de la Nueva España*, 267; A. S. Aiton, *Antonio de Mendoza: First Viceroy of New Spain* (Durham: Duke University Press, 1927), 119; and Adorno and Pautz, *Álvar Núñez Cabeza de Vaca*, I, 411.

15. Quote from a letter from Viceroy Mendoza to Emperor Charles V, circa September 1539. This letter fragment was preserved only in an Italian translation made in the 1540s or early 1550s by Ramusio. See the transcription of the original Italian and its translation into English in Richard Flint and Shirley Cushing Flint, eds., *Documents of the Coronado Expedition, 1539–1542* (Dallas: Southern Methodist University Press, 2005), 45–50.

16. Obregón, *Crónica*, quoted in Aiton, *Antonio de Mendoza*, 119.

17. Pedro de Castañeda de Nájera, "Relación de la jornada de Cíbola," in *Documents of the Coronado Expedition*, 387–388.

18. Quote from Castañeda de Nájera, "Relación de la jornada de Cíbola," 37. Fray Marcos de Niza claimed that the group had reached Cíbola (present-day New Mexico), but little in the diary supports such a contention. See discussion in Carl O. Sauer, "The Road to Cíbola," 29. An oral tradition among Zuni Indians seems to pertain to Estebanico's final days on earth. This tradition states that a "black Mexican" made his way into Hawikuh and that, although treated hospitably, he "very soon incurred mortal hatred by his rude behavior toward the women and girls of the pueblo." Frank Hamilton Cushing heard this Zuni oral tradition in the early 1880s and shared it with anthropologist Adolph Bandelier. See Jesse Green, ed., *Cushing at Zuni: The Correspondence and Journals of Frank Hamilton Cushing, 1879–1884* (Albuquerque: University of New Mexico Press, 1990), 335; and Adolph Bandelier, *The Gilded Man* (New York: D. Appleton, 1893), 159. Yet, as indicated earlier, it is doubtful whether Estebanico ever reached western New Mexico.

19. Quote from Dorantes de Carranza, *Sumaria relación de las cosas de la Nueva España*, 266.

INDEX

INDEX